THE PSYCHOLOGY OF SLEEP

The PSYCHOLOGY OF SLEEP

DAVID FOULKES

Member of the Department of Psychology and Philosophy,
University of Wyoming

CHARLES SCRIBNER'S SONS *New York*

In Memoriam

Joan Foulkes Layton

1927–1965

PREFACE

I N this volume it is my intention to summarize and interpret, for the interested layman as well as the specialist,
the present status of experimental research on psychological
aspects of sleep. In particular, the goal of this book is the
study of mental experience during sleep—what it is, and why
it is what it is.

The psychological side of the equation has not received
its due share of attention in a rapidly proliferating technical
and popular literature on the psychophysiology of sleep and
dreams. There are several excellent accounts of the physiological aspects of recent research on sleep and dreams, but
they have not, in general, done justice to the psychological,
or experiential, dimensions of this research. There have also
been "popular" accounts of this research, but when such treatments have not been inaccurate or misleading, they too have
succumbed to the tendency to treat psychological considera-
tions as being decidedly inferior to the sometimes admittedly
brilliant researches and speculations of the physiologist.

PREFACE

I have attempted to integrate the evidence which is now available. Developments in research on sleep and dreams are so fast-moving that it is perhaps audacious even to attempt to review the evidence, much less to attempt to tie it together conceptually. I think, however, that facts do require interpretation. Such I have tried to provide. Some of my interpretations are possibly wrong, others incomplete. But it seemed preferable to attempt to fit the pieces of the puzzle together now, on the basis of the information presently available, rather than to simply present an accumulation of isolated research findings. Ultimately, of course, it will be for the future to decide the fate of the speculations and hypotheses which are elaborated here.

This book is by no means a complete "psychology of sleep." Such a book is out of the question at the present time. For example, though there are some developmental studies of sleep patterns, there have been no published psychophysiological studies of dream content at different age levels. College students have been the most readily available research subjects, and, almost without exception, it is upon such young adults that our present understanding of mental activity during sleep must be based.

Some gaps in the present account are unavoidable, then, but I hope that justice has been done to the research findings which are presently available. It will be obvious from the many citations in the text that the real authors of this book are many—the researchers whose data are presented here. I can only hope that they will find the presentation of their findings and conclusions reasonably accurate.

DAVID FOULKES

Laramie, Wyoming

ACKNOWLEDGMENTS

S EVERAL persons have helped shape my interest in sleep and dreams, and it is with pleasure that I acknowledge them. I owe particular debts of gratitude to Joe Kamiya, in whose laboratory and under whose guidance I was first introduced to this area; to Allan Rechtschaffen, some of whose energy, enthusiasm, and knowledge could not help but seep into my system during a year of postdoctoral research at his laboratory at the University of Chicago; and to Gerald Vogel, whose clinical and psychoanalytic orientation, so thoughtfully expressed, has served as a challenge to my more experimental biases. None of these gentlemen is responsible for the book as it now stands, but without them, it would have been impossible.

The preparation of this manuscript, and some of the author's research reported herein, has been supported by the National Science Foundation, under grant GS–860. Indeed, the generous support of both NSF and the U.S. Public Health Service for research on sleep and dreaming in general must be acknowledged. Without the support of these government agencies, we would probably know very little of what is now known in this highly important area of psychophysiological research.

Allan Rechtschaffen's detailed analysis of an earlier version of this manuscript aided immeasurably in the sharpening of both form and substance in the final version. Sandra Davidson's secretarial skills have proved invaluable in the preparation of the manuscript. The assistance of several students at the University of Wyoming, particularly Terry Pivik and Ethel Meginness, has been of great help. Thanks are also extended to Gerald Meyer, Dean of the College of Arts and Sciences, and to Hugh McFadden and Wilson Walthall, Jr., professors in the Department of Psychology and Philosophy, at the University for providing an environment in which it has been my pleasure to write this book.

Last, but by no means least, acknowledgment is made to my wife, Susan. Being the wife of a professional sleep researcher or of an author is sufficient punishment for any woman; to have been both for the past year is a strain which she has carried with amazingly little grumbling, and her help and encouragement are sincerely appreciated.

CONTENTS

CONTENTS

LIST OF ILLUSTRATIONS

THE PSYCHOLOGY OF SLEEP

INTRODUCTION

THE one third of man's existence that he spends asleep
has long held a special fascination for him, and psychological experiences occurring during sleep have had much
to do with this. To primitive man it seemed as though sleep
allowed his spirit to wander from his inert body and to engage in
numerous adventures, returning safely to its usual dwelling
place at the moment of awakening. For modern man, the bizarre
and dramatic qualities of dream episodes have seemed attributable more to the activity (organized or chaotic) of his own brain
than to any supernatural phenomena. Either way, dreams have
been not only a source of interest for man but also cause for
wonderment and perplexity.

The application of scientific methods to the study of dream
phenomena, as is true of their application to human behavior
and experience in a more general sense, is of relatively recent
origin. Dreams have been of interest to the professional psychologist, however, since the very outset of his endeavors at
extending scientific methods to the study of man.

At the turn of the century, it was possible for Sigmund Freud (1856–1939), the Viennese physician, to summarize a considerable literature of scientific research and speculation on the nature of dreaming. Dream interpretation held a central position among Freud's newly discovered psychoanalytic techniques for the treatment of nervous disorders, and his intensive analyses of his own dreams and those of his patients did much to increase the development of scientific understanding of dreams. Even today, his theory of the dream process remains the major source of insights for psychologists.

Freud's investigations, and those of the investigators who were to follow, did suffer, nonetheless, from a lack of appropriate tools with which to undertake a really thorough analysis of mental activity during sleep. The researcher was dependent for his sample of dream specimens upon either delayed daytime recall—quite probably an unreliable and distorted transformation of the dream experience—or awakenings from nocturnal sleep caused by accidental or systematically biasing factors. In view of these limitations, it is not surprising that for many years after Freud's pioneering efforts there were few genuinely new developments in the psychology of dreaming.

Quite recently, however, this situation has radically changed. New techniques have been found that have enabled psychologists and other scientists to initiate a systematic investigation of the workings of the human mind during sleep. A professional organization devoted at least in part to this goal, the Association for the Psychophysiological Study of Sleep, has held annual meetings since 1961, and its membership now numbers in the hundreds. Government-financed laboratories for the study of sleep and dreams, sometimes attached to universities and in other cases associated with hospitals or research institutes, now dot the country from coast to coast.

Recent developments in the physiological investigation of sleep are directly responsible for this newly opened possibility of examining the nature, functions, and meaning of mental activity during sleep. Approximately fifteen years ago, scientists discovered that dreaming occurs during sleep characterized by a particular patterning of electrical activity of the brain and by rapid movements of the eyeball, as if the eye were "watching" the pictorial content of the dream. When awakened from this stage of sleep, which occurs periodically through the night, human subjects almost always are able to recall a vivid, perceptual, *hallucinatory* (at the time it seemed "real"), and somewhat distorted drama that would unhesitatingly be called a "dream."

This discovery that dreaming is associated with a particular kind of sleep has made it possible for scientists to make precise determinations of how often and for how long one dreams and also to observe the effects of differences in personality and daytime experience upon the amount of dreaming sleep a person experiences. More important for the psychologist, with knowledge of when a person is dreaming, it becomes possible to awaken him at these times and collect relatively complete samples of his dream experiences. This, in turn, permits a systematic investigation of why people dream the things that they do. Can it be shown, for example, that events of the previous day, a frightening experience, for instance, will radically affect the nature of the dreams that subjects report from *rapid eye movement* (REM, pronounced rĕm) sleep? Can it be shown that accidental noises or bodily sensations occurring during sleep itself are related to the content of REM-sleep dreams? Is there any support for the

Freudian hypothesis that personality, one's particular constellation of hopes, fears, unfulfilled desires, and unrecognized anxieties, determines the kinds of dreams experienced throughout the night? Experimental evidence has been collected to answer each of these questions as well as many others that had seemed incapable of yielding reliable or definitive solution.

In addition to the discovery that dreaming occurs during REM sleep, it has also been found that mental experiences of a distinctive sort occur in other phases of sleep as well. These experiences are generally more thoughtlike and less dramatic, perceptual, hallucinatory, and bizarre than full-blown REM-sleep dreams. While it is a matter of semantics as to whether these quasi-dream experiences should be called "dreams," it is important to note that they are different in quality from the typical REM-sleep mental products to which the label is most usually assigned. These non-REM (often abbreviated to NREM in writing) mental experiences assume importance, not only in their own right, but also as they seem to provide part of the mental context out of which the more vivid REM dream emerges.

The transitional, or "twilight," zone between wakefulness and sleep has also been found to be associated with distinctive kinds of mental experience. Sleep-onset mental activity seems more dreamlike that that occurring during NREM sleep, but it is briefer and more superficial in character than REM dreaming.

The various states of drowsiness and sleep, then, seem to be filled with a variety of mental experiences, and there are physiological indicators that serve as reliable signs of the form such mental activity may assume. Thus the human mind is far more active during sleep than has been hitherto suspected. The reliable correlation of physiological indexes with the nature of this activity, moreover, demonstrates the manner in which physiological recordings may contribute to a psychological analysis of the operations of the mind during sleep.

The evidence of recent years seems to indicate that it will not only be possible, but also quite necessary, that psychology devote a fair share of its attention to the period of sleep. Findings of qualitatively varying kinds of mental experience during different phases of sleep indicate that sleep is far from a psychological void. The lack of significant overt behavior during this state can no longer mislead us into accepting the notion that it is primarily the concern of the physiologist. No one with an interest in mental processes can afford to ignore the variety, richness, and complexity such processes demonstrate during the relative behavioral quietude of sleep.

The evidence indicating that there is considerable mental functioning during sleep inevitably raises the question of why such activity is not suspended with sleep onset. By analogy to purely physiological phenomena, it might be suggested that sleep is never a state of complete suspension of organismic activity. Our hearts do not stop beating nor our lungs breathing during this state. In the case of these physiological phenomena, however, it is clear that the maintenance of steady bodily functioning is necessary for life itself. One can never awaken from a "sleep" that has been without heartbeat or inhalation-exhalation. But what of that mental activity accompanying sleep? Is it an accidental or incidental phenomenon without any significance for the organism's over-all adaptation? If so, why is it present during sleep? It would seem so much more efficient to simply "shut down" the mental apparatus.

Does its very presence perhaps indicate that mental activity is more than an insignificant by-product of the state of sleep, that it is, in some sense, as essential to the organism as the beat of its heart or the rhythmic action of its lungs? Do we *need* to dream, much as we have obvious needs for circulatory and respiratory activity during sleep?

Freud's observations led him to postulate that dreaming was a meaningful and motivated activity, one that fulfilled basic needs of the human organism. He felt that the dream protected sleep by transforming stimuli that might awaken the dreamer—for instance, bladder tension—into hallucinatory perceptions—imagining the act of urination, perhaps—compatible with the continuance of sleep. Rather than replying to the stimulus with an appropriate motor response that would necessitate awakening, the dreamer imagines an appropriate action and maintains his state of sleep.

Freud also felt that dreaming serves functions beyond those directly concerned with the state of sleep. He assumed that the very maintenance of waking personality integrity depends upon the harmless discharge in dream content of tensions or impulses whose appearance in waking life would be most inappropriate or harmful. Better to dream that one harms a friend or commits an indecency than really to perform such actions while awake.

Recent studies employing the rapid-eye-movement method of dream detection have seemed to some observers to provide a measure of support for Freud's hypothesis that dreaming is an essential human activity. The hypothesis has been tested by observations of subjects who are systematically prevented from experiencing REM sleep and, presumably, the dreaming associated with it. Marked deterioration in personality functioning has sometimes been observed as an apparent consequence of this *dream deprivation*. While the meaning of these particular findings is not yet totally clear, they do illustrate the potential value of physiological techniques of dream detection in determining the functions of mental activity during sleep.

Many of the most basic questions man has asked about dreaming, then, now seem more open to research than ever before. The introduction of physiological methods has created new techniques for the careful experimental study of the psychological features of sleep. As systematic study of mental activity during sleep has become possible only very recently, many aspects are still shrouded in mystery. It is now possible, however, to state some preliminary findings and to draw some tentative conclusions concerning the psychology of that portion of life spent in the state of sleep. This volume is intended as a map of the presently known psychological features of sleep as revealed by contemporary psychophysiological research. It is also hoped that it may serve as a guide to further exploration of the as yet uncharted features of this same terrain.

Chapter 1

SLEEP

THE NEED FOR SLEEP

All human beings sleep. To be sure, some sleep more than others: infants and children more than adolescents, adolescents more than adults, and some adults more than others. But a periodic alternation of sleep with wakefulness is universal among members of the human species. That all men sleep, whatever the diversity of their heredity, social background, or other activities, suggests that it fulfills a basic biological need of the human organism.

Many different theories of sleep have attempted to explain its recurrence and apparent necessity.[1] Some stress nervous fatigue or exhaustion; others, the accumulation of metabolic waste products in brain or body; still others, hormone accumulation and discharge. In spite of the fact that much is now known about the mechanisms immediately responsible for the onset and maintenance of sleep,[2] it is still unclear *why* humans must sleep and why they need as much as they do.

That they need sleep is an undoubted fact, however. The sentry on continuous night watch and the automobile driver who travels day and night find the pressures toward sleep irresistible, although their lives depend upon their staying awake. The effects of prolonged sleep deprivation are well known: a loss of efficiency in mental and physical functioning, irritability, and tendencies toward perceptual distortion and ideational confusion.[3] Experimenters who have deliberately sleep-deprived animals report that the animals may actually die after ten or more sleepless days, and there is sometimes an indication in postmortem analyses that such sleep deprivation has produced degeneration in the tissue of the brain and other bodily organs.[4] Sleep-deprivation research using human subjects has, understandably, rarely been pushed to these limits, but there is no question that even shorter deprivation periods seriously impair the person's adaptation to his environment. Indeed, deliberate attempts to produce such impairment, for example "brainwashing," seem to rely heavily upon sleep deprivation as a technique for breaking down established patterns of thought and behavior.[5]

THE NATURE OF SLEEP

In behavioral terms, sleep might be defined as a period of relatively low responsiveness to sensory stimulation and of relatively little goal-directed motor activity. The person attempting to fall off to sleep "tunes out" all but the most insistent of external stimuli. He closes his eyelids to occlude visual-stimulus input. He turns off his radio and attempts to induce other family members to maintain relative silence. When he is successful in achieving sleep, he shows few indications of complexly motivated behavior; his tosses and turns and his occasional grunts seem random and purposeless.

The behavioral definition of sleep is not entirely satisfactory, however, for both selective responsiveness to external stimulation and goal-directed behavior can appear during sleep—in some rather varied and complex forms. It has also seemed to most observers that behavioral changes in sleep are but symptoms of the more basic alterations that must be taking place in internal bodily, particularly brain, processes.

In fact, it has been studies of the brain physiology of the sleeping human that have proved most useful in defining the state of sleep and in charting its intricate and complex internal organization. Although this is a book dealing with the psychology of sleep, it is necessary to consider certain aspects of the descriptive physiology of the bodily state in which the mental activity of sleep occurs. This physiological evidence will indicate that sleep is not uniform, but, rather, that it conveniently can be analyzed into several different stages, each with its own physiological peculiarities. This evidence is of considerable psychological significance, for these physiologically defined stages have proven to be highly predictive of the particular form assumed by mental activity during sleep.

ELECTROPHYSIOLOGICAL EVIDENCE

The brain is a continuously active electrical medium. It is possible to make recordings of its electrical activity without establishing physical contact with the brain surface itself. Tiny metal-disk electrodes are affixed to the scalp, usually with a collodion-impregnated gauze pad. These electrodes are sensitive to *brain potentials*, that is, moment-to-moment shifts in energy level between adjacent cells or regions of the *cerebral cortex*, the convoluted covering of the largest lobe of the human brain.

The recording input of these electrodes is fed into a biomedical apparatus known as an *electroencephalograph*, which amplifies the very small electrical potentials, being measured in units of *microvolts*, or millionths of one volt, with sufficient power to translate them into a written record that can be read by the human eye. This graphic record is called an *electroencephalogram* (EEG) and, in popular terminology, provides tracings of a person's "brain waves." The EEG is of relatively recent origin, although it is now well established as a useful diagnostic tool in clinical neurology and as a research technique in electrophysiology and experimental psychology.

Recordings of brain waves during sleep were first reported about thirty years ago,[6] but a coherent picture of the electrical activity shown in the EEG during sleep did not appear until much more recently, when continuous night-long recordings were collected by Eugene Aserinsky, William Dement, and Nathaniel Kleitman of the Department of Physiology at the University of Chicago.[7] Their research revealed that there was a cyclic pattern of four different states of EEG activity spanning the entire sleep period.

To appreciate the shifting EEG patterns accompanying a full night's sleep, imagine an experimental session in a laboratory devoted to the electroencephalographic study of sleep. The experimenter, who may be a psychologist, physician, or physiologist, attaches the recording electrodes to various points on the face and scalp of the subject, who is most likely a paid volunteer. In addition to electrodes positioned on the forehead and scalp to record brain waves, two or more are attached lateral to and/or above the subject's eyes to register changes in

FIGURE 1

The experimenter monitors the subject's brain waves and eye movements. The electroencephalograph amplifies the electrical potentials being recorded from the subject so that they deflect the pens in the ink-writing apparatus. A roll of moving paper is fed through the ink-writing apparatus during the entire night. On a typical night, some 700 or more feet of paper will be used to obtain a continuous record of the subject's brain waves and eye movements during sleep.

voltage associated with movements of the eyeball in its socket. When all electrodes are in place, the subject goes to a nearby sleeping room and gets into bed. The experimenter then gathers together wires from all the electrode disks and connects them to receptacles on a box at the head of the bed. The wires are sufficiently long so that the subject is free to toss and turn from side to side without affecting the electrode placements. From the box at the head of the bed, a cable leads to the electroencephalograph in the experimenter's room. The lights in the subject's room are turned off, and the experimenter retires to his room to begin his all-night monitoring of the continuous physiological record that the subject is producing. The accompanying drawings show the conditions of a sleep experiment such as this.

At this point, there might be some doubt that the subject can fall asleep or experience anything approaching natural sleep, given the fact that he has a number of electrodes pasted all over his face and scalp. There is also the possibility that he may be fearful of an electrophysiological recording technique that he only vaguely comprehends. It is true that during the first night in the laboratory many subjects experience some difficulty in falling asleep, but most of them soon come to feel quite comfortable there and can not only fall asleep with ease at the start of the night but can also return to sleep quickly after any awakenings that may be made during the course of the night—testimony to the seemingly limitless adaptability of human behavior.

Incidentally, one of the most interesting findings of EEG dream studies is that *physical* discomfort very rarely results in a total failure to fall asleep. Subjects have slept not only with EEG electrodes on their face and scalp but also, in various studies,

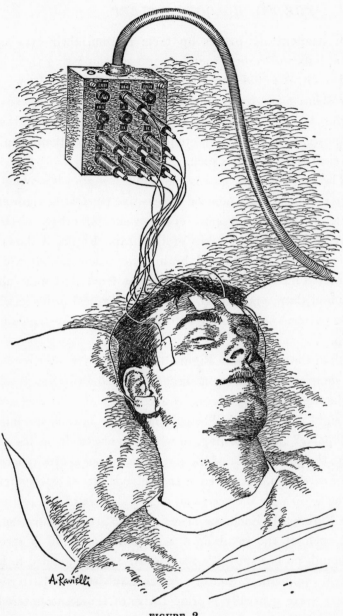

FIGURE 2

A subject in a sleep experiment. Electrodes are tiny metal discs which lie flat over various areas of the face and scalp and which are held in place either by elastic bandages or by collodion-impregnated gauze pads. Wires lead from each electrode disc to a receptacle in a "terminal box" at the head of the subject's bed. From this box a cable runs to an adjacent room where the electroenceph-alograph produces a "write-out" of the subject's brain waves and eye movements.

with temperature probes up their rectum, their eyes taped open, bulky ultrasonic sound devices encompassing their head, and so on. It would seem that difficulty in falling asleep generally stems more from *psychological* factors—such as anxiety during the first night in a new environment or expectation or reminiscence of exciting daytime events—rather than from any physical discomforts as such.

The experimenter spends the night scanning a moving roll of paper on which a number of sensitive pens write vigorously. Some of the pens record eye movements, others electrical activity from various areas of the brain. Figure 3 shows the various eye-movement and brain-wave tracings that are encountered during the subject's journey from alert wakefulness to sound sleep, and Figure 4 shows the typical order in which these patterns occur throughout the course of an average night's sleep.

All of the examples in Figure 3 were taken from the record of the same subject during a single night. The two pen tracings at the top of each specimen are recordings of the movement of the right and left eyes. The bottom tracing in each specimen is a "bipolar" EEG recording, in which an electrode on the scalp above the *parietal lobe* of the cerebrum, rather centrally located in the cerebrum, is referred to an electrode placed on the surface of the scalp near the *occipital*, or visual, area of the cerebrum (see Figure 7). Each specimen is of 2.5 seconds duration, so that each of the small lined segments represents .5 second. Although no one subject's EEG record can be assumed to be a perfect duplicate of that of any other subject, the patterns in Figure 3 are generally representative of those encountered in research with normal, young-adult subjects.

Specimen *A* in Figure 3 shows a record taken at the begin-

FIGURE 3. EEG and eye-movement patterns

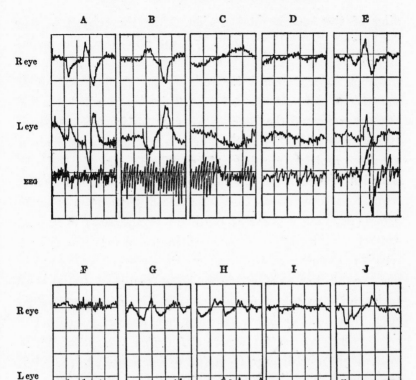

A. Low-voltage, fast EEG; REM; awake, eyes open.
B. Alpha EEG; REM; awake, eyes closed.
C. Alpha EEG; SEM; drowsy.
D. Low-voltage EEG, theta waves; NREM; EEG sleep descending stage 1.
E. K-complex; NREM; EEG sleep stage 2.
F. Sleep spindle; NREM; EEG sleep stage 2.
G. Spindles with delta waves; NREM; EEG sleep stage 3.
H. Delta waves; NREM; EEG sleep stage 4.
I. Low-voltage EEG, theta waves; moment of ocular quiescence; EEG sleep ascending stage 1 (REM sleep).
J. Alpha EEG; REM; EEG sleep ascending stage 1 (REM sleep).

ning of the experimental session, while the subject is still awake and alert and while his eyes are still open. The EEG is of relatively low voltage, reflected by the height of the pen tracings. As a standard for judging the absolute voltage of the various EEG patterns in Figure 3, it may be noted that the average value of the regular wave forms in specimen *B* is 40 microvolts (.00004 volt). The EEG tracings in specimen *A* are not completely regular in form. The absence of regularity is called *desynchrony,* since it is sometimes assumed that a regular pattern reflects the fact that adjacent brain cells are *firing* (reaching a phase of maximum excitability) in unison, while irregular patterns occur when the firing of adjacent cells is not synchronous.[8] What regularity may be observed in the EEG tracing is of relatively high frequency (number of *cycles,* or wave peaks, *per second*—cps; in this case, over 20 cps). The eye-movement tracings are recording horizontal motion whenever the two pens converge upon (an eye movement to the right), or diverge from (an eye movement to the left), one another. The eye movements in specimen *A* are rapid eye movements (REMS), and the sharply pointed spikes indicate fixations achieved at some particular place in the subject's visual field.

The next set of tracings, specimen *B* of Figure 3, was taken after the lights were turned out in the subject's room. The EEG is of greater amplitude now, and a regular wave form, a 10 cps, or *alpha, rhythm,* dominates the record. The subject's eyes are closed, and yet they still reveal rapid movements such as those associated with shifting eye-open perceptions. It has been known for some time that active and voluntary imagining is often accompanied by eye movements appropriate to the perception of the real object or situation being thought of,[9] and it has been demonstrated recently that REMs accompany semivoluntary daydreaming.[10] Specimen *B* shows, then, that the subject is probably engaged in some kind of voluntarily controlled reminiscence or imaginative thought or that he has lapsed into mind wandering or semivoluntary daydreaming. Eye movements with the eyes closed are sporadic rather than continuous, and their presence or absence probably depends upon the role of visual imagery in the subject's thought processes.

In specimen *C* of Figure 3, the alpha rhythm persists, although without the continuity or regularity observed in *B*. The behavior of the eyes is strikingly different from that heretofore observed, however. A slow, rolling drift has replaced the REMs, and fixation points are no longer obvious. The subject has lost voluntary control over the movement of his eyes, and they are rolling slowly back and forth in their sockets. Two recent studies have shown that subjects experimentally "awakened" from a period characterized by alpha-rhythm EEGs in association with such slow eye movements (SEMs) most often report that they were either "awake but drowsy" or "drifting off to sleep" immediately prior to the "awakening." [11]

A subject can reach the stage portrayed in specimen *C* even when his eyelids have been artificially taped open.[12] The movement of his eyes is likely to give an observer the feeling that the subject is slowly scanning the room and that he must, of course, be aware of all that he "sees." This impression appears to be erroneous, however. Recent research has demonstrated that the subject with eyes taped open is, during the alpha-SEM phase, likely to be functionally blind.[13] That is, he is quite unable to report the nature of various objects that the experimenter may wave before his open and slowly moving eyes.

Dement and Kleitman's pioneering investigations at the

University of Chicago indicated that the many and varied EEG tracings observed during sleep could be sorted efficiently into four classes, to which they assigned the labels "stage 1," "stage 2," "stage 3," and "stage 4." [14] Their classification system is now almost universally followed. Thus, some understanding of this system is essential to the comprehension of the findings of modern sleep research.

Specimen *D* of Figure 3 presents the tracings of a stage-1 sleep EEG: the alpha rhythm has disappeared and has been replaced by a low voltage, irregular pattern, with occasional 4–6 cps, or *theta*, waves of low to moderate amplitude. Slow eye movements may persist, or the eye tracings may reveal almost total quiescence. Subjects awakened from this phase most often report that they were "drifting off to sleep" or in "light sleep" immediately before their arousal.[15] The EEG stage 1 occurring at sleep onset is called *descending stage 1* (a "descent" from wakefulness to sleep), to distinguish it from the *ascending stage 1* (an "ascent" from sound sleep toward arousal) that terminates each sleep cycle (see Figure 4). One immediate difference between the two is that REMs are seldom, if ever, observed at sleep onset, while they almost invariably accompany ascending, or nocturnal, stage 1.

Specimens *E* and *F* of Figure 3 present two EEG and eye-movement tracings representative of stage-2 EEG sleep. Specimen *E* includes a *K-complex*, a sharp, high-voltage EEG slow wave with a "tail." The K-complex may be evoked in several EEG phases as the brain's reaction to, for example, an auditory stimulus sufficiently loud to elicit brain activity but not any observable signs of wakefulness. During stage 2, such complexes occur "spontaneously," that is, in the absence of any clearly defined external stimulation. Specimen *F* includes another EEG pattern characteristic of stage 2, the *sleep spindle*, a moderately low-amplitude wave whose usual frequency is 12–14 cps. Stage-2 sleep is defined electroencephalographically as that sleep stage characterized by the presence of K-complexes and sleep spindles and by the absence of both the alpha waves of wakefulness and the *delta waves* (1–3 cps, high-voltage waves) that define the more profound stages of sleep. Stage 2 seems, in many respects, to be intermediate or transitional. Subjects awakened from stage 2 generally describe their state prior to awakening as having been "light sleep." [16]

Specimens of *G* and *H* of Figure 3 portray, respectively, the EEG and eye-movement patterns of EEG stages 3 and 4. The common characteristic of these two stages is that both contain considerable delta-wave activity. As is true of the sleep spindle, delta waves are totally absent in the waking record of normal persons; unlike the spindle, however, they are sometimes seen in the waking records of persons suffering from chronic brain damage or in other states of impaired consciousness. Where a differentiation is made between stages 3 and 4—it is now common to treat the two stages as one—it is along these lines: in stage 3, spindles are still evident and delta waves, though present, are not overwhelmingly predominant; in stage 4, the record is essentially nothing but delta waves. Subjects aroused from EEG stages 3 and 4 are apt to be confused immediately upon awakening but usually assert that they have been in "light sleep." [17]

EEG stages 2, 3, and 4 are without REMs, indeed, without much significant ocular activity at all. What is noted in the eye tracings during these sleep stages is merely a *spillover* of brain-wave activity into the eye-movement record. Such brain-wave spillover is easily detected, since the tracings of both eyes follow the same pattern as that of the EEG rather than diverging from, or converging upon, one another, as they would when this particular method is used to record horizontal eye movements. Vertical eye movements would register in the same direction on both eye-movement channels, but they would produce much larger deflections there than in the EEG tracings, so that even these eye movements are distinguishable from brain-wave spillover. The several sleep stages portrayed in Figure 3 are often summarized dichotomously, with descending stage 1 and EEG stages 2, 3, and 4 (specimens *D–H*) described as non-REM (NREM) sleep and distinguished from ascending stage 1, in which REMs do occur intermittently.

Specimen *I* of Figure 3 is from this ascending stage-1 sleep that developed from sleep rather than from wakefulness. It looks very much like specimen *D*. There is a low-voltage EEG tracing with occasional theta waves. The eyes are relatively quiescent, and there is neither the alpha rhythm of wakefulness nor the K-complex, spindle, or delta activity of NREM sleep. Specimen *J*, however, reveals that the *ascending* period of stage 1 is qualitatively different from descending stage 1 in several immediately measurable aspects: REMs occur intermittently throughout the period as does alpha-rhythm activity—the latter more for some subjects than for others, but to a certain extent for most subjects. In these two respects, the ascending stage-1 REM period is more similar to certain forms of wakefulness (see specimen *B*) than to any other sleep stage. From behavioral observations, however, it is clear that the subject is asleep during ascending stage 1. He is generally immobile, relatively insensitive to external stimulation, and may be very difficult to wake up. Moreover, when he does awaken, he is likely to feel that he has just been in "deep sleep." [18] There is also a physiological difference between REM periods and wakefulness that can be detected; note, for instance, that the alpha rhythm is relatively slower, 8 cps, in specimen *J* than the waking tracing of 10 cps in specimen *B*. REM periods also contain certain "saw-toothed" EEG waves (not illustrated) and a sharply diminished tonus of neck and face musculature characteristic of neither wakefulness nor descending EEG stage 1.

There are four discriminably different phases of sleep, then— five if one distinguishes, as should be done, descending stage 1 from ascending stage 1. Stages 2, 3, and 4 are characterized by particular combinations of spindle, K-complex, and delta waves that are seldom if ever observed during wakefulness, and are accompanied by no rapid eye movement. Descending, or sleep-onset, EEG stage-1 sleep lacks the wave forms characteristic of other NREM sleep stages, but is also without rapid eye movement; ascending stage-1 sleep, however, features not only EEG patterns superficially similar to wakeful or drowsy EEG tracings, but also rapid eye movement much like that seen during wakeful, eye-open perception.

Figure 4 shows the order in which the several sleep stages are likely to occur over the course of a subject's night of sleep. It is an idealized picture, based upon group data reported by several investigators, rather than upon any one subject's actual sleep pattern on any given night.[19] It is, for this very reason, however, a better guide to what might be observed over an extended series of nights than any one particular night's pattern would be. It should be noted, however, that the apparently smooth transitions between sleep stages are somewhat misleading as applied to individual records. Abrupt changes in EEG stage, particularly

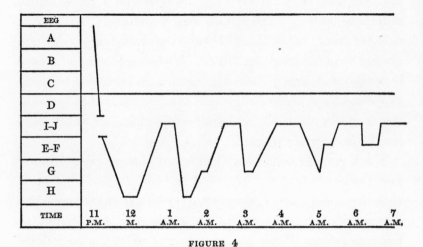

FIGURE 4

Distribution of EEG Activity in a Typical Night of Sleep. The letters
identify the same EEG and eye-movement patterns as in Figure 3.

in the ascending phases of the sleep cycle, for example, the
transition from stage 4 to stage 2, are often observed in individual subject-nights in the laboratory.

The most obvious revelation of Figure 4 is that a night's
sleep includes a recurring cycle of stage 1 to stage 2 to stage 3
to stage 4 to stage 3 to stage 2 to stage 1. An eight-hour sleep
period generally includes from four to six such cycles. The first
is completed an average of one hundred minutes after sleep
onset. Subsequent cycles take approximately the same time. It
is also clear from Figure 4, however, that the distribution of
stages within a cycle shifts during the night. In particular, later
cycles differ from early ones in two important respects: (1) A
greater proportion of each cycle subsequent to the first will be
spent in stage-1 REM sleep, with correspondingly less time spent
in NREM stages 2, 3, and 4. The first stage-1 REM period is

approximately ten minutes long; the second may be about twenty minutes in length; and, toward morning, these periods may persist for as much as forty to sixty minutes of a ninety- to one-hundred-minute cycle. (2) The nature of NREM sleep between these stage-1 REM periods also changes. Stage 4 will generally be experienced only in the first and, perhaps, the second cycles. Toward morning, the cyclic alternation may simply be stage 1 to stage 2 to stage 1.

It is apparent, then, that we do not simply sleep in some undifferentiated sense, but rather that during the course of the night we move through a recurring cycle that includes several different stages of sleep. This finding of qualitatively varying kinds of physiological sleep raises the question of the relative depth of these stages. For, although the detailed picture of these cyclic variations offered by electrophysiological recording techniques is new, the concept of different kinds, or "depths," of sleep is not. It is natural to inquire, therefore, which EEG stage is "light" sleep and which "deep" sleep.

Unfortunately, there seems to be no simple answer to this question. As has been noted, subjective judgments offered by the sleeper immediately following his arousal from the various sleep stages identify ascending stage-1 REM sleep as deep sleep and NREM sleep, including descending stage 1, as light sleep. But, as also noted, the stage-1 REM period looks, in terms of EEG and eye movements, as much like wakefulness as anything observed during sleep, while NREM sleep includes EEG wave forms that are rarely, if ever, observed when subjects are awake. In other words, the sleeper's subjective judgments identify as the deepest sleep that physiological stage apparently most similar to wakefulness.

A number of studies have been performed that are of some

value in clarifying this discrepancy between subjective impressions of sleep depth and its classification in terms of similarity of physiological responses to those observed during wakefulness. These studies employ one of three methods.

In the first approach, recourse is made to other physiological data collected during sleep. In which sleep stage, for instance, do heart rate, respiration, and so on most closely approach waking levels of intensity and variability? In which sleep stage are such variables most depressed as compared to wakefulness? The other two approaches return to the behavioral definition of sleep in terms of insensitivity to sensory stimulation and of minimal bodily motility. That stage of sleep will be deepest in which the sleeper is most insensitive to external stimulation and most immobile. Evidence relating to these three approaches to sleep depth—other physiological variables during sleep, sensitivity to external stimulation, and motor behavior—will not only put the question in sharper focus, but also add, in a more general sense, to our knowledge of the topography of sleep.

AUTONOMIC PHYSIOLOGICAL VARIABLES

The EEG is a measure of the functioning of the brain, the integrative center of the *central nervous system,* consisting of brain and spinal cord, which provides the organismic basis for mind and the means of integrating incoming sensory stimulation and of effecting voluntary motor responses. Many of the more vegetative functions of the human organism, however, are under the immediate regulation of the *autonomic nervous system,* a motor system innervating visceral organs such as the glands in eye, mouth, and throat, the heart, the lungs, the liver, the pancreas, the kidneys, the colon, and the bladder. The responses of these organs are less voluntary in the sense that one does not deliberately have to "will" one's breathing, heartbeats, and so on. Activities such as these are performed automatically, in normal circumstances in any case. Students of sleep have for some time been interested in the functioning of the autonomic nervous system during sleep. Such interest has been intensified since the discovery of the EEG sleep cycle, and there has been much research on the relationship of the autonomic variables of heart rate, blood pressure, respiration, skin resistance, body temperature, and peripheral sexual response to sleep stages defined in terms of central-nervous-system physiology, that is, EEG sleep.

Heart Rate.

In one of the most extensive EEG studies of sleep yet conducted, Joe Kamiya, a research psychologist now at the Langley Porter Neuropsychiatric Unit in San Francisco, observed twenty-five subjects for ten nights each.[20] In addition to taking continuous EEG recordings, he also registered the heart rate, respiration rate, and electrical skin resistance of a number of his subjects during sleep. He reported a trend of decreasing heart rate over the course of a night's sleep. Superimposed on this general decrease, however, was a significant tendency for heart rate to increase by an average of about 5 per cent during stage-1 REM periods as compared with heart rate during immediately preceding episodes of NREM sleep. This increase did not seem to be attributable to any changes in body motility. Kamiya also reported that heart-rate variability increased during stage-1 REM sleep and that this increased variability was also independent of body motility. Other scientists have reported data that fully confirm Kamiya's observations on heart rate and heart-rate variability.[21]

Blood Pressure.

It has also been reported that the basic trend during sleep for systolic blood pressure is an early fall followed by a sustained rise over the remainder of the sleep period.[22] Superimposed on this long-term trend is an increase in average level and variability of systolic pressure with the onset of stage-1 REM periods as compared to values computed from the preceding period of NREM sleep.

Respiration.

Kamiya also reports an over-all decline in respiration rate over the course of a night's sleep, but, as was also true for heart rate, the average value increased in stage-1 REM periods (by an average of one to two breaths per minute) as compared with the preceding period of NREM sleep.[23] Again, this rise in a measure of autonomic functioning was clearly independent of changes in body motility. Kamiya's observations have been confirmed, and a rise in respiratory variability with the onset of stage-1 REM periods has also been observed.[24]

Electrical Skin Resistance.

Electrical skin resistance is an inverse measure of the conductivity of the skin. Conductivity increases, and resistance decreases, with the experience of emotion, a fact that explains the use of skin-resistance measurement in "lie detectors." * It is customary to measure two separate aspects of skin resistance—the basal level and moment-to-moment change. The latter is sometimes associated with the presentation of specific stimuli (*galvanic skin responses,* or GSRS). At other times it appears

* For a discussion of skin resistance as an indicator of emotionality, see R. S. Woodworth and H. Schlosberg, *Experimental Psychology* (New York: Holt, Rinehart & Winston, Inc., 1954), chap. vii, pp. 185–191.

without any clear indication of a particular stimulus to which it might be a response ("spontaneous" GSRS).

Kamiya reports that skin resistance rises initially at sleep onset and that this rise is followed by a steady, though less rapid, increase in resistance over the rest of the night.[25] Kamiya was unable to demonstrate that conductivity, generally thought to be associated with arousal, increased during REM periods in the same manner as did the other arousal measures of heart rate, respiration, and so on. He reports that in NREM stages 2, 3, and 4 rather large GSRS were observed, ranging from a drop of 1,000–10,000 ohms in skin resistance. These large variations could not be traced to known external stimuli and hence were classified as nonspecific, or spontaneous, GSRS. Such sudden increases in conductivity did not occur during REM sleep.

Body Temperature.

Body temperature reflects basic metabolic processes. Since sleep is a state of relative inactivity, it might be expected that body temperature would be lower during sleep than wakefulness, and this expectation is substantiated by several studies.[26] In one, it was reported that rectal temperature reaches a low point sometime in the early morning and then starts to rise back toward waking levels.[27] However, rectal temperature is only "negligibly" higher during stage-1 REM periods than during NREM sleep.

Allan Rechtschaffen, psychologist at the Sleep Laboratory of the University of Chicago, and his associates, however, have found a striking and almost invariable increase in the brain temperature of cats at the onset of REM sleep.[28] It has also been discovered recently that cortical blood flow "increases markedly" during REM sleep.[29] Both of these responses indicate heightened cerebral metabolism during REM sleep and hence are central- rather than autonomic-nervous-system associated; but they are both further signs of an "aroused" quality of REM sleep.

Peripheral Sexual Response.

Other researchers reported recently that erections of the penis almost regularly accompany the REM phase of sleep in adult males and that the duration of the erection is generally coextensive with the duration of the REM period.[30]

Autonomic Physiology: Summary Statement.

The stage of sleep that, by superficial EEG analysis, appears to be most like wakefulness is also, by most autonomic criteria, the most activated, or aroused, state of sleep. During EEG stage-1 REM periods, there are increases in the average value and in the variability of heart rate, respiration, and blood pressure. Peripheral sexual arousal, in the form of penile erections, is observed. Data on the conductivity of skin tissue are an apparent exception to the trend of increased autonomic arousal during this sleep stage. In general, however, if an aroused condition of the autonomic nervous system is used as a criterion of "lightness" of sleep, stage 1 with accompanying REMs must be adjudged "light" sleep and NREM stages 2, 3, and 4, "deeper" sleep. Data on the central nervous system-associated variables of brain temperature and cerebral blood flow also seem to support this conclusion.

RESPONSIVENESS TO SENSORY STIMULATION

Several lines of evidence, then, lead to the classification of stage 1 as light sleep and of stages 2, 3, and 4 as deep sleep. Recent evidence on the determination of *sensory thresholds*—

which are the lowest intensity values of a stimulus which reliably elicit a reaction from an organism—during sleep, however, has made the classification of stage 1 as light sleep seem somewhat more uncertain. The stage 1 experienced at sleep onset is almost unequivocally light sleep—only relatively low-intensity stimuli are needed to elicit responses during this stage. But ascending stage 1 accompanied by REMs seems to defy any attempt at simple classification in terms of sleep depth. The present tendency is to conceive ascending stage 1 as "a neurophysiologically unique phase of sleep" [31] that is light in some respects but deep in others. Many of the light-sleep characteristics of ascending stage 1 have already been described. Now, briefly, to turn to evidence giving rise to the inference of deep sleep during this period.

Harold Williams, a psychologist at the Walter Reed Army Institute of Research in Washington D.C., and his associates, have measured "evoked responses" of the cerebral cortex of the brain to auditory stimulation ("click" sounds) during various sleep stages.[32] They found that the brain was most sensitive to such external stimulation—that is, gave the most evoked responses—in descending stage 1 and in stage 2, and was least sensitive to such stimulation—that is, gave the fewest evoked responses—during ascending stage-1 REM sleep. They conclude "that events from an external stimulus tend to be occluded" during stage-1 REM sleep.[33] In another study, Williams and his associates measured the EEG response, manifested, for example, in K-complexes, to an auditory stimulus in various sleep stages.[34] In sleep stages 2 and 3 there was consistently more EEG responsiveness to the external stimulus than there was during either ascending stage 1 with REMs or stage 4. By this criterion, then, both stage 4 and ascending stage 1 were deep sleep. The authors of this study employed another index of sleep depth: the performance of a behavioral response within fifteen seconds of the presentation of a stimulus. The subject was instructed that, whenever he heard an auditory stimulus during the night, he was to press a microswitch taped in the palm of his right hand. The percentage of responses to a tone of a given intensity was consistently high for sleep stages 2 and 3 relative to sleep stage 4 and ascending stage 1. The behavioral-response criterion also leads, then, to the classification of stages 1 (ascending) and 4 as deep sleep.

The search for an answer to the question of the relative depth of the several different stages of EEG sleep leaves one in some confusion; for by superficial EEG appearance and by signs of autonomic-nervous-system arousal, the REM phase of sleep seems to be lighter than the NREM phases, but by data of subjective classification of psychological state and of the responsiveness of the brain to external stimulation, REM sleep seems to be deeper than most NREM sleep.

These apparently discordant observations can be reconciled, however, by reference to the results of the study of Edward Evarts, a physiologist at the National Institute of Mental Health, of the activity of nerve cells in the brain during sleep.[35] Evarts inserted tiny microelectrodes in the visual cortex of the brain in several cats. These made it possible to record the spontaneous activity of single nerve cells, or *neurons*, in different stages of sleep. Evarts found that the mean rate of spontaneous discharge of neurons was significantly higher during REM sleep than during either NREM phases or wakefulness. This means that the relative unresponsiveness of the brain to external stimulation during REM sleep does not necessarily signify any depression of brain-cell activity; on the contrary, spontaneous firings exceed the rate achieved in total wakefulness.

These findings may be interpreted as follows. When one is attentive to something, he is less likely to be distracted by extraneous stimuli than might otherwise be the case. The child watching television with avid interest quite literally may not hear his mother calling, although she is speaking loud enough to be heard and understood by those less engrossed.* In this example, insensitivity to external stimulation is not indicative of mental lethargy; to the contrary, it reflects a high degree of attentiveness to the television program. During sleep no such attention-getting *external* stimulus exists to account for insensitivity to incidental external stimulation. But the high rate of spontaneous nerve activity in the brain and the elevated brain temperature suggest that an *internal*, or imagined, stimulus may be playing the same role during stage-1 REM sleep as does the television program for the waking child.

The hypothesis—based on spontaneous neural firing, cortical blood flow, and brain-temperature data—that during stage-1 sleep mental fantasy is especially vivid leads to an explanation of the four separate and somewhat contradictory aspects of stage-1 REM sleep: insensitivity to external stimulation—the subject is highly attentive to his internally generated fantasy and not easily distracted; judgment of sleep depth—the subject is highly engrossed in this sleep fantasy and thus feels his mental

---

* For an experimental demonstration of how attention to one aspect of the environment may induce "deafness" to another, see R. Hernández-Peón, H. Scherrer, and M. Jouvet, "Modification of Electric Activity in Cochlear Nucleus During 'Attention' in Unanesthetized Cats," *Science*, 123 (1956), pp. 331–332.

state to be deep; EEG—looks like wakefulness because the subject is mentally active in weaving fantasies; and autonomic-nervous-system arousal—the imagined mental experiences are exciting. If this analysis is correct, ascending stage-1 REM sleep should be characterized by especially vivid mental experiences, and, as shall be seen in the subsequent chapter, this expectation is amply justified by data collected in the last decade or so on the association of mental activity with EEG sleep stage. Also, if this analysis is correct, stage 4 is deep sleep and stage 1 is activated, or light, sleep. However, the inner focus of stage 1's activation leads to a paradoxical similarity to stage 4 when criteria of sleep depth involve responsiveness to distracting external stimulation.

Williams and his associates have recently reported evidence providing some support for the notion that the ascending stage-1 phase is light sleep in spite of the fact that subjects in this sleep stage are sometimes quite unresponsive to external stimulation.[36] These researchers showed that subjects who responded (by pressing microswitches taped to their hands) only very seldom to a tone stimulus presented during REM sleep under standard conditions were capable of much greater responsiveness when some special importance was attached to their noticing the tone. The experimenters made it a significant stimulus for subjects by attaching certain unpleasant consequences to a failure to attend to it. When the experimenters began "punishing" subjects' inattentiveness to the tone by sounding a loud fire alarm, flashing a light, and giving electrical shocks to the leg when the subjects failed to respond within four seconds of the tone presentation, subjects reacted to the no-longer irrelevant external stimulus at a rate comparable to that achieved during other EEG stages of light, low-voltage sleep.

Before leaving the topic of sensitivity to external stimulation during sleep, it might be well to consider briefly the frequently made allegation that we discriminate between meaningful and nonmeaningful stimuli during sleep. It is said, for instance, that a mother will hear her baby's slightest whimper while sleeping through incessant traffic noises from a nearby street. In an experimental test of perceptual discrimination during sleep, Ian Oswald, the British physician, and his associates played a tape containing many names for their sleeping subjects.[37] K-complexes, indicating the brain's responsiveness to external stimulation, were significantly more frequent and better formed when the stimulus was the subject's own name than when it was the name of another person or even his own name said backwards. These results were obtained from NREM stages 2 and 3 and indicate that, even in these moderately deep stages of sleep, the brain can carry out perceptual discriminations of some complexity.

MOTILITY

Body movements during sleep may be measured as artifacts in EEG recording (every time the subject moves the recording pen flicks back and forth violently) or by separate recording devices attached to the springs of the subject's bed. From analysis of extensive data it has been concluded that motility during sleep is common. To sleep like the proverbial log is an apparently unattainable, or at least unmet, standard. Since body movements do occur during sleep with some frequency, it is natural to inquire in which EEG sleep stages they are most, and least, likely to occur.

Kamiya reports that there are frequent body movements during sleep and that the body-movement rate is related to EEG sleep stages.[38] By and large, stage 4 is a period of relatively little motility. As sleep lightens, in stage 3 and especially stage 2, body movements increase, and motility is especially prominent just before the onset of, and at the conclusion of, ascending stage-1 REM periods. Motility during REM sleep is considerably greater than that observed in stage 4, but is less than that of the NREM sleep just prior to and subsequent to the REM period.

These data are in accord with the picture of sleep depth evolved above. Stage 4 is a deep, immobile sleep; stages 2 and 3 are lighter sleep and characterized by increased motility. Ascending stage 1 contains much motility, as befits a light period of sleep, but when compared with the immediately preceding and succeeding NREM sleep, it contains less motility, as is consistent with the notion of a focus of interest on inner reality. Think again of the child raptly watching television: he is less likely to fidget than one who is attending nothing in particular. When ascending stage-1 REM periods are compared with the over-all NREM stages, rather than with those portions of NREM sleep coming just before and after REM sleep, the correlation of motility with sleep depth is perfect. Oswald and his associates report that major body movements are most likely to occur in stage 1 sleep and least likely to occur in stages 3 and 4, with the frequency of movements in stage 2 intermediate between these extremes.[39] They note that "in so far as one would use the adjective 'deep' to describe sleep associated with few major body movements" these results are "consistent with the traditional classification of sleep depth." [40]

This motility is normal. Everyone tosses about during sleep. Other motor responses that are less frequently observed are talking and walking. The major study of "sleep talking" in relation to sleep stage was done by Allan Rechtschaffen, in collaboration with Donald Goodenough, a psychologist, and Arthur Shapiro, a physician, both associated with the Downstate Medical Center of the State University of New York.[41] These authors found sleep talking to be distributed throughout the night in a somewhat random fashion with respect to time but not with respect to EEG sleep stage. Sleep talking occurred predominantly in periods of NREM sleep, especially stage 2. Only 8 per cent of eighty-four sleep-talking incidents occurred during ascending stage-1 REM periods, while 63 per cent of such incidents occurred in stage 2. Sleep talking in NREM sleep almost always occurred with major muscle artifacts in the EEG, while REM sleep talk occurred without such artifacts. This suggests that muscle inhibition, in addition to an internal focus for attention, may account for the relative infrequency of overt speech during REM sleep. In this connection, it is interesting to note that there is a sudden drop in the tonus of neck muscles at the onset of REM sleep.[42] Since general body motility and trunk and limb muscle tonus persist into the REM period, there must be a selective inhibition of certain, predominantly neck and facial, musculature in this stage of sleep.[43] Kamiya's earlier data on sleep talking are in accord with those of the Rechtschaffen group: sleep talking generally occurs outside REM periods and is accompanied by general body motility; however, when an episode does occur during REM sleep, it may occur without any such movement.[44]

Sleepwalking, or *somnambulism*, has been studied by Allan Jacobson, of the Department of Anatomy at the University of California, Los Angeles, and his associates.[45] Of seventy-four incidents of coordinated movement recorded from nine subjects, only nine actually involved walking. In the other cases, the subject performed such reponses as sitting up and putting his feet on the floor. In every instance, activity began during the slow brain-wave patterns of NREM sleep, and, when the incident was of brief duration, there was no noticeable lightening of sleep. If a lighter sleep did occur, as was the case with longer incidents, it never included a REM phase. The segregation of sleepwalking from REM sleep was further seen in the concentration of somnambulistic episodes early in the night when REM sleep is at its minimum frequency.

In two studies of the performance of a previously learned motor response during sleep, subjects were to press a switch to diminish or avoid an unpleasant stimulus, such as a loud noise or electric shock.[46] In both cases, it was found that subjects responded during all stages of sleep. Although careful experimental studies of *sleep learning*,[47] the acquisition of new responses during a state of sleep, have produced negative results, it is still an impressive accomplishment of the sleeping organism to be able to perform, in a situationally appropriate manner, responses acquired during wakefulness and to be able to do so even during the deepest stage of sleep. As the authors of one of these studies note, such observations, in conjunction with the previously mentioned demonstration of perceptual discrimination during NREM sleep, "lend support to the idea that the 'higher mental states' continue to operate at some level of the nervous system even during *deep* sleep." [48]

Sleep, then, consists of a recurring, regular alternation of several different patterns of nervous activity of the brain, as indicated by EEG patterns. During one of these stages, ascending stage 1, there are numerous indications of physiological, and, presumably, psychological arousal: an EEG with characteristics also observed in wakefulness; intermittent rapid eye movements like those observed in wakeful perception and during certain kinds of wakeful mental activity; autonomic nervous system (heart rate, blood pressure, respiration, body temperature, sexual response) arousal; a high rate of spontaneous firing by individual neurons in the cerebral cortex of the brain; and a relatively high frequency of gross body movement. This regularly recurring stage of light sleep becomes increasingly predominant in later hours of sleep, and would seem likely to be capable of sustaining relatively intense mental activity.

Other phases of EEG sleep, particularly stages 3 and 4, seem to involve less organismic arousal than is commonly found during ascending stage-1 sleep. Autonomic variables, for example, are depressed relative to values achieved during either wakefulness or REM sleep, and body motility is relatively low. And yet, even during these phases of deeper, non-rapid-eye-movement sleep, there is ample evidence of the possibility of complex mental functioning: the brain is sensitive to external stimulation, as demonstrated by evoked responses, and is capable of reliably discriminating between meaningful and meaningless patterns of stimulation; relatively complex motor habits may be performed on appropriate cues; and such integrated, voluntary behavior patterns as walking and talking may be initiated. Even in deeper phases of the sleep cycle, then, it seems quite possible that meaningful mental activity may occur.

The next four chapters contain a detailed examination of the kinds of mental activity occurring in the different physiological phases of sleep described in the present chapter. The method of the studies to be reviewed is simplicity itself: the subject is awakened from various stages of EEG sleep and asked to report what, if anything, was passing through his mind immediately prior to having been awakened. The findings indicate a far more varied and intricate mental life during sleep than has been generally recognized and promise to open new paths to the study of the mind and personality of man. Chapters 2 and 3 consider data on mental activity during REM sleep; Chapter 4, data on mental activity during NREM sleep; and Chapter 5, data on mental activity during the sleep-onset period.

Chapter 2

MENTAL ACTIVITY DURING
REM SLEEP

R ECENT physiological discoveries, summarized in the previous chapter, indicate that there are several qualitatively different kinds of sleep. Most important, there is a diffusely activated phase of sleep accompanied by rapid eye movements and there is a non-rapid-eye-movement phase of sleep in
which various indexes of body functioning proceed at a slower
and more steady pace. The isolation of different kinds of sleep
has opened the way to the systematic study of mental processes
during sleep.

The physiological state that seemed the most probable locus
of vivid mental processes during sleep was ascending EEG stage 1

with its accompanying REMS. From evidence amassed in the past fifteen years or so, it is now clear that this stage of sleep is associated with those vivid, hallucinatory, and distorted mental dramas called dreams. The establishment of this association has made it possible to provide reliable answers to many of the perplexing questions that have always arisen concerning dreaming. By making careful observations of the characteristics of the sleep stage in which dreaming occurs, it is now possible to state with some certainty, for instance, how long dreams last and how often we dream.

What is now known about mental activity during REM sleep can be traced back to the investigation of the sleep patterns of human infants conducted during the early 1950's at the University of Chicago by Kleitman and Aserinsky. Kleitman had devoted much of his scientific career to the study of sleep, and so, for him, this particular investigation was but another step in his efforts to describe and explain the nature of this physiological process. It was a study to have more far-reaching implications, however, than any other he had ever made, for in the course of it, the cyclic nature of eye-movement activity during sleep was discovered—and, in the wake of this finding, came practically all of the physiological and psychological research findings that are the subject matter of this book.[1]

The occurrence of "peculiar rapid eye movements" [2] during periods of low-voltage brain-wave activity, an apparent "light" sleep stage, suggested to Aserinsky and Kleitman that such eye movements might be associated with a visual form of intense mental activity—dreaming. This hypothesis was tested in a subsequent study with adult subjects, who were awakened after intervals of sleep with and without REMS. The results of this study were that:

Twenty out of twenty-seven replies from individuals who were awakened after rapid eye movements had been observed, yielded detailed dream descriptions in contrast to 19 out of 23 replies from persons awakened in the absence of eye movements, which revealed a complete failure to recall dreaming. . . .[3]

Although no attempt was made to secure a thorough account of the recalled dream events during the extremely brief interrogation, there were reports revealing strikingly vivid visual imagery, especially after the subjects were awakened following the eye movements. It is indeed highly probable that the rapid eye movements are directly associated with visual imagery in dreaming.[4]

The probability of this last assertion seemed even higher, when one recalled the studies several decades earlier showing the involvement of muscular (including oculo-muscular) activity in thinking processes. Edmund Jacobson, the American physiologist, had shown that when a subject was told to "imagine" bending his right arm, *action potentials*, indications of changes in the electrical potential of muscle tissue, could be recorded from the right biceps; but action potentials could not be recorded from the right biceps when the subject was told to "imagine" bending, or to actually bend, his left arm.[5] The failure of some subjects to show action potentials in the biceps when imagining activities involving the arms led Jacobson to investigate the action of the muscles controlling eyeball movement; the hypothesis was that such subjects might be visualizing, rather than implicitly performing, the imagined act. During visual imagination suggestions, his recordings indicated tension in the muscle units controlling the movement of the eyeball. Furthermore, the direction of ocular activity was found to be associated with the content of the imagination performance:

For instance, the pattern for imagining Eiffel Tower is practically identical with the patterns of the same subject for looking upward. Evidently in imagining the tower, the subject's eyeballs move upward, somewhat as they would upon actually seeing a tower.[6]

Such results were consistent with a then current hypothesis, the "motor" theory of John B. Watson (1878–1958), founder of behavioristic psychology.[7] Watson stressed that thinking was an implicit form of overt behavior. He imagined that thinking "out loud" (by speech) is the natural thing but that in the course of development the child learns (or is forced) to "keep his thoughts to himself." Watson predicted that traces of this overt, or active, muscular nature of thought might still be observed in the throat muscles of adults who seemed to have completely mastered the skill of silent thought. He had suggested that deaf-mute subjects, since their speech mechanisms (hands) are so much more accessible to observation than the speech mechanisms of normals, would provide interesting data concerning the peripheral-muscular basis of thought; and he had reported some preliminary observations:

> I have collected considerable evidence that those deaf and dumb individuals who when talking use manual movements instead of words, use the same manual responses they employ in talking, in their own thinking. But even here society forces minimal movements so that evidence of overt responses is often hard to obtain. . . . Dr. Samuel Gridley Howe, Superintendent of the Perkins Institute and Massachusetts Asylum for the Blind, taught the deaf, dumb, and blind Laura Bridgman a hand and finger language. He states (in one of the annual reports of the Institute) *that even in her dreams Laura talked to herself using the finger language with great rapidity.*[8]

In 1935, an experimental test of this anecdotal observation was provided.[9] Action potential bursts were recorded from the arms of nineteen deaf-mute subjects. The subjects were tested as they were about to fall asleep and during sleep. All showed a decrease in action potentials as they drifted from wakefulness to sleep, although, in most cases, the potentials did not entirely disappear. In thirty-three instances, large action-potential bursts were noted during sleep. Subjects were awakened during these periods, and in thirty cases dreams were reported. Of sixty-two awakenings made during periods of relative muscular quiescence, only nine produced reports of dreams. Tests on normal control subjects showed no instances of action potentials in either arms or legs, yet dreams were reported by them following awakenings from such periods of muscular quiescence. Since normal subjects neither talk nor think, in general, with their hands, it would not be expected that their dreams would be detectable through changes in action potentials of the arm. But the findings with deaf-mutes did suggest that the dreams of normal subjects might well be detectable when electrodes were placed to record action potentials from muscular groups involved in normal imaginative thought, for example, the ocular muscles when thinking is conducted in the form of visual imagery.

These experiments bolstered the plausibility of Aserinsky and Kleitman's speculation on the association of visual dream imagery and REMs during sleep; they also indicated that their observations were, in a sense, long-overdue extensions to normal subjects of the findings with deaf mutes. In any event, the immense potential value of having a reliable sign of dreaming sleep now suggested to Kleitman and his co-workers, William Dement and Edward Wolpert, that the association of dreaming with REM sleep must be further investigated until it could be asserted beyond any reasonable doubt.

CONFIRMATION OF THE ASSOCIATION OF REM SLEEP WITH DREAMING

ASSOCIATION OF REM SLEEP WITH DREAM REPORTS

Dement and Kleitman awakened each of nine subjects several times every night that they spent at the laboratory.[10] Awakenings were sometimes made during ascending stage-1 REM periods and sometimes during NREM sleep stages 2, 3, and 4. Their criterion of dream recall was as follows: "Subjects were considered to have been dreaming only if they could relate a coherent, fairly detailed description of dream content. Assertions that they had dreamed without recall of content, or vague, fragmentary impressions of content, were considered negative." [11] By this criterion, 80 per cent of the 191 REM awakenings produced dream recall. A recent review demonstrates that the association of a high frequency of dream reports with REM sleep is now established beyond any possibility of doubt.[12] In this review the findings of the original Chicago studies and many subsequent ones were pooled, thus producing a sample of over two hundred subjects and of over two thousand REM-period awakenings. The proportion of dream recall from REM sleep in this pooled sample was 83.3 per cent.

LENGTH OF DREAM REPORT AND LENGTH OF REM PERIOD

The above data suggested that dreaming is an ongoing process during REM sleep, but they did not actually demonstrate such an association. It was possible that the dreams occurred at some other time, but were, for some reason, better recalled during ascending stage-1 REM periods. Confronted with this possibility, Dement and Kleitman sought additional evidence to demonstrate that REM sleep is dream sleep, not just dream-recall sleep.

If the dream actually did occur during REM sleep, it would be expected that the longer the REM period prior to the experimental awakening, the longer the dream report should be. Dement and Kleitman awoke each of five subjects on a random basis either five or fifteen minutes after the onset of the REM period.[13] Subjects were able to guess accurately, on the basis of the length of their dream narrative, whether they had been dreaming for five or fifteen minutes. In addition, Dement and Kleitman showed that for each subject, the length of the dream narratives (number of words) significantly increased as the duration of REM periods from which the narratives were elicited increased.

REPORTED VISUAL IMAGES AND PATTERNING OF REMS

REMs do not occur continuously throughout ascending stage-1 sleep, and, when they do occur, they may be either horizontal movements to the left or right or vertical movements up or down. These facts make it possible to investigate whether the REMs the subject does have are related to particular visual images experienced during REM sleep. For example, if he reports pre-awakening mental experiences of shifting visual imagery only following periods of ocular activity and if the directional quality of the shifting visual fixation in the reported dream corresponds with the preawakening eye-movement direction, then it would seem clear that his eye movements are executed in association with the visual characteristics of the dreams he reports. It would also be clear that the dream experiences actually occurred during the periods of REM activity just prior to his being awakened from ascending stage 1.

Dement and Kleitman aroused subjects when one of four different patterns of REM activity had persisted for at least one minute.[14] These were: (1) predominance of vertical eye movements; (2) predominance of horizontal eye movements; (3) mixture of vertical and horizontal eye movements; and (4) essentially no REMS at all. Subsequently elicited reports proved to bear a relationship to the preawakening REM patterning.

The first and second patterns were rare, but when observed, they were associated with reports appropriate to the eye movement. In one instance of predominantly vertical movement, "the dreamer was throwing basketballs at a net, first shooting and looking up at the net, and then looking down to pick another ball off the floor." [15] During predominantly horizontal eye movement, a subject dreamed that he "was watching two people throwing tomatoes at each other." [16] Reports of dreams during the third category of eye movement were of the subject actively inspecting and interacting with people and objects perceived close-up, while reports in the fourth category "all had the common property that the dreamer was watching something at a distance or just staring fixedly at some object." [17]

Dement and Wolpert extended the analysis of the relation of the direction of eye movements to dream content by further classifying vertical movements into "up" or "down" and horizontal ones into "left" or "right." [18] Of thirty-nine dreams collected from six subjects, the last dream event was recalled well enough in twenty-three cases to permit a comparison of dream content with the direction of the last eye movement prior to awakening. These authors report that the last eye movement was identical with the last reported visual fixation in the dream narrative in seventeen cases, a value much in excess of what would be expected by chance were there no real association of eye movement direction and dream imagery.

Moreover, in dream narratives obtained following periods of much REM activity, the dreamer tended to play an active role, while dream narratives obtained following periods of little REM activity tended to cast the dreamer in a more passive role.[19] These results are what might be expected were the REM activity of the subject to correspond to his hallucinated dream activities, although a more precise hypothesis would have attempted to relate eye movements to the amount of perceived movement or of visual scanning in the dream. In a similar vein, it has been reported that the vividness of dream content relates positively to the frequency of REMs prior to REM-period awakenings.[20]

Other researchers have confirmed the association of the amount of REM activity with the hallucinated role of the subject in his dream.[21] When there are many REMs, the dreamer's role tends to be active; when there are few REMs, his function tends to be passive. The association of the timing and directionality of REM activity with alternations in the timing and directionality of the dreamer's subsequently reported hallucinated visual behavior during sleep has also been confirmed.[22] There can be little doubt, then, that dream reports elicited from REM sleep are reports of mental activity actually experienced during such sleep, and that REMs are often executed in association with the nature of such mental activity.

OTHER REM-SLEEP PHYSIOLOGICAL/BEHAVIORAL INDEXES AND DREAM CONTENT

It also has been demonstrated that certain other measurable aspects of REM sleep are correlated with the nature of REM content. Dement and Wolpert [23] reported that gross body movements during REM sleep provide the demarcation point between separate episodes in the dream, a finding confirmed in a second investigation.[24] An awakening at the moment of such movement may produce a report that a dream has just ended, while arousal a few minutes after such movement may produce a report of a short dream preceded by a separate, but related, longer dream. A more specific relationship between muscular response and dream content has been reported by Wolpert.[25] He showed that action potentials in wrist muscles during REM periods tended to be associated with dream reports including the recent hallucination of wrist-involved activities, such as picking up something with the hand.

It has been somewhat more difficult to demonstrate that autonomic physiological activities during sleep are correlated with subsequently obtained dream reports. That is, although vivid mental activity (dreaming) occurs in association with an autonomically activated stage of sleep, variations in its intensity are apparently not reliably related to variations in amount of autonomic arousal during this stage of sleep. In one study, no association was found between the excitement value of dream content and heart or respiratory rate.[26] Similarly, the data of another study fail, with one exception, to show a relationship between autonomic arousal and dream intensity.[27] This one relationship is in the reverse direction from that expected, *lower* rectal temperatures associated with more exciting dreams. If recalling a dream versus not recalling one is considered to constitute a scale of dream intensity, however, it should be noted that more respiratory variability has been reported before recall-producing REM awakenings than preceding no-content REM awakenings.[28]

A final technique for determining whether reports following REM-period awakenings represent mental activity that actually occurs during REM sleep involves the application of external stimuli during this stage. In a series of experiments in which the effects of external stimuli on dream content were observed (for a fuller account, see Chapter 7), it sometimes happened that the stimulus failed to awaken the subject.[29] In such cases, he was aroused a short time afterward. The authors report that, in these circumstances, the narrative might incorporate the stimulus but include subsequent material of a duration that approximated the actual time between stimulus application and awakening. For instance, a subject was sprayed on the back with cold water and awakened thirty seconds later. The last portion of his dream report, involving a theatrical production, was:

> I was walking behind the leading lady, when she suddenly collapsed and water was dripping on her. I ran over to her and felt water dripping on my back and head. The roof was leaking. I was very puzzled why she fell down and decided some plaster must have fallen on her. I looked up and there was a hole in the roof. I dragged her over to the side of the stage and began pulling the curtains. Just then I woke up.[30]

Thus, there seems to be little doubt that the stimulus intruded upon an ongoing REM-sleep dream that continued from the point of stimulus application until awakening.

This line of evidence secures the already well-supported hypothesis that the high frequency of dream reports observed on REM-sleep awakenings reflects ongoing dream activity indigenous to this stage and closely correlated with its physiological manifestations. With an apparently reliable sign of the occurrence of dream activity, it became possible for researchers to try to tackle many of the persistent questions about dreaming that had hitherto lacked any reasonably well-confirmed answers.

SOME PERSISTENT QUESTIONS ABOUT DREAMING
HOW LONG DO DREAMS LAST?

Folklore has it that dreams occur instantaneously or that their duration is, at any rate, much briefer than that of the real-life events they purport to portray. Such contentions are not borne out by research on REM-period dreams. These periods are rarely less than ten minutes long and may last for an hour or more. That this time is devoted to dreaming one dream or one series of related episodes, rather than hundreds of "instantaneous" dreams, is suggested by several lines of evidence. It has already been noted that the length of the subsequently retrieved dream narrative is proportional to the amount of REM sleep prior to the subject's awakening. Furthermore, Dement has shown that the acting out, in waking life, of the content of the dream narrative takes about as long as the duration of the REM period from which the dream was reported.[31]

HOW OFTEN DO WE DREAM?

This question can now be translated into: how often do we experience REM periods of sleep? The answer seems to be that there is an average of four or so REM periods in the course of a typical night's sleep. As Dement has argued, the occurrence of body-movement demarcated episodes within most REM periods means that the number of dream episodes is even greater than the number of REM periods.[32] As shall be seen in subsequent chapters, the occurrence of some dreaming outside REM sleep means that any estimate of dream frequency based on this stage of sleep alone is still likely to be an underestimate. It must be concluded, then, that we dream very often, spending much of each night's sleep in dreaming. The best estimate of the proportion of sleep spent in REM periods for young-adult subjects is 24 per cent for a six- to seven-hour sleep period.[33] During childhood and adolescence and during periods of life subsequent to the young-adult stage, the proportion of sleep spent in REM periods is slightly lower than this.[34]

DO SOME PEOPLE DREAM ALL THE TIME, OTHERS NEVER?

Everyday observations suggest wide individual differences in the frequency of dreaming. If ten acquaintances are chosen at random and asked how often they dream, the answers are likely to range from several times every night to once every two or three months. When individuals who claim they dream often ("dreamers") are compared with those who claim they seldom, if ever, dream ("nondreamers"), however, it turns out that these groups do not differ in the number of REM periods they experience while sleeping in the laboratory.[35] Furthermore, nondreamers do report dreams after many of their REM-sleep awakenings,[36] so it appears that dreaming does accompany at least a fair proportion of their REM-period sleep. On the basis of evidence such as this, it is now commonly held that the apparent widespread differences in dream frequency that might be encountered in such an informal poll are actually variations in memory of dreams rather than differences in dream frequency.

THE FORGETTING OF DREAMS

The evidence above suggests that dreaming is a much more pervasive activity than is usually imagined. Why is this so?

Why are we aware of only a small fraction of our nocturnal dream life? Actually, two separate questions are raised by experimental evidence on REM-period dream recall: (1) why do we, all of us, seem to forget so many of our dreams? and (2) why do some of us seem to forget many more of our dreams than do others?

THE FORGETTING OF REM-PERIOD DREAMS

There is one additional argument for associating REM sleep with dreaming: awakenings made during NREM sleep only a few minutes after the termination of a REM period produce very little dream recall. Dement and Kleitman report that: "The incidence of dream recall dropped precipitously almost immediately upon cessation of REMs." [37] In another investigation, it was reported that, during ascending stage-1 sleep, 85 per cent of awakenings produced "detailed recall," while awakenings made within five minutes after the termination of ascending stage-1 sleep produced no instances of "detailed recall." [38]

It is obvious, then, that unless a subject is awakened during a REM period, he is likely to forget the mental content then experienced. Much of everyday dream recall probably comes from REM periods that happen to be experienced just before waking up. Since one is seldom awakened during earlier REM periods, a natural process of forgetting their mental content occurs. One of the great values of the experimental study of dreaming when the EEG is used is that many of these early-night dreams, which would otherwise be almost totally forgotten, can be detected, and, when awakenings are made, their content recorded.

Though it is obvious that REM-period dreams are forgotten with the termination of that stage, it is far from clear why this is so. It has been suggested that NREM sleep does not provide adequate neural conditions for the memory traces of REM mentation to "consolidate." [39] A like process may be observed when a blow on the head apparently interferes with neural processes and causes *retrograde amnesia*, the forgetting of events experienced just prior to receiving the shock. In both cases, it is alleged that neural processes are in some manner not adequate for the transformation of short-term memories into long-term ones. Modern theory, however, stresses that failures of memory are less often due to the absence of relevant memory traces than to failures to make such traces available to conscious memory. Under extraordinary circumstances, for example, direct electrical stimulation of the temporal lobe of the brain,[40] vivid memories that have been hitherto inaccessible may be retrieved. One wonders whether trace unavailability rather than trace absence might not be the case with REM-period dreams as well. There are suggestions, in the reference sometimes made in subsequent dreams to previous ones, and in apparent *déjà-vu* experiences—those feelings that one has encountered a situation before, although he is not sure when or where—in wakefulness that are later traced back to hitherto forgotten dreams, that REM-period dreams do leave adequate memory traces. There must be something, still unknown, about the way in which these traces are "filed" that renders them generally inaccessible to consciousness unless wakefulness intervenes very soon after the original impressions are experienced.

INDIVIDUAL DIFFERENCES IN THE FORGETTING OF REM-PERIOD DREAMS

Certain people have nearly total inability to recall dreams while others can recall them almost daily under the generally prevailing patterns of sleep in which REM periods are only occasionally terminated by awakenings. What causes these differences? It seems apparent, from evidence already surveyed, that they are, for the most part, variations in dream recall rather than in dream occurrence. Research into the causes of the selective forgetting of REM-period dreams has focused on three kinds of variables: characteristics of the REM period itself—maybe the dreams of some people have qualities, indexed in physiological manifestations during REM sleep, that make them less memorable than the dreams of others; characteristics of the awakening stimulus—perhaps those who luxuriate in slowly awakening have an advantage over those of us who must jump up and turn off an alarm clock; and characteristics of personality of those who are attempting to recall these REM-period dreams—some people really may not *want* to recall their dreams.

REM-*Period Differences.*

"Nondreamers" have been found to have REM periods marked by more alpha EEG activity than "dreamers." [41] It has also been found that nondreamers have more eye movements during REM sleep than do dreamers.[42] By both of these criteria—alpha per cent and eye-movement rate—the REM periods of nondreamers appear, paradoxically, more aroused or wakeful than those of the dreamers—paradoxically because it would seem that a condition of arousal or relative wakefulness would promote better dream recall. But it may be that it is precisely because his psychophysiological state is more aroused and the associated content presumably more vivid or intense, that the subject is motivated to forget his dream. In any event, there are differences among individuals in the kinds of REM periods they have, and these are associated with variations in the amount of dream recall. The nature of the content to be recalled may account, in part, for differing rates of remembering nocturnal fantasy after arousal.

The Awakening Stimulus.

Several studies of the effects of gradual as opposed to abrupt awakenings on dream reporting have been conducted.[43] In a typical gradual-awakening procedure, a tone is increased in 4 decibel steps from 0 decibel intensity until the subject terminates it by lifting a phone from its cradle. On abrupt awakenings, the tone sounds initially at 80 decibels, a value sufficiently intense to almost immediately alert the subject. In general, there is a small, but *statistically significant,** tendency for gradual awakenings to produce more thoughtlike reports than abrupt awakenings. In such reports, there are fewer indications of typical dream characteristics—perceptual imagery, bizarre action sequences, and so on. So it appears that gradual awakenings are less apt to produce vivid dream recall than are abrupt arousals. To the extent that individuals habitually experience one or the other kind of awakening in their usual sleeping environment, this variable may account for a small portion of the individual differences found in everyday dream recall.

Personality Characteristics.

Several recent studies seem to indicate that nondreamers are generally more inclined than dreamers to *repress* (keep from conscious awareness) significant psychological experiences.[44] Subjects who say they dream infrequently or who fail to

* A statistically significant difference is one for which the probability of occurrence by chance alone is very slight, less than one chance out of 20, hence, a probably genuine difference and one that would recur were further samples of observations to be taken.

report many dreams while keeping a dream diary are inclined to deny anxieties and engagement in daytime fantasy and tend to score high on psychological tests measuring repression and inhibition.

In a recent study in our laboratory, it was noted that several personality traits (assessed by means of the California Psychological Inventory) correlated significantly with questionnaire responses indicating everyday impressions of dream recall, but did not correlate with actual laboratory recall after nocturnal REM-sleep awakenings.[45] The personality variables related to impressions of dreaming, but not to actual dreaming, were degree of conformity to social standards, degree of self-control, and tendency to conceal less desirable aspects of one's own personality. The nature of the relationship in each case was negative: highly conformist, self-controlled, and defensive individuals had impressions of minimal dream recall; and less conformist, self-controlled, and defensive individuals had impressions of maximal dream recall. These results are thus generally consistent with the association between repression and denial and nondreaming found by previous investigators.

A trait that we found to be associated, again negatively, with everyday impressions of recall but that was also negatively associated with actual recall in the laboratory was "psychological mindedness," assessed by the California Psychological Inventory. This finding indicated that the person who does not show much interest in his private and subjective world of thoughts and feelings in waking life (who, therefore, might be thought of as something of a represser) was a relatively good recaller of his dreams. This seems inconsistent with the other results of our study and with the results of previous investigators, all of which demonstrated that repression was associated with relatively poor daytime dream recall.

Part of the explanation of this discrepancy may lie in the fact that the trait of psychological mindedness correlated negatively not only with questionnaire responses on daytime impressions of dream recall (the focus of all previously cited findings) but also with nocturnal recall in the laboratory. As noted in Chapter 8, the actual occurrence of nocturnal dreaming, indexed by laboratory recall on REM-sleep awakenings, seems to be negatively associated with self-awareness. It might be expected that waking impressions of dream occurrence would be at least partially accurate, that is, that they would at least somewhat reflect the true occurrence of nocturnal dreaming. In fact, in our study, we did observe a significant positive association between daytime impressions of dream frequency and actual nocturnal dream recall. To the extent, then, that waking impressions of dream occurrence reflect not only waking personality but also the true occurrence of nocturnal dreaming, they may be found to correlate negatively not only with personality variables indicating waking disinterest in subjective experiences such as dreams, but also with whatever personality variables prove to be negatively correlated with the actual occurrence of REM-sleep dream recall.

The bulk of the evidence now available seems to indicate that some portion of individual differences in everyday dream recall is attributable to a waking personality dimension that might be labeled self-awareness, manifested in the relative absence of the defenses of repression or denial as applied to one's own inner thoughts and feelings. Those who generally deny or ignore their world of private and subjective experience during wakefulness seem to recall fewer dreams than do those who accept and exploit this dimension of experience. To the extent that everyday impressions of dream recall are *accurate* reflections of memory after nocturnal awakenings from REM sleep, however, these impressions may also prove to be related to whatever personality variables are tied to actual nocturnal dream recall. That is, daytime impressions of dream occurrence may reflect two rather different sets of personality variables: those associated with a waking interest or disinterest in the subjective realm from which dreams arise, and those that happen to be correlated with the actual experience of vivid fantasy during REM-sleep, as revealed by dream recall on nocturnal awakenings from this stage of sleep.

Chapter 3

THE NATURE OF
THE REM-SLEEP DREAM

THERE have been epochs in the history of Western civilization in which dreams have been treated with great reverence, as signs and portents of a spirit world or as messages from heavenly powers. There have been other periods in which dreams have been regarded as idle sputterings of the brain, meaningless bits of mental fluff to which only fools would pay attention. In our own era, under the influence of psychoanalytic theory, dreams are regarded as revelations, not of the divine, but of our own inner selves.

The discovery of electrophysiological techniques of dream detection has given renewed impetus to the attempts to account for the nature of dreams: surely an activity as pervasive as these methods have revealed dreaming to be must have some significance for man. The identification of dreaming with a particular physiological state has also made possible, for the first time, the collection of the kind of sample of a person's dreams seemingly required to establish precisely what that significance might be.

In the present chapter, the nature of the dreamlike mental content reported from rapid-eye-movement (REM) sleep is examined from the point of view of its significance or meaning. Two different approaches are followed: first, a detailed study and interpretation of particular REM-sleep dream specimens, and, then, a look at statistical findings on the general properties of the mental content reported from REM sleep. Both of these kinds of evidence make it clear that dreams, however "crazy" they may first appear, are meaningful, and, as the psycho-analyst might insist, that they reveal feelings, motives, and so on, that people often are unable to recognize when awake.

Two dream specimens follow. The first (Report *A*) was collected from a subject on the second awakening of his third night in the laboratory.[1] The awakening was made eight seconds after the initial onset of REMs during a period of ascending stage-1 sleep and thus is representative of the early formative stage of REM-dreaming. The second specimen (Report *B*) is from the next, or third, awakening of the same night. This arousal was made many minutes after the initial onset of REMs during a period of ascending stage-1 sleep and is representative of fully formed REM-dreaming. These two specimens have been selected because they reveal, in a highly concrete form, most of the important characteristics of REM dreams and because this subject's excellent memory, his articulateness, and his readiness to probe, both awake and asleep, into his own inner self yield an extensive vista of mentation during REM sleep.

TWO REM-SLEEP DREAM SPECIMENS

REPORT A

(*A*–1) Well, it seems that there were two people in the dream, me and someone else, I think my wife. I think something was being decided about us and it seems as though we were around Rockefeller Chapel, and then walked away from there, went some place, and that seemed to be what we were doing whenever you woke me up.

(*A*–2) It seemed as though we came out of the west side of the Chapel, then sort of made a big circle, starting to head east again, a big circle south and then back toward the east. I don't even know if we came out or if I was just outside waiting. It seems as though she was inside and I was alone waiting. I'm really not sure.

(QUESTION: Do you know what this was that was being decided?) I can't think of what it was that was being decided. It wasn't a decision we were making between ourselves, it was a decision that some other party was making, or some other group.

(QUESTION: And how were you to be informed of the result?) I don't really know. I guess through my wife, but I don't really know if I thought of that.

REPORT B

(*B*–1) It had something to do with this choir business. It seems as though we had been singing something and came to a break time. I guess I really wasn't singing at all, but my wife had been. Anyway I was in there during the break time, and, as I was standing there, some member of the choir, a person who was in charge of getting refreshments and things at the break, asked me to go and get something for the break. It was sort of something like these—I guess they still have them, but I remember them from a long time ago—they were these little wax bottles that you just break the top off the little bottle and drink this sweet juice that's inside. And she said to get about five dollars' worth of these and something else that was rather expensive, and so I went out to get them, and then all of a sudden the scene changed.

(*B-2*) I was somewhere near a lake front, or some sort of waterfront, which was sort of a recreation place. I mean there were people swimming and this sort of thing, and I was on some sort of a high walkway, which people were diving off of doing all sorts of fancy dives, and which was very high.

But as I walked out on this thing I recalled that I didn't have any money with me and yet this lady, who was very snobbish, had said to get it with my own money and charge it up to the books of the choir. But I was thinking what should I do, because they were waiting for me to bring this stuff back, and yet I didn't have any money. And so I walked out on this thing and there were people diving off and this thing was built up high out of boards and things, and there were kids jumping and just barely missing hitting these boards and things. I thought that it really would have been awful if one of these little kids, in jumping, had not jumped out far enough or something and hit one of the boards.

(*B–3*) Anyway, I somehow, I don't recall how, got this stuff and was heading back with it. And then, all of a sudden I was there, and while I was there I was trying to explain that I had had the money to buy this stuff, but in the meantime the scene changed again.

(*B-4*) It was sort of a place behind where the choir sung, and they had sort of monuments to members of the choir. It was sort of in a stairway that goes up to the loft in Rockefeller Chapel, where the choir practice was. Anyway, they had sort of a monument to the singers in the choir. Right at the very bottom was sort of a table, and underneath the table, this was all sort of built into the wall at the side of the stairway, they had a model of me in some sort of wax, lying there huddled under this table. It wasn't at all flattering, and it struck me that it was the work of some very disdainful attitude toward me, and I said something to the effect that, well, I guess they don't know a real artist when they see one, or something like this. Anyway, so I said something of that sort, and that seemed to be all of that dream.

(B–5) But then I was somewhere else, I seemed to be back in the store where I worked during my high school days back home. It has very big plate-glass windows in the front, and I was looking out. And, let's see, well before this dream I was dreaming—it seemed to me sort of a fragment that I can remember—I was dreaming of taking care of two babies, one was a little kid that—the little baby that was at the same place I stayed at before these people moved away. These people were very good friends of mine, and he was a very lively, very healthy little thing, and then there was another little baby, and this was a little baby girl. She wasn't nearly as cute as he was, had an odd-shaped mouth, but she seemed to be the one that I was taking care of, and she was sort of having trouble with her food. She was spitting out her food, and so it was getting all over her, and she was having trouble even breathing. I thought that she was going to choke, so I picked her up and took her to a place where there was some sort of garden spray, and stood in the midst of that stuff, and reached my hand into the water, and put it up to her mouth and wiped the goo and vomit and stuff off her mouth. And then I recall it struck me that in spite of her homeliness, she was just a tiny baby, probably just about ten months old, she was a very cute little baby. And suddenly it seemed to me that the dream scene changed again.

(*B*–6) I was alone standing in this store, before the window that I used to often stand in when I worked there during high school, and through these windows you could sort of see houses all up and down the other side of the street. And during a storm we'd walk out and see these—look above these houses—and see the heavy clouds moving.

Well, it was sort of the same setting, everything was getting dark, and it was starting to rain, as though in a storm. I was watching and everything was gray, sort of a silvery gray, and I looked off to the east and then all of a sudden I saw—I've never seen a tornado, but I saw a funnel right then come down from the sky, and I knew that this must have been a tornado. It was sort of northeast of where I was, and it started moving down the main street in the town. I knew what it would do, at least I thought I knew what it would do, follow the path of least resistance and come right down that street, which was the same street that the store was on, and so I was very much afraid. And I ducked down behind some counter, and it came down. There were gushes of wind and this sort of thing, a lot of things flying about, bricks and things flew into the glass windows in the store and smashed all of the windows, and the tornado moved on down the street.

Then I got up and looked out, and it was further over to the north, and was sort of heading back up, making some sort of a circle in a rectangular fashion, as though it were following the streets, up to the north and moving east again. It seemed as though it were taking each street separately.

(*B*–7) In the meantime, the wife of a very good friend of

mine, who is the mother of this healthy little child in the dream before, sort of came casually into the store, not seemingly minding the tornado at all, and sort of out for a walk to see what damage it had done. I was amazed that she could be so unconcerned whenever all this damage occurred.

(QUESTION: Did you recognize the settings?) The choir part was sort of as I picture Rockefeller Chapel, but I think it was, I've never been up to the choir loft. There's a stairway in the back—I only saw the bottom of it when I was there tonight, so I only know what that looks like. But that was the place where this monument to me was, right at the bottom. And I knew that there were other monuments to the singers in the choir up and down the stairway and I saw models of them singing, which was sort of flattering. But I never saw any part of the stairway in the dream except the bottom part which was where this monument to me was. Upstairs in the choir loft was sort of like a balcony where I've been before, it sort of reminded me of our high school balcony.

This business about the lake, it was sort of as though I was walking on something like the structure that a roller coaster runs on, but it didn't have any humps. There were just little kids there, some of them diving off each side, and others jumping down through, since it was two rows of heavy, high beams with crosspieces running parallel to each other, and two other pieces running perpendicular to them, so that, from the top, it would be built like a square, almost like an elevator shaft, only it was, of course, open to the air on the sides. As I walked across there, there was some very good diver. There was a diving board to the right of this thing and a diving board to the left of this thing, and then this platform came out from this diving board. As I walked across, I had to stop a minute, because a guy dove from the diving board on the right clear over this platform into the water on the left side of the platform. He seemed to have control of himself, he knew how to dive and all this sort of thing. But then as I walked out I saw these little kids who didn't really know what they were doing, just barely missing the platform. (QUESTION: You didn't recognize any children or this man?) No, I didn't. (QUESTION: How about the lady who sent you out for the wax candies?) She was a member of the choir, of the university choir. She's a secretary that my wife auditioned before [before] she went to sing in the choir. She's, to me, anyway, a snob-type person, pseudosophisticated and that sort of thing, which I very much dislike.

(QUESTION: Were you aware that you were just dreaming these things?) No, I don't think I was. (QUESTION: Did these dreams seem coherent to you at the time you experienced them?) Yes, I didn't have any feeling that something was wrong.

AN ANALYSIS OF DREAM SPECIMENS A AND B
Sources of the Dream Material.

On the evening prior to the elicitation of these two reports, the subject had walked his wife to Rockefeller Chapel, where she tried out (and passed a preliminary test) for the University of Chicago Chorus. While she was inside the chapel, the subject "strolled over to 63rd Street," a main street in Chicago's Negro community adjacent to the university, which is lined with gaudy bars, liquor stores, and other evidences of "sin" and wild living. He then returned to campus, and "killed time" at the student center. At 10:30, his wife's "trial" finished, he walked her home, had a cup of tea, and then proceeded to the sleep laboratory.

It is apparent, from *A*–1, then, that nocturnal dreams are not completely foreign to everyday experience. As Freud stressed, they often build upon memories of the dream-day, so-called "day residues." [2] The particular day residues selected may often, as Freud also stressed, represent rather mundane and unexceptional daytime experiences, rather than the high point of the previous day's experience.

Dream fragment A–2 also has a parallel in the subject's memories of the dream-day: "The driveway at Rockefeller is of a circular shape. I walked up it twice and away once, while waiting for my wife. Each time I thought of how unreal the chapel appeared. The *actual* experience reminded me of what the same experience would be like in a dream."

But it is also apparent that the dream, even in its early, relatively unformed stages (specimen A) is more than a simple shuffling through of memories of the previous day. As Freud noted, the day residues are "worked over," or transformed, into pieces of a dramatic sequence that was not, as such, experienced during the dream-day. The decision of the dream-day was whether the wife had been accepted by the choir director. The subject indicates that he "was very anxious for her to be—it was sort of like being on trial, awaiting a verdict." His identification with his wife, figurative in waking life, became a concrete fact in the dream—it is now a decision about both wife and husband. It is no longer confined to matters of music; it seems to be a more general decision about the future of two people. This transformation brings the more limited choir trial into a Kafkaesque situation that has far greater self-reference and personal significance for the dreamer. That is, the direction of the transformation is from the relatively trivial to the relatively vital. It should be noted at this point that the subject and his wife have been married only a month and that it may be the future of their marital relationship itself that he is contemplating.

There is also some distortion in segment *A*–2. The subject comments that he does not understand "why the dream took place on the other side of the chapel" than did his real-life walking and waiting. This may be another case of a dream statement, in concrete visual imagery, of something that would be expressed more figuratively in waking life: the idea that something is not right (with the relationship he is contemplating). Calvin Hall, psychologist and director of the Institute for Dream Research, Coral Gables, Florida, has stressed that sleeping thought proceeds at a less abstract or conceptual level than waking thought, so that, for instance, the waking conception, "I'd better lay low for a while," becomes the sleeping perception of myself on the floor underneath a bed.[3]

A comparison of specimen *A*, the REM-onset report, and specimen *B*, the fully developed REM-sleep dream, reveals that the several dreams of one night may start with the same day residues and, by implication, the same self-concerns represented by these residues. This, in turn, implies that the dream is not a randomly generated mental product but rather a purposive exploration of certain experiences and problems that occur in waking life.

A comparison of specimens *A* and *B* also reveals that the fully developed REM-period dream is far more bizarre, elaborated, and distorted than the REM-onset dream. The day residue of the choir trial, for instance, has been subjected to an elaborate and somewhat fantastic "working over" in *B* as compared to the transformation it suffered in *A*. The dreamer comments that he "can't place" the lake-front scene at all—that is, he can locate no past memories upon which it builds, so distorted is the dream's transformation of the sense data of prior experience. Yet it can be established that fantastic elaborations themselves do build upon day residues. Consider the wax model episode with the choir (*B*–4), for instance. The subject comments:

> Upon seeing *some* members of the choir last night, I was impressed by their pseudosophistication, and a sort of sissified snobbishness. The woman I mentioned in the dream I especially disliked. The "snobbishness" seems to be responsible for my receiving the job of errand boy and for the unflattering model—both of which aroused hostility in me during the dream.

Note that the transformations again demonstrate a shift of abstract to concrete: the subject perceived that the choir members assumed a haughty, statuesque pose, hence in the dream they *are* statues; they seemed to think—at least as perceived by the subject—that they were better than he, hence he is but an errand boy, and their statues are more flattering than his and are physically placed above his.

Specimen *B* reveals that as the dream progresses it comes to draw upon memories of earlier periods of the dreamer's life as well as upon recent experiences: for example, the little wax bottles of childhood ("I guess they still have them, I remember them from a long time ago"); the store in which he worked while in high school; the storms in his hometown; the baby, and its mother, from where he used to live. As the scope of the dream enlarges, it draws upon memories from all periods of the dreamer's life. These older recollections, however, are as subject to distortion and elaboration as are day residues from the dream-day, for example, the unusual path of the tornado and the second, homely, but later beautiful, baby.

THE PSYCHOLOGY OF SLEEP

As Freud suggested, day residues from the dream-day may often serve the role of contacting older, related memories. For instance, hurricanes and tropical storms had been reported in the newspapers for several days prior to the subject's night in the laboratory, and he indicates that this is why he thinks he dreamed of the tornado in *B*–6, which reminded him of "how it rained for about four days straight when Hurricane Hazel struck my hometown some years ago and the way we looked out at the clouds—the darkness of those days."

One characteristic of day residues that seems to heighten the likelihood that they will become elements of dream content is an incompleteness of the daytime impression. For instance, the chapel scene in *B*–4 includes the stairwell of which the subject had, on the dream-day, seen only the bottom. Such an incompleteness of daytime impression perhaps leaves unresolved tension in a human organism that strives to complete its experiences in order to resolve its tensions.* What was the rest of that scene really like? The subject does not know, but he wonders. In the dream any tension is resolved. His waking vista is expanded by drawing upon his own relevant past experiences—he constructs a balcony for the chapel (which he has not seen) like that of his high school auditorium (which he has seen).

Organization of the Dream Material.

One of the impressive features of dream thinking is that associative channels seem to open much more freely and widely during sleep. For example, the word "break" serves as a link

---

* This hypothesis parallels Bluma Zeigarnik's argument (discussed in R. S. Woodworth and H. Schlosberg, *Experimental Psychology,* 2nd ed., [New York: Holt, Rinehart & Winston, Inc., 1954]) with respect to the finding that uncompleted tasks are better recalled than completed ones, and has been suggested for dreams by Otto Poetzl (see Chapter 6).

72

between two events quite unlikely to be associated in waking thought, taking a "break" and a particular "break" refreshment, wax bottles that you "break." It is as if the necessity during wakefulness to reason logically and coherently normally keeps our thinking "on the track," blocking out interesting, but less than totally meaningful, associations. But during sleep no such active inhibition keeps thought from ranging far and wide over numerous illogical—by waking standards—channels. There are certain waking reveries or daydreams where this decreased inhibition operates to a lesser extent. These are situations in which we are free to ignore outer reality (most likely there is no one else around), and suddenly find that we have engaged in a long chain of logically somewhat disconnected thoughts and images. We catch ourselves and may wonder "Now why did I ever think of *that?*" In sleep, such awareness of the process is generally lacking and consequently it operates to a much fuller degree. It is no accident that the psychoanalyst's technique of having his patient *free associate* to dream content has often proved helpful in untangling the meaning of the dream —such a spontaneous flow of mental content simulates the fluidity of association achieved during the process of dreaming in the first place.

It would be incorrect to assume that fluidity of association is a sufficient explanation of dream content, however. If the dreamer's recall of memories of past experience is outside the typical constraints of wakeful, logical control mechanisms, it is still under external constraint of another variety. Memories are being activated selectively, embellished, and distorted so that they cohere in the form of a good story. Indeed, it is a major paradox that the dream can demonstrate both looseness of association and tightness of thematic organization. Fluid association is harnessed to a particular purpose, the construction of an internally coherent hallucinatory drama. Formal constraints thus operate selectively upon potential associative thought material.

But of all the potentially well-formed stories, why does a particular one emerge—why this particular story content, rather than some other one equally satisfactory from the point of view of good form? Particular story content is selected on the basis of its potential for representing, in a pictorial and dramatic manner, matters of considerable ego reference. It is selected, that is, as the vehicle of rather probing self-evaluation that transpires while the dreamer is freed from the necessity of conforming to an outer world, from external monitoring, and even from responsibility for his own thoughts (we believe that dreams "happen" to us, rather than recognizing them as mental products for which we must bear total responsibility). These conditions of freedom from the necessity of conforming and from the burden of responsibility, in conjunction with a physiological state permitting intricate and activated thought processes, afford an opportunity for self-examination unlike any available during wakefulness. It is not necessary to assume that a motive of self-evaluation initiates mental activity during the REM period, only that the conditions of stage-1 REM sleep permit self-examination and allow it to exert an organizing influence upon the thought processes characteristic of this state. This influence can be documented by casting an interpretive eye upon dream specimens *A* and *B*.

Interpretation of the Dream Material.

The subject has spent his evening in a passive role, waiting for his wife. She has been the member of the family aspiring to achievement in the larger social world outside the boundaries of family life. The subject could achieve in this manner only through identification with her more active quest (hence, in dream *A*, the decision about *us*). She is inside the chapel, "in" on the decision, while the subject waits alone outside, presumably for her to carry the news to him.

Remember that at the time the subject had these two dreams he had been married for only a month. In such a circumstance, it might be natural for him to ponder his future with his wife. His passivity and inability to contribute to the solution of the problem in the dream, however, stem from several special circumstances in his recent experience. He had just lost his job at school—had, in fact, entered the dream experiment because it paid five dollars a night; thus he had recently experienced something of a blow to his sense of husbandly adequacy. Moreover, as the school term was about to resume, the contrast between his wife's position and his own promised to become greater. She would continue working all day, while he, an English major, might spend a typical afternoon reading novels. On the dream-day, in fact, he had been at home during the afternoon, reading a novel, while his wife had been at work. Wonder about the future of his marriage comes to focus upon doubts of his own adequacy to sustain his role in the relationship. In dream *A*, these doubts are represented by his passive role as contrasted with his wife's more active one. In dream *B*, they are represented in a number of different ways, but however expressed, they pervade the entire narrative.

In this second dream, his passive identification with his wife proceeds further. He is inside the chapel now, with her, although he apparently has no distinctive role there; he doubts that he is singing with the rest of the choir. The apparently wish-fulfilling element of getting inside the chapel now yields to reality—what precisely is his role to be? It is immediately defined as passive and dependent—he is asked to assume a minimal part as errand boy for the group. But note that the nature of even this menial task—providing for, among others, his wife—is one that has exceeded his capacity for execution in real life. His dream role, then, serves as a means of representing a waking role and as a means both of chiding himself for his failure at it and of exploring his potential for filling it.

The role is not one he actively seeks. It is one thrust upon his passivity by the self-assured choir director. This passivity is defined in the culturally deviant act of accepting orders from a woman. Her self-confidence annoys the subject, who perceives that he is lacking in it, and makes him feel inferior (as shown in the dream by the role he adopts with respect to her). She treats him, in fact, like a child, and his response to her request is also childish—he will secure wax candies enjoyed by small children. There is perhaps a measure of security in this flashback to the dependence and childish luxury of times past. But, again, wish fulfillment yields to reality—the candies cost money, five dollars, his earnings in the sleep laboratory this night, plus more (this is not enough of a job to support the responsibility). Once more his inadequacy as provider is thrown into his face.

Freud stressed the wish-fulfilling aspect of dream content,[4] but what is most striking about this dream, and dreams in general, is that tendencies toward wish fulfillment yield to a harsher reality. No one can fruitfully explore his life if he is to fool himself and hallucinate all sorts of events that cannot be solutions to his problems. Hallucinated wish fulfillments do appear in dream content, but they are not the key to its nature. They are recognized by normal persons (perhaps less so by

Freud's neurotic patients) as inadequate answers to real-life problems and thus are quickly discarded.

In *B–2*, the theme of inadequacy shifts to another, more highly symbolized, realm. This is the section of dream *B* of which, on the next morning, the subject says he can make very little sense. Self-exploration is now delving deeper, into areas where internalized cultural taboos are stronger, hence the more highly symbolic treatment.

The recreation setting identifies a shift from a concern with the subject's inadequacy in work experiences to a consideration of the more pleasurable areas of life. In this sense, the introduction of the beach may be a regressive wish fulfillment, regressive in the sense that it refers back to an era in which it was unnecessary to be concerned with the workaday world. The degree of symbolism in this regressive segment reflects the intrusion of the tabooed topic of sex, for recreation here also signifies procreation. For instance, the sexual connotations of diving into the water have been shown by noting that nocturnal emissions often accompany the male's dreams of swimming, diving, and so on.[5] The elaboration of a recreational, or pleasure, setting supports the sexual interpretation of water in this particular dream.

The subject reveals his particular conception of sexual pleasure by his particular structuring of a widely employed dream symbol.[6] He is on a high walkway over the water, and the task of diving is portrayed as rather dangerous. There are others in the dream doing all sorts of fancy dives, but the subject is, by implication, not up to this kind of performance. As he walks along, the inadequacy theme returns in a manifest sense, manifest because it no longer directly expresses, although it now carries the additional meaning of, sexual inadequacy: he remembers the snobbish lady, his menial chore, and his lack of the means with which to perform it. As he watches the children dive, and his childlike dream role leads him to intense identification here, he realizes how difficult is the achievement of personal, especially sexual, competence. He ponders the many risks of its pursuit as he sees the children barely miss disaster. At this point, incipient panic develops—about the children of the dream, but more basically about himself. There are demands to achieve sexual competence, and not the least of these spring from the exhibitionistically displayed success of others. Note how the subject omits this detail in his first account of the dream; note also the parallel between the self-confident diver of B–2 and the self-confident choir director in B–1. Feelings of self-inadequacy—now in the sexual sphere—arise. The episode closes at this point, not because any resolution has been achieved, but rather because the self-exploration is probing too deeply to be pursued comfortably beyond this point.

The story picks up again just where it was before the subject became overly concerned about, and projected his own anxiety into, the boys' diving. Note that, for all their alleged "craziness," dreams generally do have coherent plots. Events are not left "up in the air" or unresolved (and when they are, this is a matter of interpretive interest rather than a reflection of some general incoherence of sleeping thought). The subject had been commissioned to do an errand, and he now returns to that task. Not only does he now tie the story together, he worries about the loose ends remaining, for example, his attempt to explain to others how he was able to afford his purchases.

The nature of his resolution in B–3 of the episode that began in B–1 is characterized by sketchiness of detail and a predominance of simple wish fulfillment. This may be viewed as a response to the incipient panic of *B*–2. The subject is a success, not inadequate; he does what was required of him—it does not matter how. This magical restoration of adequacy is not intended as a final solution, but rather as a stopgap to regain composure before any further serious explorations of the predicament.

B–4 reopens the whole question of inadequacy once more. The chapel view ties this episode to *B*–3 but also builds upon new day-residues, particularly the subject's impressions of the choir director and, by association, others in the choir as pseudosophisticated snobs. They flatter themselves and assume the lofty mien of statues. In dream thought, this is concretely visualized —they are statues. The conceit of the choir members is again relative, rather than absolute. That is, they seem to feel that they are better than the subject is, and this is the subject's concern. Their regard of him is symbolized by the physical placement, an exceedingly reasonable concrete representation of the abstraction "status difference." They are arranged going up the stairs, while in the very lowest position, outside their series altogether, the subject is found, portrayed in fragile wax, "lying there huddled under the table." This last phrase suggests not only that he perceives his supposed low status in the eyes of others but that he accepts it rather abjectly. Upon seeing this recognizably unflattering pose, the subject sees in his own abasement grounds for the disdainful attitude he feels others have of him and that he no doubt also must hold of himself. But again, the probe has sunk, however accurately, too deeply. *Defense mechanisms*, those ways we have of forever delaying self-confrontations, waking or sleeping, are activated. The subject tries to pass off his confrontation with a glib remark, the content of which reveals his first line of defense when his self-adequacy is threatened. *They* are not real artists, but hacks—I'm the real thing, a sensitive artist, and we are always persecuted by those of less genuine talent. And yet the glibness of this remark reveals that the subject can't quite make this defense ring true, even to himself. His persistent tendency to return to reality once more overrides an inclination to distort that reality to make his predicament seem more palatable. At this impasse, the scene ends.

B–5 is a resumption of the dreamer's efforts at self-definition. Like *B–2*, however, it is more disguisedly symbolic than the episode preceding it, and this very fact sensitizes us to the presence of somewhat more provocative and threatening, hence censorable, thematic material. As was also true of *B–2*, regressive or developmentally primitive content is the focus of attention. There are two babies. One is that of a friend, who is represented by a lively, healthy baby. The other is in the charge of the dreamer, who is represented by an unattractive baby quite literally having difficulty maintaining life.

Once again, a comparison with another leads to the judgment of personal inadequacy. The friend's baby and its vitality are concrete evidences of his adequacy. A second baby, a concrete symbol, is evolved to represent the subject for comparative purposes and, in particular, to express his difficulties and inadequacy.

Why this recurring theme now attaches itself to a comparison with this particular friend is somewhat obscure, and the subject was not pressed to associate to the friend's name when later discussing the dream. Without such associations, or some other form of waking investigation of a dream element's meaning to the subject, it is difficult to decipher the meaning of that element, because symbolism is often a personal matter. The previous symbolic interpretation of diving into water relied upon assessment of the general meaning of this element to members of our own culture, bolstered by certain contextual elements pointing to the validity of this interpretation for the particular subject in one dream. But with the symbol of a particular person, known to the subject but not to us, it is difficult to assess connotative meaning without enlisting the subject's active aid. The presence of such particular symbols and the possibility that even more general ones vary in precise meaning from person to person are the reasons why the trained psychoanalyst hesitates to apply interpretation arbitrarily to dreams collected from subjects of whose life history he is ignorant. One of the most depressing occurrences for the trained interpreter of dreams is to watch an amateur, fortified by a reading of a popular exposition of psychoanalysis, essaying interpretations, in the absence of any associative data, of dreams collected from casual acquaintances. It may be fun as a parlor game, but it is not dream interpretation as the trained practitioner understands that task.

The person in the subject's charge in B–5 is an infant and a female, both symbols of passivity, and his own role (mothering) is also feminine in character. The degree of regression indicated by the dreamer's choice of a symbol for himself is shown in the focus upon the infant's oral behavior. Freud stresses that the infant's earliest mode of relating to the world is oral in character.[7] It is in this stage that the self is in a passive, dependent relation to others rather than vigorously acting upon the environment. There is more than a touch of wish fulfillment in the subject's symbolism here, the wish being a desire to escape from the problems of present-day reality and return to a passive, dependent role that is socially sanctioned. Yet once more, tendencies to childish wish fulfillment are in conflict with reality orientation and a more mature approach to present-day life. The baby (subject) is unhappy in his passive, dependent role, literally cannot stomach it. The subject's very survival as an integral personality, he correctly perceives, is threatened by the continued assumption of such passivity, and he rebels (vomits), rejecting the passive incorporation of nurture from others.

Such rebellion brings guilt in its wake, and the subject cleanses himself by wiping away the emesis (undoing the act of rebellion) and the baby (a passive, dependent role) now seems attractive, at least on a provisional basis (he rationalizes that the baby is still tiny, that is, time is needed before growth may reasonably be expected). By understanding this guilt over rebellion and this rationalization we begin to appreciate the strength of the subject's defenses against psychological growth.

In his own associations to this curious segment of dream B, the subject interprets the vomit as "a manifestation of my hostility aroused by the choir scene," which is consistent with the interpretation of a rejection of a passive-dependent role, and he interprets the outcome as "a sort of unconscious decision 'not to let it bother me,' " that is, acceptance of, rather than rebellion toward, such situations. The subject's suggestion of a link between B–1 and B–5 suggests a connection on another level: rejection of passive dependence is a rejection of mother. It is a maternal (older female) figure in B–1 who treats the subject as a child and demands passive obedience, and a dependence on mother is characteristic of the oral stage prominent in B–5. Thus to refuse to accept passive nurture is to refuse to accept a maternal offering, hence the guilt.

It would be natural for problems of dependency and passivity to be felt most acutely toward parent figures, particularly toward the mother. As the subject described his family in a brief life-history interview, it was one characterized by maternal dominance. His mother was described as devoutly religious—hence she is a leading figure within the chapel in B–1, and the subject himself has with difficulty been trying to redefine the religious beliefs he inherited, one gathers, somewhat forcefully from his mother. The problems of passivity, and consequent adult immaturity, and dependency now begin to appear in a particular causal nexus—dependency upon a dominant mother.

A familiar correlate of dependency upon the mother is the formation of an identification with her or with other female, particularly maternal, figures. In this context, it is interesting to consider: the subject's ready identification with his wife (a possible maternal figure for the subject—most likely this is the kind of figure a passive, dependent male would choose for a mate) in A–1 and B–1; his role in B–5 as nursemaid, and his assignment to a female child, which represents himself; his being inside a building (a general female sexual symbol, according to Freud) with a smashable window in front that is destroyed by a funnel-shaped (phallic) object moving down the narrow channel of the street; and so on. The identification with female figures suggests a feminine conception of sex, for example, the passive reception of cataclysmic events originating from without in the tornado episode, and this in turn suggests something that is consistent with the subject's passivity, his doubts about his masculine adequacy, his self-characterization in B–4 as a sensitive artist, and his waking behavior (shyness, soft-spokenness, and so on): homosexuality, probably repressed and latent rather than subject to expression in daily life. Such an hypothesis may also account for the recurrence of reversed direction or turning-back-on-the-self themes in both dreams A and B (for instance, ending up, in A–2, on the wrong side of the chapel—often a feminine symbol, according to Freud; the swimmer in B–2 who ends up on the wrong side of the dangerous "boxlike" (female genital) structure; the curious path of the funnel-shaped tornado, which turns back on itself in B–6.

Cast in this light, the subject's recurring negative reactions to the assumption of a passive role and his panic when confronted by the strangely twisting diver in B–2 and tornado in B–6 represent his fear of one major threat to his sense of masculine adequacy—his own homosexual impulses.

Returning now to the interpretation of B–5, the resolution of this segment is patently unsatisfactory, even to the subject who constructed it. One must grow up and face reality, rather than adopt a childish role and decide "not to let it bother" you. In B–6, reality intrudes once more upon an unrealistic resolution: the subject has grown up somewhat (he is in his high school years), and the familiar storm vista of the hometown setting represents his perception of a world whose demands are once again threatening his survival. The threat is now perceived in terms of more explicit ego reference: the storm as a symbol of a demanding and threat-filled world follows a path of least resistance to that person least prepared to cope with such danger —the subject himself. That the forces against him are seen as real and potent is suggested by the destruction for which the storm is responsible, and that he feels his response will be inadequate is symbolized by his hiding from the storm, whose curious path suggests that it will recur—it is not a one-shot catastrophe, but a symbol of cyclic (sexual?) pressures to which the meek and passive self will ever be exposed.

In B–7, the dreamer's role is again subjected to a contrast. Even the mother of the lively baby is unafraid and unconcerned;

84

even a female peer is ready to face life rather than shrink from it. In her maternal role, the female peer perhaps signifies the strong mother as contrasted to the timid son she has produced. In any event, the subject is left with his problems—no magic solution has appeared during sleep, nor has any hallucinated escape from them proven to be satisfactory even to his sleeping self. However, if the subject has provided himself with neither magical solace nor reflective solution, he has used his dreams to explore his predicament with a reasonable degree of realism and candor and tentatively sought to define his self and his role as they are manifested in waking life.

Interpretation of dreams *A* and *B* might proceed much further, particularly had more extensive associative reactions been obtained from the subject. But we have perhaps gone sufficiently far to demonstrate the nature of the motives and mechanisms that underlie the REM-sleep dream.

The Validation of Dream Interpretation.

One concern sure to arise whenever dream interpretation is attempted is how the results are validated. Are there any checks against the introduction of arbitrary and unreasonable meanings into the analysis by the interpreter? How is one to know that dream interpretations are correct? These questions are particularly important because of the tendency to project one's own needs, values, and preconceptions into ambiguous thematic material. This is the basis underlying *projective tests* of personality in which the subject's interpretations of thematic material are used to arrive at conclusions not about the material but about the interpreter. Dream interpretation, in fact, has served as a projective test of personality.[8]

All this implies that the dangers of arbitrary interpretation are very real indeed, but the situation is by no means hopeless. There are several criteria by which the reasonableness and accuracy of a particular dream interpretation may be assessed.

The first of these is one of internal consistency, both within a single dream and within a series of dreams collected from the same subject. *Personality* refers to an organization of behavior, and to the degree that dreams reveal personality, there should be some agreement of the interpretations made of different dream elements and episodes. This is not meant to imply that manifest content will be parallel, but rather that its separate strands should be interpreted so that the "pieces fit together." Since the interpretation of a series of dreams offers a greater opportunity for such comparison, it is to be preferred to the analysis of an isolated dream.[9] The first dream in such a series may be used to form hypotheses that are later tested and modified as the content of subsequent dreams is analyzed. In this manner, the subject, by way of his tendency to produce recurring dream elements and interactions, provides a constraint upon the interpreter's tendency to project his own fantasies into the subject's hallucinatory narrative.

The second criterion is one of contemporary external consistency. Although for research upon the nature of the interpretive process it may be valuable to analyze dreams *blind* (in the absence of any other information about the subject), this is rarely the way dream interpretation proceeds in the clinic. There the interpreter fortifies himself with life-history data and with knowledge, derived from the patient's verbalizations and overt behavior, of the patient's waking perceptions of self and world, his significant conflicts, and so on. Generally speaking, the interpretation of dreams should produce hypotheses consistent with these nondream data. Occasionally, however, valid

dream interpretations may produce results apparently inconsistent with waking behavior and experience. This is to be expected if dream interpretation is to have any unique value, over
and above the subject's waking performances, in assessing his
personality. In such cases, the interpretation must serve to
integrate or explain apparent inconsistencies in the subject's
behavior, that is, it must provide a new focus that is useful in
evaluating the waking personality.

A final criterion is consistency with future, as opposed to
contemporary, nondream behavior. In the clinic, the therapist
has one potent check against arbitrary and invalid interpretation. This analysis will not stimulate his client to new insights
and it will not lead him to spontaneously express thoughts and
feelings hitherto repressed. It will, in fact, lead nowhere in
terms of developing the psychotherapeutic relationship—it
simply will not work. In any long-term relationship, such as
psychotherapy, in which dream interpretation is employed to
stimulate self-insight, the question of validity of the interpretation can be translated into the question of whether the therapist's
analyses do, in fact, seem to be producing the desired goals. To
the extent this enterprise is failing, the therapist knows that he
must change his interpretations, or if he does not recognize this
fact, the client soon comes to see that he must change his therapist.

The manner in which inferences about waking behavior that
are made from dream content receive external validation is
subtle, rather than direct. Since dreams allow self-exploration
in a context of relative freedom, their content is likely to present
aspects of self-conception and motivation that are not directly
revealed in waking behavior, where there is the constraining
presence of others and of a more active conscience (or inter-

nalization of others' standards of evaluation). It is the relative freedom from typical externally imposed constraints that allows dream content to be more revealing of certain facets of personality dynamics than daytime behaviors. A man dreams of numerous attacks he inflicts upon others, revealing a facet of personality that might not be inferred readily from his waking behavior. On the other hand, this same freedom from external constraints typically present in waking life means that the interpreter should be most hesitant to conclude that the aggressive dreamer is an overtly aggressive man. It may be, for example, that it is fear of his own aggressiveness, revealed by dream evidence to be deep-rooted, that leads him to refrain from social interaction of any sort in waking life.[10]

It is in this sense, for example, that the interpretation of homosexuality in dream *B* should be understood. The interpretation is not that the subject is homosexual. He is not. But he is afraid of certain repressed, yet psychologically active, homosexual inclinations revealed in his dream content, and this fear may, complexly, motivate and help to explain certain of his waking behaviors. The necessity for subtlety in dream interpretation arises from the fact that dreams indicate motives rather than behaviors and from the fact that the motives so revealed in free fantasy may be so well controlled in waking life that their determinations of waking behavior are either indirect or inverse.

STATISTICAL FINDINGS ON
THE NATURE OF REM-SLEEP DREAMS

In several studies of REM-sleep dream content, subjects have been asked to fill out rating forms for each of the preawakening mental experiences they report. The results of one such study are presented in Figure 5.[11]

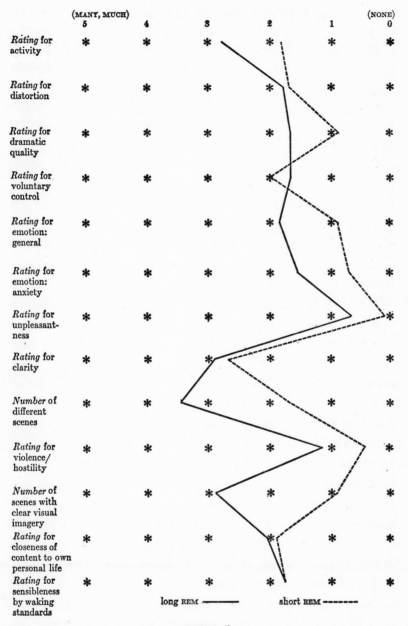

	(MANY, MUCH) 5	4	3	2	1	(NONE) 0
Rating for activity	*	*	*	*	*	*
Rating for distortion	*	*	*	*	*	*
Rating for dramatic quality	*	*	*	*	*	*
Rating for voluntary control	*	*	*	*	*	*
Rating for emotion: general	*	*	*	*	*	*
Rating for emotion: anxiety	*	*	*	*	*	*
Rating for unpleasant-ness	*	*	*	*	*	*
Rating for clarity	*	*	*	*	*	*
Number of different scenes	*	*	*	*	*	*
Rating for violence/ hostility	*	*	*	*	*	*
Number of scenes with clear visual imagery	*	*	*	*	*	*
Rating for closeness of content to own personal life	*	*	*	*	*	*
Rating for sensibleness by waking standards	*	*	*	*	*	*

long REM —————— short REM - - - - - - -

FIGURE 5

Average Dream Ratings by Duration of REM Sleep

In this particular investigation, eight subjects were awakened a number of times after varying durations of REM sleep, ranging from a few seconds to twenty-four minutes. In Figure 5, awakenings made after one minute or less of REM sleep are labeled "Short REM," while awakenings made after nine minutes or more of REM sleep are labeled "Long REM."

It is first of all apparent from Figure 5 that REM-sleep dreams are not generally the highly unpleasant, emotional, dramatic, and bizarre experiences they are popularly thought to be. The absolute mean rating on none of these scales is particularly high, showing the value of sampling all dream activity occurring through the night by means of experimental awakenings from REM sleep rather than relying upon a sample composed of dreams so highly traumatic in character that they cause us to awaken spontaneously during the night. The latter dreams (or nightmares) may indeed be highly unpleasant, but they seem not to be typical. It is, in fact, their atypicality that causes us to awaken, whereas we usually sleep through most of our other dreams, which are apparently considerably less unpleasant in character than those that awaken us.

It is also apparent from Figure 5 that there are alterations in the content of the REM process as it achieves greater duration. In this study, it should be noted, attempts were made to control for any possible effect of the time of night (relatively soon after initial sleep onset as opposed to relatively late in the morning) at which awakenings were made; neither the short nor the long REM awakenings come predominantly from any one period of the total night's sleep. With control of the time-of-night variable, it is still apparent from the separation of the two lines in Figure 5 that the REM-sleep narrative becomes more dreamlike in a number of respects as the length of the REM period increases. In particular: the average long REM-sleep dream contains more activity than the short one; it is more distorted, dramatic, emotional, anxious, unpleasant, and clear or vivid than the average short REM-sleep dream; it contains a larger number of different scenes, more scenes with clear visualization, and more socially unacceptable impulse content (violence and hostility) than the average short REM-sleep dream; and it is less under voluntary control than the average short REM-sleep dream.

As the REM period progesses, on the other hand, the mental content seems to become neither more nor less sensible by waking standards of evaluation nor more nor less close to the dreamer's everyday life. Dream specimen *B* showed the fluctuation within the REM period of highly symbolic and more typically everyday episodes, and an interpretation was made there to the effect that these fluctuations were attributable to alterations in the relative strength of the motive of self-exploration and anxiety aroused by overly intensive or revealing explorations achieved under the guidance of this motive. It is not surprising, therefore, that there are no systematic shifts as a function of time per se in these two variables.[12]

One other finding of interest with respect to the content of the typical REM-sleep dream is not presented in Figure 5. This is the very minimal occurrence, in the laboratory, of overtly sexual dreams. Such dreams, often resulting in seminal emission in the male, do occur, but apparently they are not as frequent as everyday impressions imply. The sexual dream, like the nightmare, is one during which we are likely to awaken, whereas less overtly erotic content is not so likely to arouse us. Once more, experimentally made REM-sleep awakenings may give us the more accurate picture of the *typical* REM-sleep dream.

The possibility also remains, of course, that the subject is able to suppress such socially less acceptable content while in the laboratory. While there have not been any definitive studies comparing home dreams with those during sleep in the laboratory,[13] it seems likely that the sleeper's ego is somewhat sensitive to the fact that its operations in the laboratory are to be subject to greater scrutiny, both by himself and by others. Nevertheless, it also seems likely that both nightmares and overtly sexual content are generally overestimated as factors in dreaming when estimates are based solely upon those dreams that have sufficient intensity to wake us up.

It has been noted that REM-sleep dreaming becomes more dreamlike as the individual episode progresses. What about shifts in content over the course of the night? Is that of the second REM period more intense than that of the first, that of the third more intense than that of the second, and so on? In part, this question is already answered by the finding that the content of REM periods becomes more dreamlike as the length of REM sleep increases, for duration of this stage increases, as was demonstrated in Chapter 1, over the course of the night. It is a common laboratory observation that the first REM period of the night is of brief duration, often imperfectly achieved in physiological terms (spindles or other signs of stage 2 may intrude between REM bursts), and accompanied by reports of dreams that are vaguely recalled and lacking in vividness. The last REM period of the night is, on the other hand, of long duration, without signs of NREM EEG patterns, and accompanied by reports of dreams that are vivid and well-recalled.

There is also some evidence of changes through the night in intensity of REM-period content per fractional unit of the total dream period and per constant unit of time. For example, in

FIGURE 6

Average Dream Ratings by Ordinal Position of Period of REM Sleep

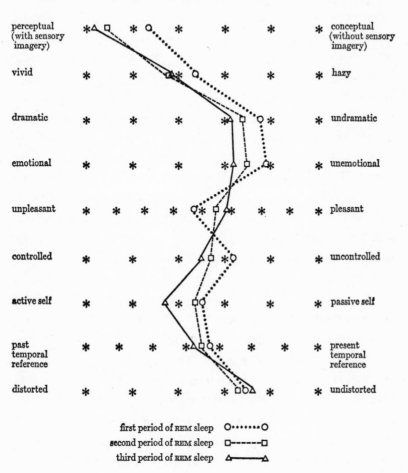

perceptual (with sensory imagery)	conceptual (without sensory imagery)
vivid	hazy
dramatic	undramatic
emotional	unemotional
unpleasant	pleasant
controlled	uncontrolled
active self	passive self
past temporal reference	present temporal reference
distorted	undistorted

first period of REM sleep ⊙·······⊙
second period of REM sleep □------□
third period of REM sleep △———△

one study, subjects were awakened five minutes after the onset of the night's initial REM period, and ten minutes after the onset of the next two REM periods.[14] Given the average figures for REM-period length cited in Chapter 1 (approximately ten minutes for the first REM period and twenty for the second), it is apparent that the first two periods were allowed to go half of their typical duration before experimental interruption. Subject ratings, therefore, of dreams from these two REM periods are of dreams of different absolute duration but presumably of an equivalent fractional unit of the total episode. The ratings of dreams from the second and third REM periods, on the other hand, are of dreams of equivalent absolute duration but differing fractional components of the total episode. The mean ratings of twenty-two subjects who recalled a dream from each of these three periods on one or two nights in the laboratory (in the latter case, a two-night average provided a single score for the subject) for selected dimensions of dream content, and the scales along which they rated are presented in Figure 6.

It is clear from these comparisons that the mental content of the initial REM period of the night differs more from that of the second period than does that of the second from the third. The first REM period is most likely to produce hazy, undramatic, unemotional reports of conceptual, rather than perceptual, mental content. Such content, however, is also most likely to be poorly controlled (*volitionally*), unpleasant, and have the self playing a passive role in the dream proceedings.[15] The temporal reference of the earliest REM period is also likely to be more recent experiences in the dreamer's life. As the night progresses, three kinds of change seem to occur per fractional unit of the dream episode or per given unit of time in the dream episode: (1) mental content becomes more intense (perceptual, vivid, dramatic, emotional) ; (2) mental content comes under better ego control (self in an active role, volitional control, pleasantness) ; and (3) temporal reference extends back to the more distant past. There are no striking changes in the distortion that elements of past experiences undergo. This again is consistent with the viewpoint that distortion fluctuates over time as a function of the waxing and waning strength of the desire for self-exploration and of the reactive motive toward self-obfuscation.

The operation of these motives over time in the manner described above has been substantiated in several studies that found, for example, that self-punishment or a comparable reaction might occur in a dream following one in which the dreamer has acted out an anxiety-provoking impulse, such as sex or aggression.[16] The more general relationships of the content of successive REM-sleep periods may best be illustrated with the presentation of a series of REM dreams collected by Dement and Wolpert [17] from one subject on one night:

1. The dreamer was in a swimming pool, with everyone admiring his body. He sees a possible competitor for the attentions of a friend (sex undetermined), but "for some reason I wasn't as afraid as I ought to have been. I seemed to have some sort of metamorphosis. I became just like a strong-muscled Greek god." He excels in a series of diving demonstrations, once almost losing his bathing suit in the process. The dream ends with the subject waiting to watch a TV program featuring a prominent Hollywood actress.

2. The subject is in a room with two Hollywood entertainers, one of whom fires his gun at the door causing it to collapse. A half-visible man walks in, demanding the "plans." He walks

over to the gun-shooting entertainer and begins to choke him. But the dreamer attacks the assailant, and knocks "the hell out of him. . . . I remember standing there in kind of a triumph."

3. The dreamer is trying to enter a room by way of the window, because he lacks a key to the door. An acquaintance standing by the door gives the subject two sandwiches, the "worst" ones imaginable. The two go in, but the subject is not satisfied with what he sees and wants to leave. "And there was something about nitroglycerine. . . . The last thing was somebody throwing a baseball."

4. The dreamer is making inquiries concerning the underground movement during World War II. At dinner time, he asks his mother about it and also asks her "Don't you think we can settle the question?"

5. The dreamer watches an argument erupt during a classroom economics lecture. The lecturer continues as two male students argue about the danger of inflation.

Conflict is a recurrent theme in this dream series, as is the expression of hostility. In the first and second dreams, the subject is magically successful in conquering rivals and enemies. In later dreams, however (as was demonstrated in the earlier treatment of the notion of wish fulfillment in dreams), it is evident that these magical solutions have not resolved the subject's problems or discharged their associated tensions: in the third dream, hostile forces impinge upon him—being given the worst sandwiches, nitroglycerine, and somebody throwing something; in the fourth dream, there is concern with past conflicts (World War II) and apparent reference (in the second query to his mother) to a more contemporary dispute; in the fifth dream, a verbal dispute is the main subject matter.

Several points may be made with respect to the content of this dream series, and, more generally, to the content of the numerous dream series investigated by Dement, Wolpert, and others:

1. As implied above, the subject seems to be working at defining his relationship to a common problem in the successive dreams of this series. With one exception, which may give a clue to the historical roots of the present problem, all of the dreams involve conflict with males. Although the surface content of male-male relationships is hostile-aggressive, there are indications, in the dreamer's symbolism, of sexual conflicts toward male objects (swimming, diving, admiration of one's own body, losing one's bathing suit, someone firing a gun at a door in the close company of males, being unable to penetrate a room through the usual means for lack of a key but being conducted into the room by a male, the "danger of inflation" in the context of a male-male relationship, and so on.)

2. Although the core problems treated may be similar in the several dreams of a series, the actual dream content is not. REM-period dreams are rarely, if ever, exactly replicated. Each period produces its own idiosyncratic exploration of the predicament of self, one conditioned by previous sleeping self-explorations but not identical with any of them. Such variability, of course, is to be expected given the task in which the sleeping ego is engaged during REM sleep. The stereotyped repetition of one conceptualization of the sleeper's conflicts would be of little value in exploring his predicament.

3. Although the manifest content of dreams is not repeated in its entirety, particular elements of manifest content in the successive dreams of a single night, particularly of adjacent

dreams, seem to recur on a basis above that to be expected by chance alone: for example, "Hollywood" in the first and second dreams; food or eating in the third and fourth dreams; and so on.

The content of a dream occurring during any REM period following the first on a particular night, then, might well be a function of: (1) basic problems the dreamer is encountering in his waking adjustment and their motivational bases, (2) the kind of solution or exploration that problem has received in preceding REM-period dreams on this same night, and (3) the particular elements or settings in terms of which that problem has been symbolized in preceding REM-period dreams of this same night. It is perhaps because in the first such period the subject lacks any orientation or framework deriving from previous nocturnal REM-period content that the ego is least successful in mobilizing its resources at this point—for instance, there is minimal voluntary control, maximal unpleasantness, and a vagueness in recall that suggests a desire not to register what has been transpiring.

Chapter 4

MENTAL ACTIVITY DURING NREM SLEEP

Dement and Kleitman's findings indicated that REM-sleep awakenings almost invariably produced dream reports while arousals during non-rapid eye movement (NREM) sleep did so only very seldom.[1] Their criterion of recall, however, was "detailed" dream description. The failure of NREM awakenings to meet this criterion did not imply that NREM sleep was without mental content of any sort, only that it was without content meeting this criterion, but the earliest feelings of dream researchers seemed to be that NREM sleep was, in fact, altogether devoid of significant psychological experience. In more recent years, however, it has become clear that this is not the case; mental content of a distinctive quality *can* be reliably elicited from NREM sleep, and the nature of this content may be one key to the understanding of the REM-sleep dream.

In the first independent confirmation of the Dement and Kleitman findings on the association of REM sleep with dreaming, a much higher proportion of NREM recall of dreamlike mental experiences was reported (53 per cent for subjects with a high rate of recall of dreams outside the laboratory) than would have been anticipated on the basis of Dement and Kleitman's figure for NREM recall (7 per cent).[2] The authors, however, attributed the NREM recall, as had Dement and Kleitman, to the memory of previous REM-sleep dreams rather than to the recall in NREM sleep of ongoing NREM mental activity. In this manner, the hypothesis of the unique association of REM sleep with significant psychological activity during sleep was preserved.

The issue of NREM mental activity, however, did not lay dormant for long. Kamiya's extensive study of mental activity during sleep (502 REM-period awakenings, 404 NREM awakenings) produced not only the expected high value for REM recall (86 per cent) but also an unexpectedly high value for NREM recall (46 per cent).[3] His criterion was the recollection of any specific topic, action, scene, idea, and so on, and so was broad enough to include reports that would have been classified negatively by Dement and Kleitman. When a stricter criterion, one more similar to that employed by Dement and Kleitman, was applied, the NREM recall figure dropped to 28 per cent, indicating that this difference in recall criterion in the two studies accounted for at least part of the difference in NREM rate of recall. The 28 per cent figure, however, was still substantially higher than Dement and Kleitman's 7 per cent, and Kamiya demonstrated that NREM recall as memory of previous REM-sleep dreams failed to account for his NREM recall values. NREM awakenings made *before* the occurrence of any REM periods (either since sleep onset or since the last awakening) produced

43 per cent recall by the more lenient criterion and 21 per cent recall by the stricter criterion, both values very much like the over-all NREM values. Since no prior REM periods had occurred in these cases, the conclusion seemed inescapable: ". . . dreams can occur outside of rapid eye movement periods as well as during them, although they apparently occur with much less frequency than during the rapid eye movement periods." [4]

My doctoral thesis at the University of Chicago, completed in 1960, was the first study to deliberately examine the question of NREM mentation.[5] Eight subjects were tested for seven nights each, with both REM and NREM awakenings made on each night. I sought to determine the extent of NREM (and REM) recall in nocturnal interviews in which the subject was requested to report on his mental experiences in general rather than on his "dreams." This change in interview technique seemed desirable in light of previous evidence that NREM mentation might be less dreamlike than REM mentation and consequently would be unreported by the subject if he felt that the experimenter were interested only in his "dreams." In addition, recordings were made during the nocturnal interviews of the subject's answers to a number of standardized questions concerning the quality of reported mental experiences—for example: Did you have any feelings or emotions? Was the imagery clear?—and the subject also filled out a rating form the next morning for each such experience. These answers and ratings made possible a comparative analysis of the nature of NREM and REM mental content.

REM-sleep recall, with 108 awakenings, was found 87 per cent of the time, and NREM-sleep recall, with 136 awakenings, was found 74 per cent of the time. The difference between these values was statistically significant, but not large. The recall criterion employed in this comparison was similar to Kamiya's "lenient" one: recall was counted if the subject reported any item of specific mental content. When claims, substantiated or not, of mental content as well as actual reports of mental content were considered, 92 per cent of the REM awakenings and 87 per cent of the NREM awakenings seemed to be associated with some mental activity. The difference between REM and NREM mentation with this latter criterion was not statistically significant.

This very high index of mentation in NREM sleep, compared with Dement and Kleitman's very low index of the same variable, immediately raised a number of questions. Was this NREM recall memory of something other than NREM mental activity? Was it, in particular, recollection of experiences that occurred during REM sleep? My findings demonstrated that the NREM recall rate was identical whether awakenings had been preceded by an uninterrupted REM period or not. The hypothesis that NREM recall consisted of prior REM content thus could not explain NREM reports of mental activity. Did this NREM recall come predominantly from EEG stage-2 sleep adjacent to REM sleep, or was it evenly distributed through the NREM portion of the sleep cycle? Recall from ascending stage 2 was high (74 per cent), but that from stages 3 and 4 (70 per cent) was almost equal to it. Apparently, the entire NREM period was capable of sustaining mentation. How had earlier experimenters failed to achieve the high levels of NREM mental activity obtained in this study?

Part of the difference in findings on the rate of reported NREM mentation may stem from unknown differences in the subjects employed in the several investigations of such mental activity. Dement and Kleitman's study employed only nine subjects, five of whom contributed the bulk of their data, and my research used only eight subjects. With samples as small as these, subject variability, which seems far greater for NREM recall than for REM recall, becomes particularly important. Kamiya's study, with its large number of subjects and awakenings and its NREM value midway between mine and that of Dement and Kleitman, probably yields the most generally representative value of the incidence of reportable NREM mental activity.

In addition to subject variability, however, the difference in findings on NREM mentation is also probably due, in part, to differences in interview technique and in recall criterion, as discussed above. The key element in both of these cases seems to lie in qualitative variations between REM and NREM content. Because NREM mentation is less dreamlike than REM mentation, it was less apt to be elicited in interviews in which subjects were asked to report their "dreams" than in interviews in which they were asked to report their mental experiences in general, and it was less apt to be classified as "recall" (dream recall) by experimenters.

QUALITATIVE DIFFERENCES
BETWEEN REM AND NREM REPORTS

Table 1 indicates some of the major dimensions along which my subjects' REM and NREM reports proved differentiable. There was, first of all, a greater incidence of thinking (conceptual) reports from NREM sleep than from REM sleep, whereas almost all REM reports were of dreams (perceptual).

NREM reports had less content involving hallucinated organismic involvement (emotional processes, in general, and anxiety and hostility-violence, in particular; visual activity; physical movement) than did REM reports. NREM reports were less elaborated than REM reports—it was more likely that there would be only one, rather than several, characters other than the

TABLE 1

Qualitative Characteristics of REM and NREM Reports

Subject replies to nocturnal interview questions:

	REM Sleep		Stage 3 and 4		Ascending Stage 2	
	PERCENTAGE	NUMBER OF AWAKENINGS/ REPORTS	PERCENTAGE	NUMBER OF AWAKENINGS/ REPORTS	PERCENTAGE	NUMBER OF AWAKENINGS/ REPORTS
"Dreaming" Content	82	108	51	37	51	35
"Thinking" Content	5	108	19	37	23	35
Emotion: self	50	88	28	25	29	24
Visual	90	93	73	26	62	26
Physical movement: self	67	73	33	15	38	13
Only one other character	34	79	62	16	50	14
Shift in scene	63	81	28	18	38	13
Median judged duration of reported mental experience	(5 min)	87	(5 min)	20	(5 min)	23
Awareness of dreaming	25	84	15	20	24	21

	MEAN RATING	NUMBER OF REPORTS	MEAN RATING	NUMBER OF REPORTS	MEAN RATING	NUMBER OF REPORTS
Occuring just before bell?	98	91	88	25	96	24
Work/school themes	15	94	19	26	50	26
Continuation process	11	62	35	23	35	17
Memory process	1	94	8	26	23	26
Makes sense to dreamer in terms of recent experience *	48	93	69	26	75	24

Subject ratings of dream characteristics (scales 0 to 5):

	MEAN RATING	NUMBER OF REPORTS	MEAN RATING	NUMBER OF REPORTS	MEAN RATING	NUMBER OF REPORTS
Anxiety	1.19	87	.71	17	1.00	16
Violence-Hostility	.71	89	.12	17	.59	17
Dramatic	1.10	87	.65	17	.76	17
Distortion	1.68	87	1.12	17	.41	17

* Question asked on postsleep questionnaire rather than during nocturnal interview.

subject; the narrative was less likely to contain several different scenes or parts and less likely to be rated as dramatic in character.

NREM reports showed a greater manifest correspondence to recent events in the subject's life than did REM reports (greater presence of themes from the subject's daily routine—school or work; more likely to represent a continuation of material reported on a previous awakening; more likely to be an undistorted re-creation of some recent event, thought, or situation; more likely to "make sense" to the dreamer in terms of a manifest reference to some recent experience in his life; and less likely to be rated as distorted.)

Table 1 also indicates several dimensions along which NREM and REM reports were not differentiable: median judged length, awareness of unreality of the content, and time of occurrence relative to the awakening stimulus. These findings will prove helpful when considering certain questions about the status of NREM reports.

The main outlines of my findings on the qualitative characteristics differentiating REM and NREM reports have been independently verified by Rechtschaffen and his associates,[6] and have more recently been almost totally confirmed by the findings of myself and Rechtschaffen [7] in a study in which a much larger number of subjects, twenty-four, was employed.

Although statistical evidence may give a rough idea of NREM reports, a full feeling for their nature can come only through acquaintance with actual examples. To this end, the following series, obtained from an adult male subject who was employed by the Internal Revenue Service, is presented:

1. He asked an acquaintance at work for a hammer, so that he could fix something in his apartment (NREM).

2. He was thinking of a point made in his tax class, that you have to provide over half of a person's support to claim him as a dependent (NREM).

3. He received a phone call in the middle of the night from a girl identifying herself as from the University of Chicago. She said that it was time for his "35-day evaluation." He chided her for calling so late at night. She replied that it was the only time they could get him in (REM sleep, 3 minutes after REM onset).[8]

The first two reports, which are typical of this subject's NREM reports, have an everyday quality which the third one lacks. In commenting on the thirty-five-day evaluation by the University of Chicago, with which his only connection was his service in this dream study, the subject noted that he was in a ninety-day probationary period in his new job. He was to receive thirty-five dollars for his services as a dream subject. It seems, then, that experimental and work experiences have been fused in the REM-period dream so that neither is portrayed with complete accuracy. In the second NREM report, however, the subject is re-experiencing, in a completely undistorted manner, the recent event of considering one of the details of his new job. The purely conceptual quality of this report was a fairly typical NREM characteristic for three of my eight subjects.

The others generally had somewhat more "dreamlike" NREM reports. The following samples are from such a subject, an undergraduate major in English literature (and, incidentally, the same subject whose REM reports were examined in detail in the preceding chapter):

1. He pictures Anna Karenina. She is sitting at a table, then gets up, turns to the left, and walks away (NREM).

2. He is in a sleep laboratory, filling out a pencil and paper form. Someone passes by commenting that the task is a stupid one (NREM).

3. In the first scene, he is standing on a street corner, holding his bicycle and talking to someone about a girl who wanted to be a striptease dancer.

In the second scene, he is in a doctor's study with two women and the doctor. They are discussing two books. The heroine in the first book was a striptease dancer, but is no longer this, but a nurse. The women are discussing how much hardship she has as a nurse. A discussion then ensues of a second book, by John Steinbeck, in which the main character, also a nurse, did not, apparently, endure similar hardship. The women discuss this avidly, as if they were going to go into "this sort of thing" (REM sleep, 3 minutes after REM onset).[9]

The first two reports of this series seem to be tied much more clearly and with much less distortion to recent manifest behaviors or concerns of the subject. In the first, he brings to life a character of a novel that he is reading; in the second, he takes notice of the questionnaire that he must fill out each evening at the laboratory and makes, through a vaguely identified figure, a comment as to how he views this labor. Although these NREM reports are more detailed and dreamlike than those of the previous subject, there is still a striking difference from REM content in terms of distortion and elaboration.

Many more NREM than REM reports were continuations of the theme of a prior narrative. For example, consider the following two reports, the first collected from ascending stage 1, and the second from descending stage 2 as the subject fell asleep following the first awakening:

1. It was about the parkers who are going to this school, letters being sent to all of them. I saw the office with the files of all the people whose name begins with DEL, and then I saw another file, with the L's, with all this taken out, only other names still in there. Letters were going to be sent to those people with the L's.

2. It was about the L people at the University who want to be sent mail. This person had complained because they hadn't gotten the mail, and sent a complaining letter to the registrar. When I was with the person who was writing the letter, it was sort of a gaily rebellious feeling.[10]

The NREM report clearly takes up where the ascending stage-1 dream was broken off. Note that the NREM dream contains the subject's negative reaction to being interrupted the first time, just as the letters were to be sent out. The subject feels "gaily rebellious" as the would-be recipient files his complaint with the registrar (experimenter). Both of these dreams were also scored in the work-school category as well, since the subject had a clerical job in the University Registrar's office that involved the regulation of student parking.

The following report serves as an example of an NREM report that was rated a memory process:

I was thinking about this phone call from home tonight. I got a long-distance call from home, and my parents were very angry with me because I haven't written. They really gave me hell for about twenty minutes on the phone tonight, which bothered me no end. I had been thinking of that this last time you rang the bell, and I had a very unpleasant feeling about it. I was rehearsing their conversation in my mind.[11]

The nature of the qualitative differences between typical NREM and REM content should now be fairly clear. The former is, in Freudian terms, more like secondary-process, or everyday rational, thinking while the latter is more like primary-process, or fanciful and unrealistic, thinking that does not labor under nearly so many constraints imposed by external reality or by inner standards derived from external reality.*

It is important not to overestimate the differences between REM and NREM mentation, however, even though all these points of statistical differentiation have been established. Although most undistorted memory processes occur in NREM sleep, most NREM reports are not undistorted memory processes. Although most themes derived from an everyday routine of work or school occur in NREM narratives, most NREM awakenings do not produce such reports. Although REM reports are rated as more distorted than NREM reports, most of the latter contain some distortions. Although most "thinking" reports come from NREM sleep, most NREM reports are of "dreaming" (a visually hallucinated, dramatic episode). And, although the typical NREM report is less dreamlike than the typical REM one, some NREM narratives get very dreamlike indeed:

I was with my mother in a public library. I wanted her to steal something for me. I've got to try and remember what it was, because it was something extraordinary, something like a buffalo head that was in this museum. I had told my mother previously that I wanted this buffalo head and she said, all right, you know, we'll see what we can do about it.

---

* For more on Freud's distinction between primary and secondary process thinking, see E. Hilgard, "Impulsive versus Realistic Thinking: An Examination of the Distinction between Primary and Secondary Processes in Thought," *Psychological Bulletin,* 59 (1962), pp. 477–488.

And she met me in the library, part of which was a museum. And I remember telling my mother to please lower her voice and she insisted on talking even more loudly. And I said, if you don't, of course, you'll never be able to take the buffalo head. Everyone will turn around and look at you. Well, when we got to the place where the buffalo head was, it was surrounded by other strange things. There was a little sort of smock that little boys used to wear at the beginning of the century. And one of the women who worked at the library came up to me and said, dear, I haven't been able to sell this smock. And I remember saying to her, well, why don't you wear it then? For some reason or other I had to leave my mother alone, and she had to continue with the buffalo head project all by herself. Then I left the library and went outside, and there were groups of people just sitting on the grass listening to music.[12]

The first suspicion about this report is that it must be of an experience that occurred during REM sleep, and this idea may well be justified: the awakening was made twenty-five minutes after the conclusion of an undisturbed REM period. Yet a nagging uncertainty persists. Why did not the customary post-REM amnesia for REM content occur? Might this not be, in fact, an NREM dream?

The apparent overlap in qualitative characteristics of NREM and REM reports, represented in extreme form in the preceding report, raises the question of the actual degree of discriminability of the two classes of reports. Lawrence Monroe, a psychologist at the University of Illinois Medical School, and his associates, have recently addressed themselves to this problem.[13] Judges (graduate students in psychology) who were instructed in the nature of the typically observed REM-NREM recall and content differences were given the task of discriminating between REM and NREM reports but were kept ignorant of conditions of awakening for any of them. The judges averaged 80 per cent correct judgments where the only information available to them consisted of the reports (both content and no-content) themselves. When controls were instituted for no-content awakenings, subject differences, night, and time of night (judges were given ninety-two content reports subgrouped into forty-six pairs, one REM and one NREM, obtained from the same subject on the same night and at the same time of that night) the judges averaged 92 per cent correct.

The slight improvement in performance when subject and time of night were held constant may demonstrate two characteristics of NREM mentation. First, some subjects have more dreamlike NREM mentation than do others (as was illustrated above), and so, while their NREM reports may be discriminable from their own, even more dreamlike, REM dreams, they may not be discriminable from the REM dreams of a subject whose sleeping mentation, both REM and NREM, is generally less intense than average. Second, NREM thought seems to have, and REM mentation definitely does have, more dreamlike properties later in the night, so that, although the subject's late morning NREM report may be discriminable from his late morning REM one, it may not be discriminable from his initial REM report (which, as we have seen, is less dreamlike in numerous respects than subsequent REM reports). The overlap between REM and NREM reports is thus likely to be accentuated if the researcher fails to institute controls for two variables, in addition to REM versus NREM sleep, that influence dream intensity: subject differences and time of night.

It is apparent from the degree of accuracy achieved by the judges in this study that REM periods are highly diagnostic of that kind of sleep mentation that ordinarily merits the label "dreaming": experiences that are vivid, highly distorted, elaborated, and visual-hallucinatory. NREM periods generally produce a relatively more plausible, thoughtlike kind of mentation, although, here too, some distortion is the rule rather than the exception. If "dreams" are defined as any mental experiences occurring during sleep, then dreaming is not localized to any one phase of physiological sleep. It is not likely to be fruitful, however, to blur the numerous differences between the mental activity occurring in NREM sleep and that occurring in REM sleep by assigning a common label to them. So, it seems justifiable to continue to refer to REM sleep as dreaming sleep. In assigning this label, however, it is no longer possible to imply that NREM sleep is altogether without mental content. Nor is it possible to imply that NREM content consists solely of low-intensity, everyday thinking processes. The typical NREM report is somewhat dreamlike, merely less so than the typical REM report.

NREM REPORTS AS AWAKENING EXPERIENCES

NREM reports do not seem explicable in terms of the recall of previous REM-sleep dreaming. In particular, they are not more likely to occur in the NREM sleep following an undisturbed REM period than in NREM sleep without such a prior period. It has also been demonstrated that NREM content reports are not significantly more likely to consist of "dreaming," as opposed to "thinking," content when there has been a prior undisturbed REM period.[14]

The authenticity of NREM reports, however, will be in some doubt until preawakening physiological landmarks can be correlated with the content of subsequently elicited NREM reports as preawakening eye-movement patterns have been associated with visual imagery reported by subjects after REM-sleep awakenings. NREM sleep is, by definition, without rapid eye movements, and no NREM physiological variable of comparable potency has appeared as a predictor of the nature of post-awakening reports. It has been suggested, therefore, that NREM reports may be not of NREM sleep mentation at all, but rather of mental experiences occurring during the *hypnopompic,* or awakening, state.

At present such an hypothesis can be neither definitively supported nor definitively refuted. The weight of the evidence, however, appears to refute it. In particular, for example, with respect to the data of my study of NREM mentation:

1. Awakenings were made with a loud bell, ensuring reasonably rapid arousal by the subject.

2. Recall was very rarely obtained when the subject was difficult to arouse, that is, had a longer awakening period.

3. As noted in Table 1, the median estimated duration of experiences reported from stages 2, 3, and 4 was five minutes, identical with the value for experiences reported from REM-sleep awakenings (made at points ranging from REM onset to twenty-four minutes after REM onset) and much in excess of NREM awakening times, which averaged but a few seconds.

4. As also noted in Table 1, subjects most often felt that NREM mentation, like REM mentation, was occurring just *before* the application of the awakening stimulus, and most often felt that it was totally hallucinatory, as is true of most REM mentation but not, perhaps, of most hypnopompic experiences.

5. Much of the NREM content in this study, examples of which were noted above, seems too well-organized and coherent to be the product of the psychic confusion that often accompanies the process of waking up.

Goodenough and his co-workers have been investigating the effects of gradual versus abrupt awakenings, in part to determine the extent to which NREM reports might be awakening experiences. There data indicate in general that "thinking" reports more often accompany gradual awakenings than abrupt ones.[15] When NREM awakenings were made thirty minutes after the termination of a previous REM period, the mean reaction time for those awakenings producing thinking reports was considerably longer (thirty-eight seconds) than the average for all such NREM awakenings (seventeen seconds). These data suggest, although they cannot prove, that some NREM *thinking* reports may be reports of awakening, or hypnopompic, experiences. NREM *dreams,* however, occurred as often on abrupt as on gradual awakenings and came from abrupt awakenings with relatively short reaction times. NREM thinking reports elicited relatively soon (five minutes) after the end of a REM period also often had short reaction times. The researchers conclude that the hypnopompic experience explanation may account for some, but not all, NREM "thinking" reports but cannot explain those of NREM "dreaming."

In addition to this negative evidence on the awakening-artifact hypothesis of NREM recall, there are a few indications in the literature that preawakening events *can* be associated with the content elicited on subsequent NREM awakenings, just as preawakening REM patterning can be associated with subsequently elicited REM content. For example, the following case has been reported:

During one NREM period (Stage 2), the following sequence of stimulation was presented to a subject: 67 seconds after the subject showed a slight body movement, a 500 cps tone was presented below waking threshold for seven seconds. This was followed in turn by 27 seconds of no stimulation, a second presentation of the tone, and an additional 32 seconds of no stimulation. Then the subject was awakened by a loud buzzer. He reported that he dreamt he was standing on a rock talking with someone, then: " . . . a little whistling tone was going on . . . and then it went off. And (the other person) said, 'Oh, you had better get things over with quickly, because you may have to wake up soon.' . . . I just said 'Oh!' to this and I think I heard the whistling noise again. . . . Then the same scene was there for some time, and I was just walking around trying to think of what was going on." [16]

In another study, a subject who found that his hand was "asleep" upon awakening from NREM sleep reported that, immediately before the awakening, he dreamed he had been trying to buy some avocados in a grocery store.[17] He said that in the dream he repeatedly tried to pick the avocados up with his hand, but found that it would not move. It appears then that some NREM reports may be tied to landmark external stimuli or to naturally occurring organismic events in such a manner to establish that the experiences reported did occur, in fact, during NREM sleep.

Furthermore, recalling the evidence cited in Chapter 1 on the behavioral possibilities of NREM sleep (performance of conditioned responses, and initiation of such complex behaviors as walking and talking), there seems to be little reason to doubt that mental experiences might occur during this kind of sleep. To be sure, some few NREM reports may represent recall of previous REM dreams, and some NREM (and some REM) reports may well be awakening artifacts. It now seems apparent, however, that most NREM reports are just what they appear to be, narratives of mentation occurring during NREM sleep.

THE RELATIONSHIP BETWEEN
REM AND NREM MENTATION

The existence of somewhat distinct kinds of mentation in physiologically distinguishable stages of sleep quite naturally raises questions as to the relationship between the NREM and the REM mentation occurring on any given subject night. It seems from the evidence now available that the nature of the NREM mentation on a given night is affected by, and affects, the nature of the REM mentation occurring on the same night. For example, NREM reports may continue the theme developed in previous REM reports.

Rechtschaffen and his associates have investigated systematically the interrelatedness of REM and NREM mentation occurring during the course of a single night's sleep.[18] Subjects were awakened during both types of sleep and asked to report on mental experiences occurring just before awakening. The following series illustrates the close relationship these authors sometimes found among the REM and NREM reports occurring on a single night:

A–1: REM Period: Time 62 [minutes since initial sleep onset] I was dreaming. I remember the feeling that the dream contained a few people other than myself—contemporaries of mine. We were all in a *boat*. I remember worrying about the boat overturning and what we would do. And I remember the thought that we would just have to swim to save our souls.

A–2: Stage 3: Time 95 I have the feeling that I was in a *boat* again, a small boat, like a rowboat. It being rather *sunny* out. . . . I don't remember thinking of what would happen if the boat overturned, as I did before. I was preoccupied with a thought. I really can't remember what it was.

A–3: Stage 4: Time 187
I had been dreaming about getting ready to take some type
of an *exam*. It had been a very short dream. . . . I don't think
I was worried about them.

A–4: REM Period: Time 223
I was dreaming about *exams*. In the early part of the dream
I was dreaming I had just finished an exam, and it was a very
sunny day outside. I was walking with a boy who's in some of
my classes with me. There was sort of a . . . break, and
someone mentioned a grade they had gotten in a social science
exam. And I asked them if the social science marks had come
in. They said yes. I didn't get it, because I had been away for
a day.

A–5: Stage 2: Time 274
. . . dreaming about *exams*, and about having taken different
exams . . .[19]

The authors conclude that discrete elements and themes
elicited in NREM reports sometimes repeat, and sometimes antic-
ipate, the content of other NREM and REM reports collected
on the same night. In particular, REM-period dreams "do not
arise *sui generis* as psychologically isolated mental productions
but emerge as the most vivid and memorable part of a larger
fabric of interwoven mental activity during sleep." [20]

In my study of NREM mentation, I sought to observe the role
that such mentation might play in the formation of REM-period
dreams by making NREM awakenings in ascending EEG stage 2,
presumably just before the issuance of an ascending stage-1
REM period.[21] Table 1 contains some of the data on the content
elicited during this pre-REM sleep stage. Note that, as compared
with other NREM mentation, pre-REM stage-2 mentation is rated
as less distorted by the subject, contains more routine, everyday

(work/school) themes, and more undistorted memories. In these respects, the mentation of pre-REM stage 2 bears a close resemblance to the Freudian concept of the day residue, to the recent memories from which dreams are presumed by Freud to develop.

Strictly speaking, the fact that day residue content is often experienced during pre-REM stage-2 sleep and that dreamlike experiences occur in the next stage of the sleep cycle, ascending stage 1, does not establish that the first kind of material is dynamically transformed to produce the second. Evidence for the "working over" of day residues at dream onset comes from the following report, elicited twenty-six seconds after REM onset:

> I was in the library and I was filing cards, and I came to some letter between "a" and "c." I was filing some, I think it was Burma, some country, and just as I put that in, there was this scene of some woman, who was sent to look for a little girl who was lost, and she was sent to Burma. They thought the little girl was going there, for some reason. This was sort of like a dramatization of what I was doing. I mean I was filing, and then this scene took place right at the same time. In the setting it was sort of like you'd imagine it, but I had the feeling it was really happening.[22]

In this dream, a scene from the subject's daily work experience —she had a job in the university library—led to an elaboration far removed from her everyday experience. The work element (filing), typical in ascending stage-2 content, preceded the unusual and somewhat unrealistic element (Burma), typical in REM-period content. The physiological recording shows a recent progression from stage 2 to a REM period. While this one example proves very little, in and of itself, it does suggest that

REM-period dreams may begin with the working over of day residues of a sort most often experienced during NREM stage 2.

This particular example also suggests, of course, the abruptness with which the intrusion of new thematic elements may occur at REM onset and illustrates the considerable differences that exist between NREM and REM mental content. Thus, while NREM content may provide some sort of a starting point for the REM dream, the REM process is strikingly different from its NREM predecessor.

Chapter 5

MENTAL ACTIVITY AT SLEEP ONSET

THE sleep-onset period, that borderland between wakefulness and profound sleep, is peculiar from several points of view. Subjectively, for example, it has often been associated with unusual kinds of bodily sensations and hallucinations. Objectively, it is characterized by EEG and eye-activity patterns (alpha rhythm in conjunction with slow eye movements and a descending stage 1 without the rapid eye movements which characterize ascending EEG stage 1) seldom, if ever, observed during either complete wakefulness or total sleep. One fact about the sleep-onset period is clear. Except in the case of patients suffering from *narcolepsy*, a disease characterized by the frequent and uncontrollable urge for sleep, REM periods do not occur at the onset of nocturnal sleep.[1] Nor does REM sleep occur at the onset of daytime naps.[2] And yet there are indications in reports in the older literature on the subject that "dreams" occur at the onset of nocturnal sleep.[3] One author, for example, reports:

> In the course of a very short sleep—two minutes at most—I found myself standing at my study window, looking out at a curious collection of long straws which some birds have, in fact, made in one of the trees in the square. The object of the collection I cannot guess—it is certainly not a nest. In my dream I was surprised to note that the trees, instead of being in the other side of the wide roadway, came up close to my window, and that the straws seemed to have turned into a roughly circular heap of sticks, resembling a nest. After I awoke, the picture remained quite clear. This was all the dream. I call it a dream because it was somewhat less fleeting than a mere hypnagogic [sleep-onset] illusion.[4]

Similarly, it has been noted that persons not infrequently assert that they dreamed as they fell off to sleep during daytime napping.[5]

In recent years, there has been a tendency for researchers to identify dreaming with REM sleep and to answer questions about dreaming with data derived solely from research on this stage of sleep.[6] But anecdotal reports of dreaming at sleep onset suggest that the REM period may not be the only locus of mentation sufficiently hallucinatory, bizarre, and so on to merit the label "dreaming," and that REM-period observations therefore may provide only part of the answer to questions concerning the nature of this process.

DREAMING AT SLEEP ONSET

With Gerald Vogel, a psychiatrist associated with the University of Chicago Medical School, I undertook a study of mental activity during the sleep-onset or hypnagogic period to determine whether dreaming does occur in association with EEG/EOG [*] patterns other than those of the ascending stage-1 REM period.[7] Nine subjects were "awakened" a number of times over a series of four nights from each of four sleep-onset EEG/EOG patterns: alpha rhythm with REM, alpha rhythm with SEM (slow eye movement), descending stage 1, and descending stage 2 (specimens *B, C, D,* and *E–F,* respectively, of Figure 3, page 17). They were asked to describe what, if anything, they had been experiencing just before the experimenter's intrusion. Upon completion of his spontaneous report, the subject was asked a number of standardized questions concerning his state of wakefulness or sleep and the sensory imagery, hallucinatory quality, and so forth, of any content he may have reported. The 9 subjects were awakened a total of 212 times: 53 from alpha REM, 54 from alpha SEM, 47 from descending stage 1, and 58 from descending stage 2.

Previous studies of the sleep-onset period had been more narrow in scope (investigations of descending stage 1,[8] the point at which descending stage 1 yields to descending stage 2,[9] or the early moments of descending stage 2 [10]) or in number of subjects and awakenings (a pilot study spanning the several different EEG/EOG stages of the hypnagogic period had been reported [11]). These earlier studies, moreover, apparently because of their investigation of varying portions of the sleeponset period, had developed a number of differing notions of the nature of hypnagogic mental activity: subjects sometimes reported nonhallucinatory kaleidoscopic visual sensations "distinctly different from an actual dream," sometimes reported dreams, and sometimes reported experience of content very sim-

---

[*] Electro-oculogram, referring to the recording of the movement of the eyeball in its socket.

ilar to typically reported NREM mentation. The pilot research spanning the several different stages of the sleep-onset period confirmed this variety of mental content, but its results suggested that there was an orderly succession of these different types of mental activity with progressive stages of sleep induction, with fragmentary visual material passing into more extended and self-involved "dreamlets" as the EEG passed from the alpha rhythm to spindle-dominance.

Since our study is the only major research to take the same subjects through the several discriminable EEG/EOG patterns of the hypnagogic period, it presents the most comprehensive picture to date of mental activity at sleep onset. Its findings, however, are in general agreement with the findings of the earlier and more limited research in the same area, particularly as to the variety of mental activity during this period and the orderly succession of different kinds of mental experience as wakefulness passes into sleep.

We found, first of all, that subjects almost invariably were able to report some kind of mental experience—not necessarily dreaming—upon being awakened during the sleep-onset period. Pooled percentages of recall of some mental experience were:

> Alpha REM   96.2 per cent
> Alpha SEM   98.1
> Descending stage 1   97.9
> Descending stage 2   89.7

Subjects were asked to judge their state of consciousness on a five-point scale (0, awake and alert; 1, awake but drowsy; 2, drifting off to sleep; 3, in light sleep; 4, in deep sleep). There was considerable variability from subject to subject in the judged depth of sleep associated with a particular EEG/EOG stage. Individual subject means ranged:

Alpha REM	.17—2.17
Alpha SEM	.50—2.67
Descending stage 1	1.25—2.67
Descending stage 2	1.67—2.67

For any one subject, however, there was an increase in judged drowsiness with the succession of EEG/EOG stages, and the medians of individual-subject means revealed the same trend:

Alpha REM	.80
Alpha SEM	1.50
Descending stage 1	2.00
Descending stage 2	2.25

It is apparent from the combination of data on reported mental experience and data on judged state of consciousness that mental activity does not suddenly cease at the onset of drowsiness or sleep. The human mind is not suddenly "turned off"; we do not suddenly plunge into the unconsciousness of deep anaesthesia as sleep impinges upon us.

What *kinds* of mental experience are reported during the sleep onset period? In terms of sensory imagery, hypnagogic experiences seem to be primarily visual in quality. (Visual images were reported on 78 per cent of alpha-REM awakenings, 81 per cent of alpha-SEM awakenings, 89 per cent of descending stage 1 awakenings, and 83 per cent of descending stage 2 awakenings.) Auditory and kinesthetic imagery were present in roughly one-quarter of the hypnagogic experiences, with little differentiation of incidence by EEG/EOG stage. The most striking aspect of the data on sensory imagery was the extent of individual differences, both in association of imagery modality with any particular EEG/EOG stage and in the shifting incidence of imagery modality across EEG/EOG stages. One subject, for instance, might report visual imagery almost all the time in all EEG/EOG stages; another might indicate increasing incidence of visual imagery and still another a decreasing incidence of visual imagery with the succession of stages. This is but the first of many indications in our data of wide individual differences in mental experience at sleep onset, a much wider range of variation than would be found during REM sleep, for instance.

In terms of *affect,** emotion during the hypnagogic period was neither as frequent nor as intense as emotion during REM sleep. Affect was neither predominantly unpleasant nor predominantly pleasant. All subjects but one reached their peak value of hypnagogic affect during the alpha-rhythm EEG.

This decrease in affect during descending EEG stages 1 and 2 was accompanied by an increase in hallucinatory dreamlike experience. Subjects were clearly hallucinating in the following way:

Alpha REM reports	29 per cent
Alpha SEM reports	47
Descending stage 1 reports	74
Descending stage 2 reports	80

If those mental experiences occurring during sleep that are at least partly hallucinatory and somewhat dramatic in quality are to be called dreams, then such phenomena were reported:

* Affect refers to the experiential, as opposed to the behavioral or physiological, aspects of "emotion."

Alpha REM awakenings	31 per cent
Alpha SEM awakenings	43
Descending stage 1 awakenings	76
Descending stage 2 awakenings	71

Individual differences in the incidence of dreams during the hypnagogic period were quite striking. Some subjects dreamed early (beginning during the alpha pattern) and frequently, others only later (beginning during descending stages 1 and 2) and less frequently. From these data, there would seem to be considerably more scope for the influence of personality variables upon dream incidence during the sleep-onset period than there is during REM sleep, from which dreams are almost universally reported (these influences are considered in Chapter 8).

Our investigation, as is often true of initial studies in any area of psychological research, involved intensive collection of data from a rather small number of subjects. Further research is always needed, in such cases, to establish the generality of the preliminary findings. A recent investigation employed thirty-two young-adult subjects in an attempt to verify the findings of the smaller subject sample in our study.[12] It confirmed that dreaming occurs fairly frequently at sleep onset, although it was found that full-blown dreaming occurred significantly more often during REM sleep than at sleep onset.

Dreamlike mental activity apparently does occur during the hypnagogic period, but in what sense are these experiences dreams? In particular, in what ways are sleep-onset dreams similar to, and in what ways are they different from, the REM-period experience that has been the most frequent referent of the term dream?

THE NATURE OF HYPNAGOGIC DREAMS

The examination of representative reports is perhaps the easiest pathway to an understanding of the nature of sleep-onset mentation. Consider, first, a series of reports collected from an early and chronic hypnagogic dreamer:

Alpha REM. I saw a girl holding a baby, standing on some steps. That created rather an unpleasant experience to me— I thought I flushed or something. The girl had black hair and a plain black sweater and black slacks. It was sort of like basement stairs. She was going down, standing about in the middle of the steps, and I was in the basement. I was observing it through my eyes. She was looking straight ahead. She wasn't looking at me. I got sort of the feeling like I was hiding. (QUESTION: Were you aware, while this experience was taking place, that you were in bed here in the Sleep Laboratory?) No. I felt myself definitely in the basement. (*Awake but drowsy.*)

Alpha SEM. I was lying with my head in a girl's lap, saw my face up against her leg. I was sort of looking at myself and the girl. It was a good feeling, a mild erotic feeling. This was out in the park or woods, a blanket there and a little grass around. I was aware, about 10 per cent approximately, that I was not completely dissociated from reality, but I would say I was definitely experiencing the appropriate feelings of the image I had seen. (*Awake but drowsy.*)

Descending Stage 1. I was looking at some teeth, as a dentist would look at teeth, at two side by side. A patient's teeth and there was a cat. I was looking first at the person's teeth and then at the cat's teeth, making some kind of comparison. (QUESTION: Did this seem to be participation or observation of something really taking place?) Yes. It seemed to have a detached sort of quality, without any apparent significance, sort of like I just fell into it. (*Drifting to sleep.*)

Descending Stage 2. I think I was just starting to climb some steps. There was somebody else in it too. I said something to him, he was standing on the bottom of the stairs, and then I started to walk up the steps. It was sort of the thought of parting, of saying goodbye. The staircase was very wide, maybe a little bit out of proportion for the setting that I figured I was in. (QUESTION: At the time I called, did you feel that you were actually out somewhere, walking up steps, rather than simply conjuring something up in your own mind?) Yes. (QUESTION: Can you recall anything else of the experience?) No, except that the Freudian imagery seems overwhelmingly obvious. (*Drifting to sleep.*) [13]

A second series of reports comes from a later and less-frequent hypnagogic dreamer:

Alpha REM. The last thing I was thinking was this is probably the last time you will wake me up. I was very pleased with the idea, I felt confident that it was true. (QUESTION: Any visual imagery?) No. (QUESTION: Did you feel that you were controlling this experience?) Yes. (QUESTION: And were you aware that you were lying here in your bed?) Yes. (*Awake but drowsy.*)

Alpha SEM. I was thinking about Russian words and I was translating them into English. I was reviewing something I had been reading earlier in the evening. I was recalling some work that I had listed for myself in a vocabulary. I was thinking of the word which means "plateau." I was pleased that I could remember. (QUESTION: Any visual imagery?) No. (QUESTION: Did you feel that you were controlling this experience?) Yes. (QUESTION: Were you aware that you were lying here in bed during the experience?) Yes. (*Awake and alert.*)

Descending Stage 1. Had something to do with a garden plot, and I was planting seed in it. I could see some guy standing in this field, and it was kind of filled and cultivated, and he was talking about this to me. I can't quite remember what it was he did say, it seems to me as if it had to do with growing, whether these things were going to grow. I didn't feel I had control over the experience. (QUESTION: Were you aware that you were lying here in bed during the experience?) No. (*Drifting to sleep.*)

Descending Stage 2. I have some sort of visual recollection that looks like you putting the equipment on my head. I didn't control the experience. (QUESTION: Were you aware that you were here, lying in your bed?) No. (*In light sleep.*) [14]

These two series not only illustrate the variety of dreamlike and non-dreamlike reports obtained during the hypnagogic period, but also the nature of the difference observed between the chronic and the occasional sleep-onset dreamer. The first subject slips into hallucinatory or quasi-hallucinatory fantasy during alpha rhythm EEG, while the second is still keeping his thinking abstract or nonperceptual, and reality oriented, both as to form—his thinking is consciously controlled—and content —the experimental situation, his attempts to master the Russian language. During descending stage 1 both experience hallucinatory and somewhat bizarre and symbolic content fully deserving of the label dreaming. During descending stage 2, the first subject continues to experience similar content, but, while the second subject's thought maintains its dreamlike form—visual and hallucinatory, its content is brought back to matters of immediate reality, such as being fitted with EEG electrodes for the sleep experiment. Differences of this sort in sleep-onset mental activity, in conjunction with observations of subjects' waking behavior, led us to propose that subjects with earlier signs of dreamlike mentation at sleep onset were less anxious and constricted in giving expression to their inner life than those who "resisted" such content during alpha rhythm EEG.

The dreamlike reports in these two series also illustrate the inaccuracy of several previous suggestions as to ways of discriminating hypnagogic mental activity from true nocturnal dreaming. Dement and Kleitman, for example, had suggested that hypnagogic experiences were neither hallucinatory nor as well-organized as REM-period dreams.[15] But the statistics in our study indicate that subjects *do* hallucinate at sleep onset. It should also be apparent from the hypnagogic dream reports quoted that the hypnagogic dream can be, and most often is, as well-organized and internally coherent as the typical REM-period dream. However, in some cases we did receive reports betraying failures of mental synthesis; for example, the subject sees the number 2081 without experiencing any perceptual or ideational context to render it meaningful to him; and, as suggested by Dement and Kleitman's data, these were seen most often during descending stage 1.

Similarly, Oswald suggested that the subject at sleep onset does not hallucinate his own participation in his mental fantasies, that is, hypnagogic dreams lack a "living in" quality present in the REM-period dream.[16] But hypnagogic dream samples quoted and statistics collected by us on hallucinated self-involvement in sleep-onset fantasies make clear that subjects most often *do* hallucinate their own participation in the fantasies they are weaving as they fall asleep.

What Dement and Kleitman and Oswald seem to be saying is that hypnagogic dreams are not as "real" as nocturnal REM-period dreams. One sense in which our data support their contention is in terms of the subject's emotional involvement. As we have already seen, affect is relatively lacking as a component of mental experience during sleep onset, particularly when such mentation becomes dreamlike. In the specimens of hypnagogic mentation quoted above, for example, the first subject commented during his stage-1 report that his experience had a "detached sort of quality"; and there was a generally greater incidence of "feeling" content in both subjects' alpha-rhythm as opposed to their descending-stage-1 and stage-2 reports.

Still other authors have suggested that true nocturnal dreaming is unique in the extent to which its images are bizarre and symbolic. The hypnagogic hallucination, according to one such author, does not "attempt to say as much as a dream," hence "it does not need to depend upon condensed hieroglyphics to express multiple meanings." [17] Many of our reports, however, including several quoted above (tooth comparison, stair climbing, and seed planting), show considerable use of *condensed hieroglyphics*, or distortion by symbolism, in the manner of typical REM-period dreaming and much more use of such symbolism than is typically observed in NREM content. Hypnagogic dream content, then, *can* be bizarre and symbolic in the manner of REM-period dream content.

If these several suggestions as to particular ways to discriminate between hypnagogic and REM dreaming have not proved adequate, the question of discrimination along similar dimensions still remains. There must surely be experiential and functional differences between hypnagogic and REM dreams, between those that develop out of wakefulness and those that arise in deeper sleep, corresponding with the obvious physiological differentiation in terms of EEG/EOG patterns associated with their occurrence.

Our data do suggest several differences between hypnagogic and REM-sleep dreams. Those in emotional involvement and susceptibility of dream occurrence to variation across subjects have been noted. In Chapter 7, there are some observations suggesting that the hypnagogic dream may, in part, be an attempt at interpreting peripheral organismic stimuli, such as pulse and respiration, in an hallucinatory manner that permits sleep induction. This suggests that such stimuli play a larger role in determining sleep-onset dreaming than that of REM sleep. Our data suggest further differentiation of sleep-onset and REM dreaming in terms of: (1) the speed with which dreaming transpires, and (2) the degree of elaboration that fantasy undergoes.

Some hypnagogic experiences, subjects assert, have an instantaneous quality that, as noted in Chapter 2, is not the case with respect to REM dreaming. The difference seems to reside, experientially, in whether continuity is visual or conceptual in form.

Most of the time, continuity in REM dreaming is visual, or movielike. Within any one episode a realistic progression of images occurs as the dreamer imagines himself moving about or scanning the scenery. As he walks up a flight of stairs, for example, the imagery changes as would the scene in the continuous movie sequence produced by a cameraman holding his camera at eye level as he climbed the stairs.

At least some hypnagogic reports, however, are of experiences that seem to lack this sort of visual continuity. One of our subjects, for example, reported a hypnagogic dream of driving from California to Tijuana, Mexico; of entering a bar there that featured a dancing girl; and of then leaving the bar in the company of this girl. In discussing this dream, he commented that his only visual experience was of three brief images—himself driving at one particular place in California; the inside of the bar; and the girl walking with him in the street. The dream as reported, and apparently as experienced, did have continuity, but not the visual continuity of the REM dream. It was more like seeing three discretely different "still" shots, with the continuity integrated in an ideational, or conceptual, rather than a perceptual, way. While such conceptual continuity may occur in REM dreaming as a bridge between different episodes, each of which is still characterized by perceptual continuity,[18] in the hypnagogic period entire dreams may be constructed with only conceptual continuity.

Such a mode of integration of brief and discontinuous perceptual experience in the hypnagogic period may allow the dreamer to condense a relatively long action sequence into an exceedingly short visual presentation. This kind of hypnagogic mental activity may be responsible for the everyday notion that dreams occur almost instantaneously.

The length of typical hypnagogic dream reports is briefer than the length of full-fledged REM-period reports. Of some four hundred hypnagogic reports that I have examined, none has, for example, approached the length or number of different episodes manifest in REM-sleep Report B in Chapter 2.[19] This fact suggests, among other things, that an individual at sleep onset is neither interested in, nor capable of, the kind of prolonged self-exploration appearing during REM sleep. The lack of interest may be attributed to the desire for sleep. To become involved at sleep onset in the condition of organismic arousal associated with REM dreaming and to experience the kind of highly personal and emotionally absorbing content experienced in REM sleep would seem to be grossly incompatible with the motives that lead us to seek sleep in the first place.

At sleep onset, the human organism seems to shy away from

disturbing thoughts and feelings, with this tendency strongest among those persons least able to tolerate such content. It may be that this is why simple wish-fulfillment dreams seem more predominant at sleep onset than during REM periods. For an individual bent upon achieving sleep, a simple wish-fulfilling fantasy may be the quickest way of disposing of inner drives that may become salient when external-stimulus input is reduced to a minimum. In our study, for example, there was an instance of a hypnagogic dream in which a subject has sexual intercourse with a girl with whom he has not had comparable success in waking life. More symbolically, the first subject quoted above gets an invitation from someone and proceeds to mount an unusually broad staircase, symbolic of the act of sexual intercourse, according to Freud.

This orientation toward sleep, and therefore away from potentially disturbing psychic content, may also be related to the contemporary temporal reference characteristic of hypnagogic dreaming. An analysis of our transcripts failed to reveal a single report with manifest reference to any event less recent than one in the month or so before the subject's appearance in the laboratory.[20] The REM dream, however, may begin with a contemporary reference, but soon works itself back into the most distant nooks and crannies of the dreamer's life.

There seems to be a sense, then, in which the hypnagogic dream does have a more limited function than the true nocturnal dream. Although the hypnagogic dream sometimes is symbolic of repressed impulses, especially for subjects capable of tolerating such content, its purpose seems to be the glossing over of such content in order that sleep may be maintained, rather than an extensive examination of it to further the goal of self-exploration. Note that the end product of the brief hypnagogic period is undisturbed NREM sleep, with its psychically undisturbing mental content.

The hypnagogic dream, then, might best be understood in the following manner.[21] As one falls asleep, by the very definition of sleep it is necessary that he remove his attention from, or *decathect*, external sensory input. At first, the shrinking scope of attention increases the relative salience of stimuli arising within the body (see Chapter 7), but soon even the stimulus input from the periphery of the organism is decathected. The only stimuli to which the sleeper now is sensitive are those generated by the brain, or mind, itself.

Without the typical constraints placed upon the mind's activity by external-stimulus input and by a cathexis of external reality (see, for example, the results of sensory-deprivation researches discussed in Chapter 7), however, thought processes tend toward incoherence of form (meaningless fragments of visual imagery) and disturbing intrapsychic content (anxieties, and socially unacceptable wishes or thoughts). Hypnagogic dreaming reflects in part these side effects of the sensory deprivation that accompanies sleep-induction. It is also, however, the means by which sleep is protected in the face of these tendencies to cognitive disorder and emotional explosion. At sleep onset, the brain weaves internally coherent fantasies to account for— in a manner depriving these stimuli of their awakening potential —the remaining stimulus input reaching the brain and to disguise by symbolism, yet partially discharge by relatively uncomplicated wish fulfillment, any intrapsychic impulses that threaten to disturb sleep.

The hypnagogic dream evidently does accomplish these goals: sleep is preserved against external interference; mental content lacks the manifest affect and the peripheral organismic involvement that characterize true nocturnal dreaming but that, at the more labile state of sleep onset, threaten to return the organism to wakefulness; and hypnagogic mentation soon yields to NREM mentation, whose lesser dreamlike properties are totally compatible with the maintenance of sound sleep.

Thus the hypnagogic dream is not to be viewed as the same kind of prolonged, intense self-exploration that occurs during REM sleep. It is, rather, a temporary expedient adopted by the organism to allow it to pass, undisturbed and with its mental apparatus relatively intact, from wakefulness to sleep. This function is served by the hypnagogic dream's denial or transformation of stimulus input to the brain and by its successful management of potentially disturbing intrapsychic factors.

Chapter 6

PRESLEEP DETERMINANTS
OF DREAMING AND DREAM CONTENT

T HE act of dreaming and the selection of particular elements of dream content are within the broad class of
human activities called *involuntary*. That is, "Because I wanted
to" is not a particularly satisfactory answer to either "Why did
you dream?" or "Why did you dream that dream?" That the act
of dreaming and the selection of particular elements of dream
content are involuntary makes the question of their determination a particularly important one. Why do we dream? Why do
we dream the strange, bizarre things that we often do? These
obviously are very large questions, and they are ones for which
there are not, as yet, definitive answers.

In the past few years, however, psychophysiological methods
of studying dreaming and dream content have made possible the

design of numerous experimental studies that, considered to-gether, provide at least some partial answers to these questions. By equating the act of dreaming with the timing, frequency, and duration of REM periods, it has become possible to investi-gate events causally related to the occurrence of dreaming. By making experimental awakenings during REM sleep, it also has become possible to initiate the systematic investigation of the determinants of particular aspects of dream content, of why one dreams what he does.

Many of these experimental studies have focused upon events of the immediately preceding day or evening. They have demon-strated that such experiences have remarkably little effect upon the occurrence of dreaming. They have also shown that, al-though dream content may include references to experiences of the dream-day, it is by no means a simple or undistorted reflec-tion of them.

PRESLEEP DETERMINANTS OF REM SLEEP

It is apparent from evidence already surveyed that the occur-rence of REM sleep is a highly regular and predictable event. Almost without exception, all individuals thus far studied have had multiple REM periods through the course of a night's sleep, and the spacing of these periods generally has followed the regular and recurring pattern of sleep stages portrayed in Figure 4, page 24. For any given individual, the timing and frequency of REM-sleep episodes are quite similar from one night to the next. Across individuals, particularly those of different age levels, there are indications of somewhat greater variation in REM-sleep characteristics, but again, it is the uniformity, rather than the variation, that is the most impressive aspect of these phenomena. This uniformity does not leave much scope for situationally variable experiences to affect the frequency or duration of REM sleep. Nevertheless, certain presleep factors have been shown to be capable of suppressing or augmenting REM episodes.

Drug Intake.

Amphetamine,[1] a psychic energizer, and barbiturates,[2] psychic depressants, both significantly depress the frequency of REM sleep. Alcohol,[3] at least in certain doses (the equivalent of 6 ounces of 100-proof liquor for a 150-pound man) and under certain conditions of administration, may reduce REM sleep time, but caffeine,[4] at least in a certain dosage range (the equivalent of 2.5 or 3 cups of coffee for a 150-pound man), seems to have no significant effect on the frequency of REM sleep.

Hypnosis and Suggestion.

Johann Stoyva, a psychologist at the University of Colorado Medical School, found that, for seven subjects who reliably dreamed elements of content suggested to them during a presleep hypnotic trance, there was a reduction in REM-sleep time as compared with control nights (those without a posthypnotic dream suggestion) obtained from the same subjects.[5] There is some suggestion in Stoyva's data that the more elements suggested, the greater the decrease in REM time. Three subjects who dreamed in accord with a nontrance, that is waking, suggestion also had a decrease in REM time. Another psychologist employed direct hypnotic suggestions that subjects dream "all night" or "not at all." [6] He found the latter suggestion had no effect, and there was only a slight increase for one of two experimental subjects given the former suggestion. In another study, similar nonhypnotic suggestions affected subjects so that they had slightly more REM sleep on nights on which they were to dream "much" (25.0 per cent of total sleep time) than on nights on which they were to dream "little" (23.3 per cent of total sleep time).[7] Although this difference was of very small magnitude, it was statistically significant.

Social Isolation.

Paul Wood, in his doctoral thesis in the Psychology Department of the University of North Carolina, found that social isolation, such as reading, studying, writing, and so on in a room by oneself all day long, lengthened REM cycles.[8] It is not clear whether social isolation, physical inactivity, or some other variable might be responsible for this increase in REM time.

Physical and Mental Exertion.

At the University of Chicago, the effects of physical and mental exertion upon the undisturbed sleep cycle during the first half of the night (awakenings are made to retrieve content during the second half of the night) are being examined.[9] When these findings become available, they should not only clarify the findings on social isolation but also provide important data on the operation of a class of presleep variables to which one might be inclined to grant considerable scope in the determination of sleep-cycle phenomena.

Experiences of Excitement or Drive Arousal.

Working with Rechtschaffen, I found no difference in time to onset of the initial REM period between nights on which subjects saw a romantic-comedy film and nights on which they saw a particularly violent western drama immediately before retiring.[10] Since differences were found in the content of dreams elicited on these nights, the failure to observe any effect on the early portion of the sleep cycle cannot be attributed to general ineffectiveness of the experimental manipulation.

Sleep Deprivation.

Generalized sleep deprivation seems to lead, on the first "recovery" night, to greater amounts of NREM, particularly stages 3 and 4, sleep and reduced amounts of REM sleep.[11] Selective sleep deprivation—awakening the subject every time he enters a certain sleep stage for a number of successive awakenings on one night or a series of successive nights, thus depriving him of the experience of that stage—leads to greater amounts of the selectively deprived stage on "recovery" nights. This finding has been verified for REM sleep[12] and for stage-4 NREM sleep.[13] In the case of REM sleep, selective deprivation is its most potent experiential determinant. Following several nights of such deprivation, subjects will often pass directly into REM-sleep episodes without the usual intervening NREM sleep, and recovery-night REM time will be elevated by as much as 50 per cent. Control nights with equivalent numbers of awakenings made at points in the sleep cycle where they would not interfere with REM-sleep episodes failed to demonstrate any effects comparable to those seen on or following selective REM-sleep deprivation nights.

Physiological Activation.

In a study of self-described "good" and "poor" sleepers it was found that the poor sleepers had significantly less REM time as a group than did good sleepers.[14] Of particular interest in the present context is the finding that poor sleepers showed significantly greater presleep activation in a number of physiological dimensions—for example, heart rate and respiration—than did the good sleepers.

Probably related to this finding is the observation that a subject's initial night in the EEG sleep laboratory shows a reliably lower REM-time value than do subsequent nights in the laboratory.[15] It is plausible that the subject, in a novel and perhaps somewhat frightening environment, cannot settle down as well on this first night as he can on subsequent ones. This "first-night effect" is one reason why initial laboratory runs are often discarded for experimental purposes and used only to adapt the subject to the laboratory.

It appears, then, that physiological activation ("spontaneous," drug induced, experimental situation induced, or, perhaps, induced by giving subjects suggestions as to tasks they are to fulfill during sleep) has a depressing effect upon the neuroanatomical mechanisms responsible for initiating and maintaining REM sleep. Central nervous system depressants seem to affect these mechanisms in like manner. Other influences on REM sleep are more difficult to evaluate. The social-isolation data could be interpreted as demonstrating a compensatory aspect of REM sleep: when deprived of significant waking experience, the subject shows an increase in vividly hallucinated experience during sleep. The results on the effects of physical and mental exertion should, when available, fill a large gap in our understanding of the effects of daytime experience upon nighttime dreaming.

All of these REM-time findings are subject to one important qualification. There is the possibility that the REM sleep-dreaming association breaks down under unusual conditions such as those under experimental manipulation in these studies. That is, there may be increases in REM sleep without increases in dreaming, decreases in REM sleep without decreases in dreaming. Without awakenings to retrieve content, which would, of course, defeat the purpose of measuring the proportion REM-time over a full night of undisturbed sleep, it is not possible to say that changes in dreaming necessarily accompany fluctuations in REM sleep.

The newborn infant, compared with the child, adolescent, or adult, has an exceptionally large proportion of REM sleep.[16] My son, for instance, at seven weeks of age spent 56 per cent of a daytime sleep period in REM episodes. In view of such data, it is questionable whether REM sleep should always be equated with dream activity. If at some point in the organism's existence there may be a dissociation of REM sleep from dreaming as we know it, then it is at least possible that the same dissociation can occur in adult subjects under conditions other than those in which the REM sleep-dreaming association was originally established.[17]

PRESLEEP DETERMINANTS OF DREAM CONTENT

A number of presleep manipulations have been found to have reliable effects on content retrieved upon REM-sleep awakenings.

Drug Intake.

Roy Whitman, a psychiatrist, and his associates at the University of Cincinnati have investigated the effects of certain drugs upon dream content. In one study, a patient on a psychiatric ward was observed in the laboratory for eight control nights, then put on meprobamate, a muscle relaxant and "tranquilizer," for a week.[18] EEG/EOG recordings were then resumed, with the subject still on the drug. Awakenings were made during REM sleep on both predrug and drug nights. Dream reports elicited from the two series of nights were not greatly different from one another in their superficial appearance, but more subtle ratings revealed some significant differences. Dreams on nights when meprobamate was taken showed increased physical motility and psychological dependency. The former increase the investigators attribute to a compensatory mechanism—with the muscle relaxant there is less actual physical exertion in the daytime, therefore an increase in hallucinated exertion during sleep. The latter increase is attributed to the oral-dependent waking relationship of receiving a drug from another person. These data should be interpreted cautiously, however, in view of the facts that: (1) data are reported for only one subject; (2) there is a confounding of treatments and the order in which they were administered; perhaps a subject given a drug for the first series and taken off the drug for the second might not have produced the same results; and (3) there was no control for oral administration, apart from the substance administered; no placebo or chemically inert substance was given.

A second study overcame several of these deficiencies of experimental design.[19] Ten subjects were studied for four nights each; the first was a basal, or control, night. Then subjects were observed for three nights, preceding each of which they had been on a certain drug for a period of three days. The drugs employed, in a random order, were phenobarbital (a barbiturate), prochlorperazine (a tranquilizer), and imipramine (an antidepressant). Imipramine was found to increase word-count measures of hostility and anxiety. The therapeutic value of this drug is attributed in part to its mobilization during sleep of these potentially harmful emotional impulses.

Hypnosis and Suggestion.

There are indications in the older literature [20] that dream content can be manipulated by posthypnotic suggestion. Stoyva, employing the EEG/REM method of eliciting dream content, found seven of sixteen subjects almost invariably (70–100 per cent of the time) produced content reports in accord with presleep suggestions given by the experimenter while the subject was in a hypnotic trance.[21] There were sometimes variations or embellishments upon the experimenter's suggestion, but it was clearly recognizable in the content of most of these dreams. Five other subjects dreamed in accord with the experimenter's suggestion 40–60 per cent of the time. Four of the highly dream-suggestible subjects were given suggestions and awakened during NREM sleep. These reports were also, more often than not, in compliance with the experimenter's suggestion. Stoyva says that waking, that is, nontrance, suggestions were less effective than trance ones, although the former did sometimes produce REM-sleep reports compliant with the suggestion.

Data from another study of the effect of direct hypnotic suggestion also suggest that REM-sleep content can be influenced by such suggestion; five of ten subjects reported dreams in accord with suggestions.[22] But it was found here that there is less compliance with suggestions in REM-sleep reports than in those of "hypnotic" dreams—dreams said to occur in the hypnotic state rather than in physiological sleep.

One question arises with respect to these data: are the reports produced by subjects on REM-sleep awakenings naratives of mental experience that occurred prior to the subjects' awakening, or do they simply represent the reactivation of a previously established relationship in which the subject is willing to say whatever he feels his hypnotist wants him to say? The fact that hypnotist and dream retriever were one and the same person in each of these two studies makes this problem of interpretation an especially troubling one.

Social Isolation.

Wood's data indicate more socially active and physically passive dream content—sitting around and listening or talking in a group—following social isolation.[23] Once more, a compensation hypothesis would seem to provide the best explanation of his results.

Physical and Mental Exertion.

Data on dream content after varying levels of physical and mental exertion are not yet available.[24] They should, once again, however, clarify the social-isolation results and tell something of the merits of the kind of compensation hypothesis that both Wood and Whitman have proposed as an explanation of the nature of dream content.

Experiences of Excitement or Drive Arousal.

In the study I made with Rechtschaffen, we found that REM dreams following exposure to a violent television film were longer in word counts, more imaginative, as rated by two independent raters, and more vivid and emotional, as rated by the subjects themselves, than REM dreams following exposure to a nonviolent television film.[25] There were no significant differences between film nights in the areas of unpleasantness or violence and hostility. The effect of the violent film was, then, the production of dreams that were more exciting or interesting without influencing specific drive expression or general pleasantness-unpleasantness. The nonspecificity of the effect of the films is indicated further by the very low incidence of manifest incorporation of film elements into REM dreams. Judges, who were given the dream reports but no indication of the film shown on the night upon which such narratives were collected, were not successful, in general, in correctly matching dreams with the film seen before sleep onset. There were only a minimal number (5 per cent of 179) of content reports, either REM or NREM, with direct and obvious incorporations of film elements. One interesting aspect of our results is the fact that neither NREM awakenings nor the initial REM awakening showed significant effects of the films on the content of mentation reported. The significant differences attributable to the films were observed only in REM-period content elicited later in the night.

Results similar to those of the television-film study with young adults have also been found when REM dreams elicited after stressful presleep personal interviews were compared with those elicited after more innocuous presleep personal interviews.[26]

Sleep Deprivation.

There are no EEG studies on dream content as a function of generalized sleep deprivation. Rechtschaffen and I sought to determine the effects of selective deprivation of REM sleep early in the night upon REM reports elicited later in the night.[27] There was some suggestion of increased REM dream intensity on such experimental nights as compared with control nights on which early night awakenings did not interfere with REM sleep, but no statistically significant differences were observed.

In conclusion, it can be said significant differences in REM dream content have been observed as a function of various experimental manipulations such as hypnosis, drug intake, social isolation, film viewing, and so on. With the exception of the hypnotic effects, which are somewhat questionable as genuine changes in the REM dreaming process, none of the factors thus far investigated, however, seems to be a particularly potent determinant of REM dream content.

THE POETZL PHENOMENON

It has already been noted, in the discussion of several REM-dream specimens in Chapter 3, that significant waking impressions, the people and events that have been thoroughly mulled over in waking life, often fail to become incorporated in dream content, while more indifferent waking impressions often constitute the recognizable everyday elements in these naratives. An important event has just happened in my life, but I fail to dream it at all, devoting my sleeping thoughts, rather, to seemingly stupid and inconsequential happenings of the dream-day.[28] Observations such as these have been made for some time, and provided the basis for Freud's concept of the innocent day residue that may disguise, represent, or contact more hidden and meaningful memories or feelings.

Otto Poetzl, a Viennese physician acquainted with Freudian theory, attempted, in an article published in 1917, to demonstrate experimentally that it is the less than fully formed visual experiences of the dream-day that become incorporated in subsequent nocturnal mentation.[29] Using a *tachistoscope*, a device that exposes slides at rapid rates, he showed unfamiliar color slides to normal subjects, who recorded all that they said they were able to perceive. The subjects were then asked to "watch" their hypnagogic and nocturnal dreams on that night. The next day, they returned to the laboratory and drew simple sketches of particular dream fragments. As judged by Poetzl and the subjects under his guidance, the sketches demonstrated a *law of exclusion*; that is, none of the consciously perceived aspects of the slide could be seen in the dream sketches, only those elements that the subject had *not* reported seeing immediately subsequent to the tachistoscopic presentation. The reader of Poetzl's monograph is likely to be impressed by the convincingness of certain of his examples, but, at the same time, deterred by the nonquantitative and subjective method of their presentation and by the susceptibility of Poetzl's design to influence by the preconceptions of the experimenter.

In the intervening years, much experimental evidence has been adduced for the "Poetzl phenomenon," [30] but it has often been as poorly designed and methodologically suspect as that originally presented by Poetzl himself. Few studies, for instance, had an adequate control condition; that is, a condition in which dreams are examined after no presleep stimulus as well as after an experimentally manipulated presleep stimulus. Without such a condition, it is impossible to make any determination of the extent to which the stimulus, as such, has influenced dream content.

In recent years, three studies with careful experimental designs and better controls have completely failed to replicate Poetzl's finding of a complementary influence of waking impressions upon subsequent waking imagery or nocturnal mentation.[31] While, as noted in a previous section, there is some evidence that what a subject does consciously perceive affects his dream content, there is little methodologically satisfactory evidence that what he, in some sense, *does not* consciously perceive has any comparable effects.

A recent episode collected by myself and Vogel[32] in our study of sleep-onset mentation, however, has served to reawaken my interest in the Poetzl phenomenon, not to the point of leading me to believe that it is a very frequent event but at least to think that it is a possible one. One of our subjects, on a pilot night, reported the following dream from sleep-onset stage 2.

> I was thinking about a painting, I guess, but I don't know what it was. We were looking at a painting in somebody's

living room. Someone was showing me, and I was with other people but I don't know who, she was showing me a painting on the wall, and it was mostly blue. I remember I liked it because it was mostly blue. It was, I guess, in her home. I sort of remember it had shoes in it, but that's kind of silly, it doesn't figure. It seems like the picture had shoes in it, blue shoes in it, seems kind of silly, but I guess it did. I think it was sort of abstract, 'cause I guess people didn't see the shoes at first, and she was saying that, you know, this painting has shoes in it. I know that shoes had to do with the painting, so I guess it had shoes in it.

Several weeks later, and before the start of her experimental series, the subject came to the experimenter with an interesting discovery upon which she had just stumbled:

The first night that I was a subject, I was puzzled by one report of being in a large room and being shown a painting that was definitely abstract. The only thing I could see clearly was a pair of blue shoes. I could think of no relationship that this painting had with any experience I had had recently.

Several days later, while at work (in a large office room) I was talking to one of my supervisors when I happened to glance over his head to a calendar on the wall. It had a very small picture on front, approximately three inches by five inches. I had seen this calendar over and over before, sometimes studying it when I was thinking, but had never understood what the picture was. On the day described I happened to look at this calendar and immediately both thought of my dream and recognized what the picture was. "Hey, Joe," I said, "those are blue shoes in that painting, aren't they?" He said, "Sure, didn't you notice that before?" I hadn't but now I saw that the painting was an abstract representation of two pairs of crossed ballet slippers, one a blue pair.

The subject still had one more surprise in store for her. She was asked to secure a copy of the calendar painting, and in the course of her inquiries discovered that the painting was meant to be erotic: the crossed feet belonged to a pair of lovers lying in a bed. She commented that she had, up to that point, completely missed the sexual significance of the painting.

Thus, in her nocturnal mentation, the subject identified an object whose nature had eluded, and on this account bothered, her during waking life. This example is surely very close to the kinds of events in which Poetzl was interested and suggests the desirability of a full-scale EEG investigation of alleged complementary influences of waking experiences on sleep mentation. (None of the previous studies of the Poetzl phenomenon, whether producing positive or negative results, employed EEG/EOG techniques.) It is interesting, in particular, that this apparent example of a *complementary* influence of daytime impressions comes from that period of the sleep cycle apparently most susceptible to *direct* influences of everyday waking impressions, the sleep-onset period. This may well be the most fruitful place to demonstrate complementary influences, if they exist, of waking impressions upon sleep mentation.

To sum up, it appears that REM sleep is somewhat susceptible to certain presleep manipulations, both experiential and physiological. The highly regular occurrence of REM sleep episodes, however, makes it unlikely that a particular kind of evening meal, a particular traumatic daytime experience, or other occasional events of this sort can explain the occurrence of dreaming sleep. Apparently, mechanisms within the organism only slightly responsive to typical variations in presleep experience determine how much dreaming, that is, REM sleep, a person has.

Dream content is also apparently somewhat susceptible to experiential or physiological presleep manipulations, but again, the effects of such presleep stimuli are not particularly large or impressive. Where effects of presleep stimuli can be demonstrated, for instance, in the study of the effects of film viewing before sleep, they are seldom of a direct nature. The dreamer does not generally depend upon presleep experience to give him his dream topics, rather he takes bits and pieces of his daytime impressions out of their original context and turns them to some other purpose. Once more, there seem to be inner mechanisms that determine the thematic material of the dream which are only minimally influenced in a direct or immediate sense by typical variations in experiences of the day preceding the occurrence of the dream.

Chapter 7

STIMULI DURING SLEEP
AS DETERMINANTS OF DREAMING
AND DREAM CONTENT

B ECAUSE of their immediacy, it might seem that stimuli
present during sleep would have a greater influence
upon dreaming and dream content than would those preceding
sleep onset. During sleep, external stimuli are by no means
eliminated. It may happen, for instance, that a housefly is
captive in the bedroom. Not only does its buzzing provide a
fluctuating auditory stimulus, but tactual stimulation will also
be produced if it chances to alight on one's forehead. Nor are
bodily sensations entirely absent during sleep. Digestive processes may continue to apply themselves to an overly rich bedtime
snack, for example, and a host of other stimulus-producing body
processes persist during sleep, as indeed they must.

Psychophysiological studies of dream phenomena have made

it fairly clear that such stimuli present during sleep as accidentally appearing sounds or occasionally appearing bodily sensations cannot account for the occurrence of dreaming nor explain the direction assumed by dream content. The innervation during sleep of a particular nervous structure in the base of the brain, however, does seem to be directly associated with the appearance of dreaming (that is, rapid-eye-movement) sleep.

DETERMINATION OF THE ACT OF DREAMING
THE ROLE OF EXTERNAL STIMULI DURING SLEEP

In older writings on dreaming, it is sometimes suggested that external stimuli that happen to be present during sleep may initiate dream episodes.[1] The dream, it is said, is the brain's attempt to interpret such stimuli. It is sometimes added that this interpretation allows the dreamer to maintain sleep, to ignore the potential arousal aspects of the stimulus. The alarm clock rings, but instead of being aware of a signal meaning "wake up," the sleeper may weave an interesting mental fantasy about this sound that allows him to maintain sleep; for example, he may dream that he is not in bed sleeping but already at work, receiving an important telephone call.

With the discovery of the association of REM sleep with dreaming, the hypothesis that external stimuli occurring during sleep cause dreams became untenable. The occasional and unpredictable nature of external stimulation during sleep seems to make it a totally insufficient explanation of the regular and predictable appearance of REM-sleep episodes. Studies of the effects of external stimuli presented during NREM phases, moreover, have failed to show that sounds, lights, and tactile stimulation, for example, applied during such sleep lead to the sudden production of the manifestations of REM sleep.[2] It is organismic events not dependent upon external stimuli received during sleep that offer an explanation of the periodic episodes of REM sleep.

There may be two classes of dreams requiring explanation: those occurring during REM periods and those that take place at sleep onset. If external stimuli do not seem to cause REM-period dreams, might they not still play some such role for the sleep-onset dream? It would appear that here the greater unpredictability, both as to whether dreaming will occur and as to when (in terms of EEG/EOG patterns) it might occur, leaves greater scope for the determination of dream phenomena by occasional stimuli.

Some hypnagogic reports do seem to be attempts at interpreting or classifying pictorially stimuli that may be present at sleep onset. A subject hears a scraping sound, for instance, and sees a picture of her father shoveling snow; she hears a low, rhythmic sound and sees an image of a diesel train speeding along.[3] Once I fell asleep during a television commercial with a monotonous and repetitive sound and pictured a parade with the monotonous left-right-left-right sounds of marching. The commercial had nothing to do with these things; the parade imagery was apparently my way of interpreting the insistent auditory stimulation being generated by the television set.

In general, however, it is doubtful that occasional *external* stimuli would play as large a role in sleep-onset dreaming as would occasional organismic stimuli, for the sleep-onset period is one during which the sleeper seems to try to "tune out" external stimulation and in which the boundaries of awareness begin to shrink from the external world to the body itself. Except, then, for cases where external stimulation is sufficiently intense to impinge upon this shrinking awareness but not sufficiently intense to awaken one, it is doubtful that external stimulation leads to "interpretive" sensory imagery at sleep onset.

THE ROLE OF ORGANISMIC STIMULI DURING SLEEP

Sleep as a "Passive" State.

A "passive" theory of sleep is one stating that sleep is merely the absence of wakefulness. Whenever the conditions responsible for maintaining wakefulness are abolished, one is asleep. No additional mechanism is needed to account for sleep; it simply results when wakefulness can no longer be sustained. The mechanism generally conceived as necessary to sustain wakefulness is intense and varied stimulus input from the external world.

Passive theories of sleep, therefore, generally stress a kind of *functional deafferentiation* [4] of the cortex as the mechanism of sleep induction. It is as if the afferent neural fibers from sensory receptors (the eye, ear, and so forth) have been structurally altered so that their messages are no longer carried to the brain. There have been no structural changes, of course, but the sensory system is functioning as if there had been, and this altered function is partially attributable to reduced and increasingly monotonous stimulus input.

Support for the passive theory of sleep comes from several sources, both anecdotal and experimental. Anecdotally, a person may observe his own presleep rituals. He turns off the lights and radio, and seeks to reduce to a low or monotonous level all those external stimuli whose higher and more varied intensities keep him awake.

Experimentally, a body of research has developed in recent

years on the effects of sensory deprivation. In a sensory-deprivation experiment, the experimenter deliberately reduces the stimulus input and stimulus variety available to his subjects. Such deprivation has been accomplished in a variety of ways.* One technique for achieving it, for instance, is to have the subject put in a tanklike respirator so that his arm and leg movement and tactile response are inhibited by rigid cylinders.[5] He lies on his back, unable to observe his own body. Other visual input is minimal, and what there is is monotonous. A constant sound from the motor of the respirator masks any other sound stimuli that might disturb or arouse him. A common result of the sensory deprivation achieved with this technique is *behavioral sleep;* that is, the subjects, in the absence of a varied or intense stimulus input, tend to be unable to maintain wakefulness.

Neurophysiological Evidence.

Finally, recent research has uncovered a system, extending from the base of the brain to the cerebral cortex, that seems to provide a neuroanatomical basis for the passive theory of sleep.[6] This system, the *ascending reticular activating system* (ARAS), arises in the brain-stem reticular formation (see Figure 7) and diffusely projects to the cerebral cortex. When incoming sensory impulses are supported by impulses passing through the ARAS, one is awake and aware of the environmental events causing the sensory impulses. When the ARAS does not support incoming sensory stimulation, a person is not aware of environmental events causing such impulses and is asleep. Lesions of the ARAS

---

* A thorough review of sensory deprivation procedures and findings may be found in P. Solomon (ed., with others), *Sensory Deprivation* (Cambridge, Mass.: Harvard University Press, 1961).

or drugs blocking it cause behavioral and physiological, NREM, *sleep*. Electrical stimulation of the ARAS during sleep awakens experimental animals. This system is, therefore, in some sense, the mechanism of wakeful consciousness. With its support of incoming sensory stimuli, one is awake and alert; without its support comes sleep and unawareness. Some combination of autonomous internal rhythms and restricted or monotonous sensory input must periodically increase the threshold of the ARAS to incoming stimuli and cause partial functional shutdown of this wakefulness system.

But there are two kinds of sleep. The NREM-sleep of decelerating physiological functioning, which attends sleep onset, may be, in part, explained by the passive theory and its neuro-anatomical mechanisms. But what of REM sleep, with its accelerating physiological functioning and its peculiarly intense

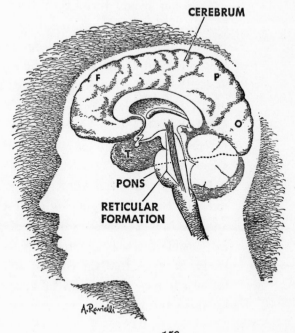

FIGURE 7
The Human Brain

The *Cerebrum* (the surface of which is the *Cerebral Cortex*) consists of 4 regions or *lobes: Frontal* (F), *Temporal* (T), *Parietal* (P), and *Occipital* (O).

The *Reticular Formation,* a network of nerve cells, extends from the base of the brain (hindbrain) through the *Pons* to the *Thalamus* in the forebrain. The reticular formation is the base from which the ARAS projects nervous impulses diffusely to the cerebral cortex.

CEREBRUM

PONS
RETICULAR
FORMATION

mental concomitants? It is doubtful that such an intense organismic state could be explained by a passive theory, and it certainly requires some explanation over and above that supplied for NREM sleep. In a series of brilliant researches, Michel Jouvet, the French physiologist, has shown that the active innervation of structures in the pontine reticular formation is responsible for, and is needed to account for, the periodic spacing of episodes of active REM sleep during passive NREM sleep.[7] In particular, Jouvet has demonstrated that destruction of a certain portion of the pons, the *nucleus reticularis pontis caudalis*, abolishes REM sleep in cats, while brief stimulation of the same structure during NREM sleep produces REM episodes ten to fifteen minutes long. It has also been shown that there is a rather unique pattern of electrical activity (4–7 cps spikes) in the pons during REM sleep.

It seems clear, then, that the active intervention of the hindbrain structures uncovered by Jouvet is associated with the periodic production of REM-sleep episodes. It is still not known, however, what causes the periodic activation of these structures —whether it is some neural, chemical, or other influence. In any event, the regular appearance of activated REM periods is attributable to the workings of these neuroanatomical structures rather than to any direct influence of presleep or sleep external stimulation.

It is my contention that findings such as Jouvet's make it unlikely that the psychological factors specified in psychoanalytic dream theories, for example, disturbing memories, are responsible for the occurrence of dreaming.[8] It is still highly likely, however, that the content of the dream period, once the latter is initiated, does reflect the psychological factors specified by these theories. That is, REM sleep may make possible the exploration of one's predicament, although pressure for such an exploration does not cause the appearance of such sleep.

DETERMINATION OF DREAM CONTENT
THE ROLE OF EXTERNAL STIMULI DURING SLEEP

External stimuli during sleep do not seem to initiate dreaming; neither, from the evidence now available, do they seem to be responsible for giving dream content its characteristic direction. The older dream literature contains numerous anecdotes of the effects of external stimuli upon dream content.[9] Such reports, however, often lack the kind of precision expected from a more systematic experimental methodology. In particular, they give us little basis for estimating how likely it is, that is, how frequently it will happen, that a given external stimulus applied during sleep will be manifest in a subsequently retrieved dream. Moreover, these early studies proceeded without knowledge of the two kinds of physiological sleep and were thus unable to apply an external stimulus consistently when it might be expected to have the most reliable effect upon dream content.

Soon after the discovery of regularly recurring cycles of dreaming sleep, Dement and Wolpert sought to determine the effects of external stimuli (a pure 1000-cps tone, a flashing 100-watt light, and a spray of cold water upon the subject's skin) applied during REM sleep upon the content of subsequently elicited REM dreams.[10] The results in general were somewhat disappointing: the tone was judged to be incorporated into dream content 9 per cent of the time, the light 24 per cent of the time, and the spray of cold water 47 per cent of the time. The awakening stimulus, a bell, was never incorporated. Incorporation refers to some manifest relationship between the externally applied stimulus and the subsequently retrieved content. The nature of the incorporation was rarely found to be direct. That is, the subject, upon awakening, almost never says, "I heard a tone." He is more likely to have embellished and distorted the stimulus, saying, for example, that before awakening, he was walking across the street when he suddenly heard an air-raid siren.

From the relative ineffectiveness of the external stimuli and from the manner of their incorporation when they were successful, it seems reasonable to draw the following conclusion from the Dement and Wolpert study: dream content is determined within the organism rather than from without. Thus, an external stimulus that cannot be woven into the already established fabric of content is ignored, and one that cannot be ignored or that lends itself somewhat to the already established pattern is redefined and shaped by the dominant inner processes before it becomes a dream element.

The relative meaninglessness of Dement and Wolpert's stimuli to the subjects might be responsible for the stimuli's failure to affect the dreams. If a relatively autonomous internal process selects elements of dream content on the basis of personal relevance, then the more meaningful the external stimuli are to a particular subject, the greater should be the likelihood of their incorporation in his dreams. Drawing upon the finding that the sleeper can discriminate meaningful stimuli, such as his own name played forward, from meaningless stimuli, his name played backward,[11] Ralph Berger, of the Department of Anatomy and Brain Research Institute at UCLA, played two familiar names, for example, the names of girl friends, and two unfamiliar names to each of his eight subjects during REM sleep.[12] He concluded from his results that there appeared to be a definite connection between the stimulus and the subsequently retrieved dream content about 50 per cent of the time.

He did not find that familiar, as opposed to unfamiliar, names had greater effects. The generally greater effectiveness of meaningful verbal stimuli than other auditory stimuli, such as a tone, however, supports the idea that the meaningfulness of a stimulus to a subject is one determinant of its potential for affecting ongoing sleep mentation.

Berger's data make it apparent, once again, that the relatively autonomous dreaming process is not the helpless captive of external stimulation applied during sleep, but rather that this process transforms these stimuli into forms compatible with its already established direction. Although his 50 per cent estimate is higher than that of Dement and Wolpert, it is clear from his results that incorporations generally appear as intrusions upon ongoing dream material. The most frequent mode of incorporation noted, for instance, was *assonance*. Here, the stimulus produces a sound-associated element rather than any indication that the person whose name has been played actually enters the dream. The name "Gillian," for example, produces the dream element of a woman from Chile (Chilean). While assonance accounted for thirty-one of forty-eight incorporations, *representation*, appearance of the named person in the dream, accounted for only three of the forty-eight incorporations.

Berger's relatively high, 50 per cent, estimate of stimulus incorporation must also be considered as reflecting rather unnatural sleeping conditions. Complex dreaming certainly occurs in the absence of the kind of systematic exposure to meaningful stimuli that occurred during the experiment; these experimental conditions cannot provide a very adequate explanation of the nature of dream content occurring under normal sleeping conditions.

Dement and Wolpert were not successful in inducing or influencing NREM mentation by means of external stimuli. Such influence has, upon occasion, been successfully demonstrated, however, and an example was presented in Chapter 4 (see page 115). The general nature of the influence appears to be identical to that which can be demonstrated in REM sleep: the stimulus intrudes upon, and its precise representation is shaped by, an already ongoing process of mental activity.

Since the intensity and momentum of NREM mentation is less than that of REM mentation, however, it seems that one ought to be able to demonstrate that the influence of external stimuli during NREM sleep is more direct than it is during REM sleep. One anecdotal observation supports this expectation: upon a stage-2 NREM awakening, a subject reported that he had been listening to some knocking on a wall down the hall.[13] There had been, in fact, noise from someone doing just that before the experimental awakening. Such a direct representation of the external stimulus would be quite improbable during REM sleep.

It may be concluded that external stimuli present during sleep cannot account for the nature of REM dream content, for such stimuli do not reliably affect such content, and, when they do have an effect, it is mediated, rather than direct.

THE ROLE OF ORGANISMIC STIMULI DURING SLEEP
Visceral Influences.

Data already considered suggest that the activity of several autonomic parameters, such as heart rate, during REM sleep is not highly correlated with subsequently reported mental experiences. This makes it somewhat unlikely that the dream is the brain's reaction to, and interpretation of, such autonomic phenomena. A possible exception to this last statement might have to be made with respect to penile erections during REM sleep. Data suggesting a correspondence of erection and detumescence with fluctuations in the erotic quality of dream content have been presented.[14] From such findings, which are still tentative, the possibility emerges that erotic dream content is caused by autonomic sexual arousal. It is also possible, however, that autonomic sexual arousal is the result, rather than the cause, of erotic dreams. In waking life, penile erections can be ideationally produced, and the same phenomenon might well occur during sleep. There is, therefore, no definitive evidence that autonomic arousal parameters are causally linked with dream content. In fact, the recent finding that quadriplegics, patients with spinal cord transections that make the experience of genital-pelvic sensations impossible, have dreams of seminal emission with orgasm imagery clearly suggests that the mind does not require genital sensations to instigate erotic hallucinations during sleep.[15]

Gastric factors have always found some favor in popular theories of dreaming. It is alleged that a rich meal and its gastric aftermath, for example, cause a dream and determine the nature of its content. The highly regular appearance of REM sleep, of course, makes the determination of the act of dreaming by factors such as this exceedingly improbable. Dement and Wolpert have investigated the effects of a related drive, thirst, upon dream content.[16] Fifteen dream reports were obtained after subjects had refrained from any fluid intake for a period of twenty-four hours. Only five of these reports contained any manifest element pertaining to drinkable fluids. There were, moreover, no instances of drinking, or even of thirst, ascribed to the self in the dream. While wish-fulfillment dreams do sometimes seem to occur in response to drive deprivation, their relative infrequency is more striking than their occasional occurrence.

Such findings, of course, are consonant with the viewpoint developed in Chapter 3 that wish fulfillment is not the primary goal of dream activity. The dreamer is apparently not particularly interested in hallucinating a wish fulfillment, for example, a glass of water, that will provide no genuine answer to his problem. These findings are also consistent with observations of the effects of systematic semistarvation upon dream reports recalled without the aid of EEG/EOG detection: there was no increase in food or eating dreams.[17] Popular mythology notwithstanding, there is no satisfactory evidence that sexual frustration produces "harem" dreams. Here, of course, the Freudian theorist might stress the need for symbolic, rather than direct, wish fulfillment, since direct expression of the sexual impulse is somewhat taboo. But why, then, cannot the thirsty person hallucinate a glass of water? What comparable taboos account for the failure of wish fulfillment to materialize in this case? It seems reasonable to conclude from the data that hallucinatory wish fulfillment simply is not the essence of dream activity.

Visual Influences.

There is, as was demonstrated in Chapter 2, a reasonably close correlation between rapid ocular movements during REM sleep and the nature of REM dream content. Do such eye movements cause dream images? Is the dream imagery the sleeping brain's attempt to integrate and interpret these peripheral manifestations? Since the unique electrical activity of the visual system characterizing REM sleep persists following removal of the eyes and extraocular muscles in experimental animals, it is clear that eye movements cannot account for this activity, and it is doubtful that they are needed for the experiencing of visual imagery.

Is the mental experience the cause of the eye movements, then? The data, cited in Chapter 2, on eye movement—imagery relationships in the waking state would seem to suggest this alternative. This cannot be the total answer, however, for eye movements are present in the sleep of cats who have had their higher brain centers removed. From this evidence, it seems unlikely that mental activity can provide an adequate explanation of the appearance of eye movements during sleep.

Certain physiological evidence suggests a third alternative: that both the dream imagery, which is presumably cortical in locus, and the response of the extrinsic ocular muscles are the independent effects of brain-stem activation.[18] If this is the case, the problem becomes one of explaining the correspondence that does exist between eye movements and dream imagery.

In any event, it does not appear likely that eye movements, undoubted concomitants of dream imagery, are in any sense its major determinant. Even were eye movements to stand in some causal relation to dream imagery, they could explain only the direction of the imagery, not its precise nature. A left-right movement of the eyeball does not "give" any particular explanatory visual image: it might be one of reading a line in a book, or one of looking up and down the street before crossing. The precise interpretation given any particular pattern of eye movement, that is, the essence of the dream content, would still remain to be explained.

If ocular movement cannot account for the precise nature of

visual imagery during sleep, it has occurred to some that patterns of retinal excitation induced by light penetrating the closed eyelid or by "spontaneous" retinal changes might determine dream imagery.[19] Rechtschaffen and I, however, have demonstrated that subjects sleeping with their eyes taped open and their pupils artificially dilated do not dream about visual stimuli presented before their eyes during either REM or NREM sleep.[20] Since such stimulus-induced retinal excitation does not seem to relate to dream imagery, it is doubtful that light-induced or "spontaneous" patterns of retinal excitation are causally related to particular elements of dream imagery.

In summary, several positions concerning an association of peripheral organismic stimulation and REM dream content fail to find any conclusive support in experimental evidence thus far collected. Dreams do not seem to be the brain's interpretation of eye movements, as the nature of these movements is conveyed to the brain by way of *proprioceptive* feedback from extrinsic ocular muscles. Dreams do not seem to be the brain's interpretation of patterns of excitation of the light-sensitive retina, as the nature of these patterns might be conveyed to the brain along afferent visual pathways. Dreams do not seem to be the brain's interpretation of impulses arising in the viscera that code the nature of autonomic nervous system arousal. Where some influence of peripheral organismic arousal can be demonstrated, it is mediated rather than direct, and where possibilities remain for demonstrating some influence, this influence is insufficient to explain more than certain very crude parameters of dream content. The nature of REM dream content thus cannot be explained adequately by patterns of peripheral organismic stimulation during REM sleep.

Hypnagogic Experiences.

As previously noted, there is the possibility that occasional, particularly occasional bodily rather than external, stimuli may influence mental content experienced at sleep onset, even if they seem to have no major influence upon REM-sleep dreaming. At sleep onset, subjects' reports often reveal a heightened awareness of bodily position, bodily sensations, states of muscular fatigue, and so on. The self seems to be exchanging its interest in the external world for concern with its own bodily processes, a shrinkage of the scope of one's interest that undoubtedly facilitates the induction of sleep. This shift in focus of interest is usually accomplished during the alpha rhythm EEG stages that appear at sleep onset but not during nocturnal sleep.

The following series of reports, elicited from one of Vogel's and my subjects during the sleep-onset period,[21] illustrates the extent to which the subject who is falling asleep may be aware of his own bodily processes and the manner in which such awareness may shape his mental experience:

2. I saw a little dog, and I guess sort of on a prairie covered with snow, standing in front of a little doghouse, and he was barking at the same rate that my pulse was beating. I could feel against the pillow from the superficial temporal artery. He looked like an impure-bred Dalmatian, or something, but he was smaller than that, and his tail was up in the air. The dog was too big to fit in the doghouse. The only thing he was doing was moving his mouth, as if he was just, you know, a sort of china dog with a moving mouth. You know, when dogs bark they usually jump around and things like that. Well, there was no animation to him at all: he was standing in the same position all the time (alpha REM).

3. I was again experiencing circulatory pulsation. I could sort of feel a pulsation inside of my stomach and then I saw the scene in the living room of my apartment, and my cat was there, and he was scratching on a scratching post but the whole image of seeing it was blurred by sort of a kaleidoscopic rotation of colors. The pulsations were real, it was just aortic pulsations, and the action in the dream was not synchronized like it was last time. It was mildly unpleasant, maybe an anxious type of feeling, just sort of an uneasy kind of feeling. It sort of annoyed me the way the cat was scratching on that post, I don't know exactly why, and sometimes those colors got in the way and I couldn't see through it too well, and when that happened was when I was feeling the most uneasy (alpha REM).

4. I was sort of hearing some wind whistling through the trees and I was also hearing, I guess I had some obstruction in my nose or something, and this wind whistling in the trees was synchronized with sort of a funny little noise that I was making on expiration. This whistling through the trees sort of came about as an amplification of this noise that I was making. The funny thing about it was that it wasn't like seeing a forest with wind blowing though it, but all I saw was about 5 or 6 little twigs, just sort of in front of me, little twigs like you gather to start a fire. The noise amplification sounded like a gale blowing through a lot of trees, and all that was there was a cloud of twigs, it was out of proportion to what you'd expect to be generating the noise. (alpha SEM).

In each of these reports, organismic stimuli have become translated into concrete visual imagery. The nature of the interpretation offered is, by the standards of waking thought, highly inaccurate, but note that it permits the subject to withdraw his narrowing scope of interest still further: hallucinated mental experiences now begin to replace actual bodily sensations. When this further shrinkage is complete (generally by descending stages 1 or 2), the subject is asleep and dreaming. It is not difficult to see the role that the substitution of hallucinated, for actual, experience might play in sleep induction, and these examples suggest that bodily sensations may sometimes be the medium through which this substitution occurs.

Another of our subjects produced a sleep-onset (descending stage 1) report indicating partial support for the determination of imagery at this point in the sleep cycle by spontaneous retinal stimulation. He reported that he saw, with his eyes closed, a spot of yellow light that then became an eye and then the eye of a black cat.

In none of these examples is the nature of sleep-onset mentation totally explained by the organismic stimulus. Why should heartbeat become a dog barking, rather than something else? Why should the dog be unable to fit into his doghouse? The apparent difference between REM and sleep-onset mentation is only a relative one. In both cases, mental content derives its unique and particular determination from factors other than peripheral organic stimuli. In the sleep-onset period, however, there seems to be a more deliberate usage of features of such stimuli to shape at least the crude outlines of mental experience.

Chapter 8

PERSONALITY DETERMINANTS
OF DREAMING AND DREAM CONTENT

Aʟᴛʜᴏᴜɢʜ organismic events spontaneously occurring during sleep seem to furnish an immediate, if not ultimate, explanation of the occurrence of dreaming (ʀᴇᴍ) sleep, the primary determinants of dream content remain to be demonstrated. Psychoanalytic theory, the most pervasive influence today upon the interpretation of dream phenomena, stresses that it is to the personality of the dreamer, rather than to transitory presleep stimuli or to stimuli that happen to be present during sleep, that we must look for any comprehensive understanding of dream content.

Personality is generally defined as the unique organization of somewhat permanent behavior tendencies and modes of adjustment of the individual. In its present usage, it refers to more permanent and internalized presleep influences than those previously considered and specifies highly idiosyncratic factors, rather than stable systems of observable traits individuals might share with one another. Although personality influences have been shown by recent psychophysiological research to be only minimally related to the occurrence of REM dreaming, they are, as psychoanalytic theory suggests, the basic determinants of REM dream content.

PERSONALITY DETERMINANTS
OF REM DREAM PHENOMENA

THE OCCURRENCE OF REM DREAMING

Previously examined evidence suggested that actual nocturnal dream frequency, even for the habitual nonrecaller of dreams, might simply be equated with the occurrence of episodes of REM sleep. In a survey of possible personality influences on the occurrence of dreaming, it is appropriate, therefore, to consider determinants of the timing, frequency, and duration of such REM-sleep episodes.

Several studies have demonstrated that there are reliable individual differences in percentage of REM sleep.[1] That is, each individual spends a characteristic proportion of his total sleep time in REM episodes that is fairly constant from one night to the next, and there are differences among individuals in the precise value of this proportion. Such variations, although stable, are of very slight magnitude, however. One study, for instance, found a twenty-subject mean of 24.2 per cent REM-time, with a *standard deviation* of only 3.4 per cent and a range of 19.4 per cent to 33.3 per cent.[2] In general, then, it appears that the range of individual differences in the amount of REM sleep is sufficiently small that any potentially responsible personality factors could still play only a minimal role in the over-all determination of amounts of REM dreaming. Nevertheless, within the small scope allowed them, personality factors have been shown to relate to the proportion of total sleep time spent in REM periods.

Monroe's investigation of self-described "good" and "poor" sleepers might be viewed as a study of "healthy" and "neurotic" personalities, in view of the striking difference between the two sleep groups in Minnesota Multiphasic Personality Inventory (MMPI) * profiles.[3] The "poor" sleepers averaged higher psychopathological scores on twelve of thirteen clinical scales investigated. The Cornell Medical Index † was also administered to all subjects and revealed a greater incidence of psychosomatic complaints and emotional disturbance for the poor sleepers. Poor sleepers, by these two tests more emotionally disturbed than good ones, had significantly less REM sleep (a similar number of REM periods, but briefer ones—this being at least partly attributable to numerous spontaneous awakenings during REM sleep) than did the good sleepers. Related to this finding, and to the finding that poor sleepers had greater pre-sleep physiological arousal, were observations of greater physiological arousal (higher rectal temperature, more frequent phasic vasoconstrictions, more body motility, faster heart rate, and increased pulse volume) during sleep among the poor sleepers than among the good ones.

* The MMPI is a personality test consisting of 566 statements with which the respondent is to agree or disagree. The individual items and the item groupings (scales) of the MMPI were originally constructed for the purpose of detecting and diagnosing personality disturbance.

† The Cornell Medical Index lists a series of physical symptoms, many of psychosomatic origin, and the respondent is to check those that he feels apply or have applied to his own physical condition.

Monroe is careful to point out that his data do not establish which of the associated variables of physiological arousal, neuroticism, and amount of REM dreaming might be cause and which effect. It might be, for example, that neuroticism causes a reduction in the amount of REM dreaming. On the other hand, greater physiological activation during sleep may cause a reduction of REM dreaming (and of the discharge of emotional tensions such dreaming is alleged to promote), thus making a person neurotic.

Rechtschaffen and Verdone found that scores on the Taylor Manifest Anxiety Scale * were positively related to the proportion of the total sleep period spent in REM phases.[4] Since this is the only one of a number of correlations between MMPI scales and REM time to attain statistical significance, however, the authors point out that it may well have resulted by chance. However, it has been found that chronic dream recallers have higher amounts of REM sleep than chronic nonrecallers [5] and earlier studies demonstrated a positive relationship between nonlaboratory recall frequency and anxiety scores.[6] It may well be, then, that anxiety scores and amount of REM sleep *are* positively related, a relationship that also embraces differences in everyday dream recall.

There seems to be a discrepancy between Monroe's findings and those of the other investigations cited above. In Monroe's study, a negative relationship emerges between psychopathology and REM sleep (the more psychopathology, the less REM sleep), and the other evidence suggests a positive relationship of manifest anxiety and REM sleep (the more manifest anxiety, the more REM sleep). It should be noted that Monroe's thirty-

---

* This is a scale of MMPI items designed to assess the frequency and severity of anxiety symptoms.

two subjects were selected from the high and low extremes of scores on a questionnaire on sleep complaints administered to a group of approximately two hundred males who volunteered for his experiment. It is likely that his psychopathological scores represent the genuine incidence of emotional disturbance. The Rechtschaffen and Verdone subjects, however, were selected by criteria guaranteeing that all would be moderately good sleepers. Within such a restricted range it is likely that higher manifest anxiety scores represent greater self-awareness— greater willingness to admit to common emotional symptoms —rather than a genuinely higher incidence of emotional disturbance. The self-awareness interpretation of higher manifest anxiety scores was, in fact, invoked in the studies showing the relationship of anxiety scores to everyday dream recall.[7]

Moving from the normal-neurotic range of personality variation to the psychotic, the situation becomes still more confused, however. Dement studied seventeen chronic schizophrenics and thirteen normal subjects.[8] He reported that the patterns of occurrence and duration of REM periods "were virtually the same in the two groups." In a more recent study, it was found that actively ill schizophrenics had slightly less REM sleep (22.0 per cent) than nonschizophrenic controls (24.7 per cent) and that short-term schizophrenic patients had significantly less REM sleep (19.6 per cent) than long-term ones (24.4 per cent).[9] It will be observed from these figures that the schizophrenic-normal difference is attributable in large measure to the short-term patients, with the figures for long-term schizophrenics being essentially identical with those of the nonschizophrenic controls. This suggests a relationship consistent with that observed by Monroe—active emotional disturbance negatively correlated with REM-sleep time. However, two reports of comparisons of

REM-sleep time values between hallucinating and nonhallucinating schizophrenic patients have produced totally negative results,[10] and the REM-sleep time of child schizophrenics does not seem to differ from that of normal children.[11]

In none of the above studies has there been an indication of a positive relationship between psychosis and dreaming, which is the relationship that many personality theorists might have predicted. Such theorists would have expected that the breakthrough of disturbing impulses, memories, and so on, that produce psychosis would also result in increased attempts at psychic discharge of these quantities during dreaming sleep. Researchers have reported the case of a patient who "precipitously developed an acute paranoid psychosis" that seems to support this expectation.[12] The amount of his REM-dream time immediately after the psychotic breakthrough was 50.1 per cent, much higher than his prepsychotic average. Unfortunately, there may be a confounding of drug effects (the patient was put on a new medication just at the onset of his psychotic symptoms) with behavioral changes in this case, and its interpretation is therefore somewhat ambiguous. A related negative observation is the failure of a group of scientists to find any increase in REM-sleep parameters at the onset of adolescence.[13] The authors, on the basis of clinical dream theory, had expected "an increase in the per cent of dreaming at puberty, along with the general upsurge in sexual drive at this time," but this prediction was not borne out by their data.

Drawing conclusions from a body of evidence as ambiguous and contradictory as the preceding is hazardous. It seems, however, that emotional disturbance is not positively, but may be negatively, related to REM-period frequency and duration. That is, maladjustment does not seem to be associated with increased

REM sleep and may, in fact, be associated with decreased REM sleep. Since other sources of sleep disturbance, for example, psychic energizers such as amphetamine, "spontaneous" physiological activation, and so on, seem to depress REM sleep, it would not be surprising were emotional disturbance ultimately to prove to be negatively related to the amount of REM sleep—the direction suggested by the somewhat scanty and inconsistent data now available. The need for further studies of the relationship between occurrence of REM sleep and personality in which the contributions of activation and poor sleep are separated out is obvious. It is worth recalling once again, however, that whatever the nature of their effect may be, personality factors do not, and could not, exert any *sizeable* effect upon the occurrence of REM sleep.

THE CONTENT OF REM DREAMING

Clinical Observations.

The demonstration of the role of personality factors in the determination of dream content is most convincing in the long-term case study of particular individuals. It is in such a setting that the entire network of experiences and associations in which any particular dream must be placed to be fully understood is uncovered. As yet, however, the EEG/EOG technique of dream detection has been employed only rarely as an adjunct to intensive case studies, and EEG/EOG researchers have usually failed to collect the kinds of associative responses necessary for the total understanding of particular elements of manifest dream content.

Yet in the few cases where interpretation has been applied to systematically collected REM-dream content, it has been readily apparent that it is in personality factors, rather than in accidental or transitory presleep or sleep stimuli, that the most adequate explanation of the particular nature of REM dream content is found. I have attempted to illustrate this with the limited analysis of dreams *A* and *B* in Chapter 3.

The same point has been illustrated more systematically by William Offenkrantz, a psychiatrist at the University of Chicago Medical School, in collaboration with Allan Rechtschaffen.[14] Offenkrantz analyzed the experimentally elicited REM dreams of a patient undergoing psychotherapy, a thirty-six-year-old bachelor with problems of drinking, sexual impotence, and an inability to devote himself steadily to his work. Over an eight-month period, the patient was seen for some eighty-three hours by his therapist, Offenkrantz, while he also spent fifteen nights in Rechtschaffen's laboratory. There his REM dreams were interrupted at their conclusion and their content recorded.

One of the patient's dreams, together with his associations to its content, was as follows:

> I was in a library, waiting for a book to come in. I had a pleasant chat with a girl on line who tells me how she frequently rides horses. A fellow I know comes in and they begin to talk to each other. He's bigger than me and ignores me. I thought she was inviting me to her place to lunch, but she wanted lunch bought for her.

> *Associations:* In the dream he felt frustration at the library, "hostility to the guy" who came in, and "pleasure at talking to the girl." He said, "The guy in the dream reads too much. The girl's eyes were like my mother's. She rode her horse near where I lived back home." [15]

The particular imagery of this dream, as is true of the imagery of most dreams, cannot be understood apart from knowledge of: (*a*) the dreamer's contemporary waking life, in particular the conflicts, anxieties, and tensions which have recently assumed a salient position in his waking adjustment; (*b*) the historical roots, in the dreamer's earlier experiences, of his present difficulties; and (c) the dreamer's other dreams of the same night.

Let us begin consideration of this dream by starting from *c*. The experimenter, by describing how satisfactorily his own work was proceeding, had, on the evening on which this particular dream specimen was collected, stimulated the patient to question his own work adequacy and also to a hostile kind of competitiveness, which in turn aroused fears of these feelings and of retaliation from others. During his first REM period—the dream specimen quoted is from the fourth REM episode—the patient awoke spontaneously in fright. He had been questioning the validity of his own work and felt quite uncertain of it. The experimenter further sharpened the patient's feelings of inadequacy and competition by making a concise summary, during the association period subsequent to the report of this dream, of thoughts the patient had been unable to verbalize with any degree of precision.

In his second REM dream of the night, the patient finally retaliates openly against the forces he feels pressing upon him. He receives news that "my rival had suicided after I outwitted him." In the third dream, the victory is even more explicit as to the immediate object of his competitive strivings, although it is now less violent in form; he imagines the experimenter doing a menial intellectual task under his own supervision.

These three dreams provide the immediate context in which the fourth must be understood. From them it would appear that a presleep stimulus, the competitive encounter with the experimenter, provides a large part of the explanation of the content of the patient's dreams on this night. This presleep stimulus, however, was effective only because it made contact with some of the basic aspects of the dreamer's personality. It served to high-light his own inner conflicts over his feelings of aggression toward others—should he be aggressively competitive with others or passive and impotent? This was a question that touched upon many of the immediate waking problems that brought the patient into psychotherapy in the first place, and it was, consequently, much discussed in the interviews conducted during the course of the therapy.

Moreover, it is not the immediate presleep stimulus but rather the historical roots of his present disturbance as aroused by this stimulus that account for the particular form assumed by the fourth dream. In this dream, the patient is again in a competi-tive situation with a male, and, as was true in the third dream, the competition is intellectualized rather than being as explicitly hostile as it was in the second dream. The early familial sources of the patient's present-day problems are seen in this fourth narrative, however, in a manner not so clearly visible in any of the previous dreams of the same night. The fellow in the dream is "bigger than me" and he "reads too much." The discrepancy in size suggests a difference in status, that is, a superior-inferior relationship, such as a father-son relationship. The patient had, in fact, previously described his father as a man "who read too much." The girl's eyes are reminiscent of his mother's, and the girl is associated with the patient's childhood home. The dream suggests, therefore, the triangular relationship of patient-father-mother as a basic source of conflict in the patient's life. The father is seen as aloof and disinterested, the mother seems inviting but ultimately proves quite demanding, and the pa-tient's behavior consists of identification with the feminine figure and a passive and repressed competitiveness toward the male.

There is, of course, much more interpretive sense that could be made of this dream, and the interested reader is referred to the Offenkrantz and Rechtschaffen report for their account. This brief discussion is perhaps sufficient to demonstrate, however, that although situational presleep stimuli may be partially responsible for the content of REM dreams, it is the more basic and internalized aspects of personality that are ultimately required for the comprehension of dream content. It is such factors that dominate the expressive symbolism of dream imagery. REM dreams, rather than simply reflecting presleep stimuli in some nonpurposive manner, express, by means of symbolism that may employ such stimuli, the individual's conflicts and his conceptualizations of his difficulties and their possible sources.

It is for this reason that the interpretation of dreams plays a large role in many kinds of psychotherapy. Freud, in particular, speaks of dreams as the "royal road to the unconscious," [16] that is, to those aspects of personality lying beneath the surface of the patient's overt behavior that ultimately account for that behavior, and psychoanalysts are particularly inclined to give dream interpretation a central role in their therapeutic practice.

In Freud's theory, as stated in *The Interpretation of Dreams*, the dream is seen as an outlet for the discharge of accumulated psychological tensions that fail to achieve expression in waking life. It is, in particular, sexual tensions that must find an outlet in dreams because these tensions are the most usually repressed in waking life. The visual imagery of the dream is conceived by Freud as an attempt at hallucinating the gratification or fulfillment of such repressed impulses or wishes. Because of the taboo nature of sexual impulses or wishes, however, Freud stresses the use of symbolism as a means of disguising their true nature. An incestuous wish toward one's mother, for instance, is something the direct contemplation of which the conscience, even the sleeping conscience, could not abide. The visual imagery of walking up the stairs to meet one's mother, however, which to Freud might represent this same wish, disguises it so that it may receive partial gratification without arousing anxiety or disgust. In psychoanalytic therapy, then, the therapist uses dream interpretation to uncover the nature of the socially unacceptable and repressed wishes that are present in disguised form in the patient's dreams and are thought to underlie his waking neurotic symptoms as well.

Freud's theory of dreaming is by no means the only viewpoint which clinicians have adopted. There are other theories of dreaming, for example, that of Alfred Adler (1870–1937), Austrian physician and founder of the psychotherapeutic system known as Individual Psychology, which, in fact, form a rather sharp contrast to Freud's position. Adler's position is stated in his treatise for the layman, *What Life Should Mean to You.* He views the dream not so much as a regressive mechanism in which the organism's taboo instinctual impulses find discharge but rather as a forward-looking form of mental activity whose goal is the solution of problems arising in the exterior social world. Adler thinks that only the neurotic who has had a pampered childhood experiences simple tension discharge in dreams, and this merely reflects his childish and unrealistic style of behavior in waking life. In general, Adler sees dreams as essentially continuous with waking forms of mental activity, while Freud stresses the differences between waking (secondary process, reality oriented) and sleeping (primary process, wishful) thought. Moreover, in Adler's view, symbols are used in sleeping thought much as they are in waking thought, as a means of expressing thoughts or feelings, not of disguising them. Dreams are used by Adlerian therapists, then, not as a key to the nature of the individual's unconscious impulses, but rather as one means of understanding his conscious problems of social adjustment.

EEG/EOG dream researchers are inclined to believe, along with most clinicians, whatever their persuasion, in the meaningfulness of dreams. They accept the proposition that dreams are expressions of profound aspects of the personality. This proposition may seem less self-evident to the layman who often finds his dream unintelligible. The symbolism and indirection of the dream's "language" are certainly such that its meaningfulness is generally not immediately obvious. With the interpretive exposition attempted in Chapter 3 as background, and with adequate knowledge of the dreamer's waking behavior, his life history, and his associations to particular elements of dream content, however, it should be possible to appreciate the extent to which many dreams are expressions and revelations of personality.

This is not to say that all REM dreams are as revealing of personality as the carefully selected examples of the clinician seem to suggest. Nor does it seem that all REM dreams fit any particular pattern, "speak the dialect" of a particular theory of interpretation, as often as a clinician's private memories or public communications might suggest. It now appears that none of the many current theories of dream interpretation will be a sufficient guide to the understanding of all the many different specimens of nocturnal mentation that can be collected from REM sleep.

In EEG/EOG dream research, for instance, one occasionally comes across a dream so beautifully Freudian in its sexual symbolism and its goal of wish fulfillment that one is struck with the neat and precise manner in which it fits into his system for decoding the content of dreams. Numerous other dreams will appear, however, that seem to fit this particular system much less clearly. EEG/EOG dream research thus has provided little comfort for theorists who seem to assert that some particular kind of feeling or thought is always expressed in dream content or some particular means always expresses it. This is not at all surprising for we can scarcely expect any simple unitary explanation of dreaming to be adequate, any more than we could trust in any simple unitary explanation of waking mental activity. Human thought processes would seem far too varied and complex for this kind of approach to ever be sufficient.

The clinical experience of those engaged in the "new" research on dreaming, then, leaves unchallenged the general position that dreams are meaningful revelations of personality, but it also indicates that the exact nature of the interrelations among personality structure, personality dynamics, and manifest dream content still remains to be demonstrated. The electrophysiological techniques of this research will, no doubt, prove useful in years to come in untangling the complex nature of the relationships that exist among these variables.

Experimental Evidence.

I have already noted the inherent superiority of the clinical case study in documenting the association between dream content and waking personality. Granted the insufficiency of statistical evidence based upon the contributions of many subjects pooled together to present the "meat" of this relationship, one should at least take note of recent attempts at statistical confirmation of this association.

Rechtschaffen and I found a positive relationship between imagination judged in a waking test of fantasy, the Thematic

Apperception Test (TAT) * and both the presence of dream recall on REM sleep awakenings and the rated imaginativeness of the elicited REM reports.[17] We also observed a significant positive association between the presence of dream recall on REM-sleep awakenings and the MMPI L (Lie) scale, a purported measure of a subject's tendency to deny unpleasant facts about himself in order to meet with approval and acceptance by others. NREM recall of content was unrelated to MMPI scales and to TAT imagination scores, and NREM imagination was unrelated to imagination expressed in the TAT. These findings provide further support for the argument that NREM recall is not something other than the reporting of mental experiences occurring during NREM sleep. In particular, it does not seem from this evidence that NREM recall consists of dreams that are actually invented during nocturnal interviews by highly imaginative subjects or by subjects characterized by the more obvious forms of striving to meet with approval and acceptance by others. If anything, it appears that waking storytelling ability and striving for social approval play a larger role in determining REM recall than they do in determining NREM recall.

Among our findings relating personality to dreaming, the major one, however, concerns the direction of the relationship found between scores on MMPI clinical (pathological) scales and various qualitative characteristics of both REM and NREM reports. Dreamlike features of these narratives (vividness, distortion, emotionality, and so on), as rated either by subjects themselves or by an independent judge, were positively asso-

---

* The TAT is a series of pictures about each of which the respondent is to tell a story. It thus provides a measure of the subject's waking imagination. In addition, the stories told by the subject are thought to reveal aspects of his own personality, which are "projected" into the characters of the stories he tells.

ciated with scores on various MMPI clinical scales. Of twenty-eight statistically significant correlations between the standard MMPI clinical scales and subject ratings of dreamlike qualities of their sleep mentation, for example, twenty-seven were positive in direction. Moreover, the word counts and rated imaginativeness of both REM and NREM reports were found, when correlated with MMPI scales, to correlate in a positive direction with these indexes of psychopathology. The kind of content reported after awakenings from REM and NREM sleep, then, is significantly related to emotional disturbance as assessed by the MMPI: longer, more imaginative, and more dreamlike reports of nocturnal mentation were produced by subjects with a greater indication, in MMPI responses, of some form of emotional disturbance. Probably related to these observations is the recent finding that "psychological-mindedness," as assessed by the California Psychological Inventory (CPI),* is negatively related to ratings of the dreamlike quality of REM reports, the less psychologically aware subjects having more intense REM-sleep mentation.[18] We conclude that our data are consistent with the belief that intensity of emotional disturbance is positively related to intensity of the dreaming process, and by inference, consistent with the hypothesis that dreams reflect or discharge the tensions or conflicts of everyday life.

We also found that no consistent relationship existed between impulse (sex or aggression) expression in waking TAT fantasy and impulse expression in REM-dream content. A significant negative correlation was found for direct expression of physical aggression (subjects with relatively extensive aggressive waking

---

* The CPI is a collection of 480 statements with which the respondent is to indicate his agreement or disagreement. The statements are grouped and scored in eighteen scales referring to different areas of personal or social adjustment.

fantasy having relatively little aggression in sleeping fantasy), a near-zero correlation for direct expression of verbal aggression, and a positive and almost statistically significant relationship for direct expression of the sexual drive. More recently, a near-zero relationship ($r = -.01$) was found between the expression of aggression in REM reports and the expression of aggression in TAT stories, while a significant positive association ($r = .40$) was observed for sexual content in the two classes of fantasy.[19]

There are evidently certain areas, sexuality, for example, in which there is some continuity in fantasy content across the wakefulness-sleep border. There are also, however, other areas, such as aggression, in which dreams reflect personality components in a manner that may differ from the way in which waking fantasy reveals personality. This, of course, is not surprising, given the differences in the structure of the situations in which waking and sleeping fantasy transpire, but it does indicate the potentially unique contribution of dream analysis to the study of human personality.

PERSONALITY DETERMINANTS
OF SLEEP-ONSET DREAM PHENOMENA

Reports of sleep-onset dreaming are not highly predictable across subjects or from particular EEG/EOG patterns. The considerable cross-subject variability allows much greater scope for personality determination of the experience of dreaming during the sleep-onset period than during REM periods. Everybody, infants and animals perhaps excluded, seems to dream during REM sleep. The same is not true with respect to the sleep-onset period, from which some subjects report dreams and others do not. Why? What personality factors might explain this difference?

Because sleep-onset dreaming cannot be predicted from EEG/EOG patterns, the answers to this question cannot be derived from research modeled after the REM-time studies surveyed above. Subjects must be awakened and questioned to determine the occurrence of sleep-onset dreaming. We have recently completed a study at the University of Wyoming in which thirty-two subjects, sixteen males and sixteen females, all young adults, were awakened four times, twice during descending stage 1 and twice during alpha SEM, to establish a value expressing their frequency of sleep-onset dreaming.[20] Subjects were "awakened" in the order: stage 1, alpha SEM, alpha SEM, stage 1. These two categories of awakening were employed as they displayed maximum intersubject variability in the study I made with Vogel of the sleep-onset period.[21]

Variables investigated for their possible relationship to frequency of hypnagogic dreaming were: CPI scales and items, TAT stories, subjects' ratings of their everyday (prelaboratory) impressions of dream recall, and ratings of REM dream content (subjects were awakened ten minutes after the onset of their second, third, and fourth REM periods, in addition to the awakenings made at sleep onset).

Two raters, unfamiliar with the category of awakening (alpha SEM, descending stage 1, or REM sleep) for any narrative, rated both hypnagogic and REM reports on an eight-point scale of "dreamlike fantasy":

1. No recall   Feels mind was blank
2. No recall   Feels he was experiencing something, but forgets what
3. Recall   Conceptual (no sensory imagery), everydayish content
4. Recall   Conceptual, bizarre content

5. Recall   Perceptual (sensory imagery), nonhallucinatory (didn't believe experience was real), everydayish content

6. Recall   Perceptual, nonhallucinatory, bizarre content

7. Recall   Perceptual, hallucinatory (believed events he imagined were really happening), everydayish content

8. Recall   Perceptual, hallucinatory, bizarre content

It was found that the reporting of dreamlike fantasy during the hypnagogic period, thus assessed, was negatively correlated with subjects' scores on a CPI scale of "socialization" and positively correlated with scores on CPI scales of "social presence" and "self-acceptance." These findings are interpreted as showing that it is the person who is oversocialized, that is, who exerts rather rigid controls over his own feelings and behavior, and lacking in social poise and self-acceptance who is least likely to report and experience dreaming at sleep onset. We feel that such a person is loath to "let himself go" when the decathexis of external stimulus input affords the opportunity for an encounter with a more highly subjective realm of private thoughts and feelings.

Sleep-onset nondreamers were, moreover, found to respond favorably to a set of individual CPI items expressing a rigid, moralistic, and repressive outlook on life, for instance:

I set a high standard for myself and I feel that others should do the same.

I would disapprove of anyone's drinking to the point of intoxication at a party.

I am in favor of a very strict enforcement of all laws, no matter what the consequences.

I feel sure that there is only one true religion.

I would rather be a steady and dependable worker than a brilliant but unstable one.

Sleep-onset dreamers, on the other hand, tended to disagree with the content of these items, to be more tolerant of shortcomings in self and others, less dogmatic in their beliefs, and less fearful of the emotional side of life.

Sleep-onset dreamlike fantasy was also found to correlate positively with several scores from the TAT. This finding indicated that subjects with the ability to exercise their imagination freely in waking life also tended to have vivid imaginative experiences during the sleep-onset period.

It appears, then, that individuals with healthier personalities tend to experience more vivid dreaming at sleep onset, while, as already noted, individuals with signs of emotional disturbance tend to experience the more vivid dreaming during REM sleep. It seems that, during REM sleep, the presence of vivid nocturnal fantasy is associated with some inability of the ego to adequately master those pressures which beset it, while the presence of vivid hypnagogic fantasy, on the other hand, varies directly with the adaptability and strength of the ego.

Chapter 9

THE FUNCTIONS
OF DREAM EXPERIENCE

WHY do we dream the things we do? This is perhaps the ultimate question for the psychologist studying mental activity during sleep. It may be approached from several different perspectives. In the preceding three chapters, this question has been considered in terms of antecedent events (presleep influences and stimuli present during sleep) that might be causally related to the appearance of particular kinds of dream content. In the present chapter, it will be examined in terms of the functions that might be served for the human organism by the experiencing of the various kinds of mental activity characterizing its sleep.

Mental activity during sleep, particularly REM dreaming, does not appear to be randomly generated but, rather, seems to be purposive in character. Although motive and function are not synonymous, it is natural to believe that such motivated behavior must have a certain functional significance for the organism. It must meet certain needs of the organism or be in the service of certain goals that it is important the organism achieve.

Prominent among the functions sometimes ascribed to mental activity during sleep are those mentioned by psychoanalysts: the protection of sleep and the maintenance of personality integrity. The dream is viewed as the means by which the continuance of the state of sleep is assured and by which potentially harmful thoughts and impulses find discharge without any interference in wakeful personality functioning. Electrophysiological studies of mental activity during sleep have, as yet, produced only the barest evidence to support or contradict these and other suggestions as to why we experience the kinds of mental content we do during sleep. Nevertheless, it does seem both possible and worthwhile to examine the evidence now available on the nature of sleep mentation to see if some educated guesses might not be made about its functions. Such an examination will also serve to tie together the various research findings on mental activity during sleep discussed in previous chapters.

THE SLEEP-ONSET DREAM

The sleep-onset dream does not seem to be a vehicle of profound self-exploration. It does not delve into the distant past that conditions our present experience and in terms of which much of our present situation is to be understood. It is of relatively brief duration. It is emotionally bland. Insofar as sleep-onset dreaming provides any solutions to the problems that beset us, they are likely to be simple and unrealistic.

The sleep-onset dream seems to be closer to the "interpretive" dream of certain earlier viewpoints. Numerous nineteenth-century writers whose work Freud reviewed in the introductory chapter of *The Interpretation of Dreams* had suggested that dream content was an attempt at an interpretation of external or bodily stimuli present during sleep. While the sleep-onset dream may reflect the partial disintegration of mental functions that occurs as a result of sleep-onset sensory deprivation, it also seems to be the organism's attempt to integrate, as best it can, the very incomplete, inchoate sense data present during this period. In achieving some kind of internally consistent, although externally invalid, explanation of these data, certain idiosyncratic and autonomous patterns of mental organization are relied upon. In this sense, personality may to some extent be revealed in the sleep-onset dream, even if the function of such dreaming is not extended self-evaluation.

Personality is revealed in a still more important respect in sleep-onset dreaming, however. With the successful dampening of external stimuli that ordinarily serve to keep our thought processes rational and well-organized, the onset of sleep is most likely accompanied by the reactivation of more personal, threatening, or taboo inner thoughts and feelings. The potential breakthrough of such content at sleep onset is an entirely plausible postulate in view of related occurrences during sensory deprivation or even during some daydreaming. The breakthrough of such content, however, is not only a threat to mental integrity but also incompatible with a continuing descent into sleep. Though why sleep is needed is not known, we do know that sleep is, in every sense, one of the basic needs of the human organism.

Such content must be "managed," therefore, deprived of its potential for disturbing and arousing the would-be sleeper.

This is accomplished partly by means of symbolic distortion of anxieties and taboo desires and partly by means of superficial, for example, wish-fulfilling, attempts at expressing or satisfying such impulses. The activation of such "dream work" mechanisms and the partial expression of the content such mechanisms are "managing," then, reveal still further and deeper aspects of the personality of the hypnagogic dreamer.

Yet, in spite of the presence of symbolic distortion and wish fulfillment for the purpose of the protection of sleep—essential elements of the psychoanalytic theory of dreaming—the brevity and relative superficiality of hypnagogic dream content tell us that this type of mentation is not likely to provide the insights into the dreamer's situation specified in psychoanalytic and other clinical dream theories and observed in REM dreams.

Sleep-onset dreaming seems, basically, to be an expedient measure, adopted as a means of escaping mental chaos and of preserving some integrity of mental functioning without compromising the passage of the organism from wakefulness to sleep. It serves those functions in a period in which there are various threats both to the maintenance of mental integrity and to the emerging state of sleep. There is residual stimulus input from the external environment and one's own body against the background of a general reduction of stimulus input to the brain. This deprives remaining stimulus input of much of its context, hence its meaningfulness. Residual stimulus input also, of course, threatens the maintenance of drowsiness and its issuance into full-fledged sleep. There is some tendency to the reactivation of those unfulfilled desires, threatening impulses, and unreasoning anxieties that an orientation to external reality can mask only so long as we attend to that reality. The sleep-onset dream masters these threats in "dreamlets," which provide some kind of internally coherent, yet hallucinatory and thus sleep-preserving, interpretation of residual stimulus input and which superficially (in the long run), but satisfactorily (in the short run), gloss over representations of basic problems in the dreamer's daily existence so that the mental apparatus is not overwhelmed by them and so that wakefulness may pass into sleep.

NREM MENTATION

The success of the sleep-onset dream in preserving some integrity of mental functioning during sleep induction may best be measured by the nature of mental activity during the succeeding period of sleep, which comprises NREM sleep stages 2, 3, and 4. NREM mentation is, generally speaking, an unemotional and rather subdued form of hallucinatory experience, the more so when the subject's capacities for dealing with his inner life are relatively strong.[1] The lesser intensity of NREM, as compared with sleep-onset, mental activity reflects the fact that the initial mental chaos attending sleep onset has now been dispelled and the fact that threats to the preservation of sleep have now been minimized. External and bodily stimuli are now almost totally tuned out. Disturbing intrapsychic factors have been met and mastered, at least for the time being. Mental operations are once more lawful, according to laws by no means totally removed from those operative during wakefulness.

NREM mentation has sometimes been compared to "background" thought in waking life, to those fragments of experience that pass along the borders of consciousness while one's focus of attention is elsewhere.[2] While shaving, to take a familiar example, one experiences all kinds of momentary, irrelevant impressions as background stimuli although the major focus of his attention is upon razor, mirror, and face. During NREM sleep the central focus of waking thought is absent: hence, such background impressions might gain in relative salience and form the basis of typically reported NREM content, which would be relatively aimless in character.

But the several NREM reports cited in Chapter 4 certainly appear better organized and more purposive than this comparison implies. The kind of aimless associative content that approaches the quality of background waking mentation may appear momentarily at sleep onset, but it is soon replaced by better synthesized and more coherent mental experience. It seems that the isolated experience of the fragmentary and disjointed content of background mentation implies a level of mental disorganization that the human organism, particularly the one lacking in the capacity to freely accept, control, and not be disturbed by his own thoughts and feelings, finds unpleasant and ultimately intolerable. For this reason, as well as because reported NREM content often demonstrates a considerable degree of mental synthesis, I am inclined to view NREM mentation as an actively produced or motivated phenomenon rather than as a passive residue of background mentation that becomes evident when a central focus of attention is no longer extended toward external reality. For these reasons I am also inclined to ascribe some functional significance to the mental experiences occurring during NREM sleep.

NREM mentation is the least disturbing psychic content of the sleep cycle, and NREM sleep is that kind of sleep upon which the organism places greatest priority. Following generalized sleep deprivation, subjects show an increase in NREM sleep and a decrease in REM sleep on the first "recovery" night as compared with base-line nights. It is only on the second "recovery" night that there is an increase in REM sleep relative to base-line nights.[3] This association of unintense mental content with that kind of sleep for which there seems to be the greatest need is surely more than coincidence. In particular, it appears that NREM mentation may function to preserve sound NREM sleep in two respects.

First, it maintains and consolidates the transfer of relatively intact processes of mental synthesis from wakefulness to sleep achieved during the sleep-onset period. This protects the organism from any upleasant consequences that might attend a total failure to exert an organizing influence upon mental experience. Such a failure is often noted after prolonged sensory deprivation, for example, where directed thought processes yield to disorganized and emotionally charged fantasies. The maintenance of synthetic mental processes during NREM sleep, then, may protect the organism in the same manner as does the successful (sleep-preserving) sleep-onset dream from the regressive and disjointed mental experiences that generally accompany a continuing state of sensory deprivation.

Secondly, it consists of ordinary, unemotional, and undisturbing elements of mental content that are more consistent with, and less disturbing to, the nonactivated state of NREM sleep than would be, for instance, REM-like elements of mental fantasy.

THE REM-SLEEP DREAM

The REM period is perhaps the most striking and unusual phase of the sleep cycle. Its physiology, often highly activated, departs considerably from the passivity and inertia generally associated with sleep. Its mental content is certainly the most distinctive experienced during behavioral sleep. It might be expected, then, that REM dream content would play some particularly significant role in over-all organismic functioning.

I have suggested that sleep-onset dreaming may be a means of maintaining some integrity of mental functioning as we pass from wakefulness to sleep and that NREM mental processes may preserve this integrity while typical NREM content may "protect" this relatively profound state of sleep. The possible role of REM-sleep dream content in relation either to the function of preserving the stability of mental functioning or to the function of protecting sleep is, however, not so immediately obvious. REM thinking is generally coherent, but in a manner quite foreign to waking standards, and its content often seems calculated to disturb the dreamer's sleep, rather than to protect it.

At present, of course, one can only speculate on the functional aspects of any kind of mental experience occurring during sleep with relation to the organism's need for sleep and its apparent need to avoid the disintegration during sleep of its capacity for achieving some degree of mental synthesis. One way of thinking of the REM dream, however, stresses the "danger" that ascending stage-2 sleep may issue into wakefulness.[4] After a person has experienced the profound sleep of NREM stages 3 and 4 for a period of time, inner self-regulatory mechanisms cause sleep to lighten. Such mechanisms are of possible evolutionary value. The animal with a periodic lightening of sleep and lowering of sensory thresholds for arousal has been provided with means to reduce total proneness to victimization by others, which is an unfortunate concomitant of the profound sleep satisfying its own biological needs. In the adult human, the lightening of sleep (to ascending stage 2) brings along with it mental content that seems the most wakeful, in its commonplace, rational content and its relative freedom from self-deceptive hallucination, of any ever experienced during behavioral sleep. A projection of the trends characterizing the transition toward light sleep beyond the point of ascending stage 2 seems to indicate the immanence of wakefulness: motility is increasing; sensory thresholds are lowering; and mental processes are moving in a nonhallucinatory and reasonable direction that ultimately must prove incompatible with the maintenance of sleep.

While the lightening of sleep once may have had survival value and indeed may still have it in less civilized surroundings, it generally seems to be in the best interests of the contemporary human sleeper, for reasons as yet unknown, that sleep be preserved beyond the point of his first NREM period, which comprises only the initial one or two hours of sleep. The progression of mental process and content toward wakefulness must, therefore, be checked. The situation becomes particularly acute as the EEG shifts further toward wakefulness, that is, into the "drowsy waking" pattern of ascending stage 1.

Thus, with the onset of this stage of sleep, mental processes turn away from the recent realistic memories of ascending-stage-2 sleep toward the bizarre and unrealistic mental content of the full-fledged nocturnal dream. This latter content abruptly replaces the typical mental content of ascending stage 2, content that is seemingly geared to proceed toward mental experience even more characteristic of wakefulness, and then to awakening itself. REM dreaming provides an inner hallucinatory focus for attention and an inner arena for the operation of thought mechanisms that, activated to this degree, are generally associated with a wakeful orientation to external reality. In this manner, the hallucinated REM dream becomes a sleeping substitute for the "real" world, attention to which and involvement in which are incompatible with sleep. It renders the sleeper less accessible to external stimulation in much the same manner as the exciting program does the rapt television viewer.

Corresponding with the change from realistic but unintense mental content to unreal but vivid mental content are: (1) a shift from the relatively high behavioral responsiveness to extraneous stimuli characteristic of stage 2 and sleep-onset stage 1 to the relatively low responsiveness to such stimuli of ascending stage 1, and (2) a relative decrease in gross body motility. Sleep has been preserved.

The mental content of REM sleep, in association with other aspects of the REM period, may, then, aid in the reversal of an ascending (pointing to wakefulness) state of affairs to a descending (pointing to the profound sleep of stages 3 and 4) state. It is of special interest, in regard to the possibility that REM dream content may serve to protect sleep, that the human infant, presumably without REM dreams as we understand them, is particularly prone to awaken from his predominantly REM sleep and is particularly prone to experience acute episodes of motility during this period.

The peculiar and distinctive aspects of REM-sleep mental activity have suggested to many observers that the REM dream fulfills a function over and above any that it might serve in and for the state of sleep. In the REM dream, the sleeper explores his life and expresses his thoughts, hopes, and fears in a manner unavailable to him in waking life. Here, unobserved by others and unfettered by input from external stimuli, he may, with a brain that is "activated" to permit intricate patterns of directed thought, engage in a kind of self-exploration unthinkable in waking life.

Freudian theory suggests that, in this manner, the REM dream serves a "safety-valve" function, that it allows the harmless and unobserved "discharge" during sleep of pent-up anxieties and cravings whose appearance in waking life would prove harmful.[5]

Dement's research on the effects of systematic deprivation of REM sleep has seemed to many to provide a measure of empirical support for the safety-valve conception of the dream occurring during this phase of sleep. His method was the interruption, by experimental awakenings made at a point reasonably close to the onset of periods of REM sleep, of such episodes so that subjects would be relatively deprived of this stage of sleep. In his earliest studies employing this method, subjects were studied for experimental series of five consecutive nights, never experiencing a single complete period of REM sleep during this time.[6] Deprivation of REM sleep was not completely effective, however, since a small portion of it would occur before the experimenter could be certain from the EEG and EOG that a REM period was in progress, hence that an awakening should be initiated. Dement's estimate is that his procedure produced a 65–75 per cent reduction in REM sleep as compared with subjects' prior nondeprivation control nights.

He reported three major effects of his experimental treatment: (1) an increase in attempts at REM dreaming during the deprivation nights (a shorter time elapsing between sleep onset and the onset of REM sleep as the number of deprivation awakenings increased); (2) an increase in actual amounts of REM sleep on recovery (noninterrupted sleep) nights following the deprivation series as compared with the amount of REM sleep on pre-deprivation nights (an average increase of 40 per cent, which is interpreted as making up REM sleep lost on deprivation nights); and (3) the presence of maladaptive behavioral symptoms on the days intervening between nights of the deprivation series (manifest anxiety, unusual increase in appetite, and difficulty in concentration).

The changes, both during and following deprivation, in the sleep cycle observed by Dement might be interpreted as indications of increased pressure for the discharge of tensions ordinarily expelled during REM sleep. The waking symptoms of deprivation might be interpreted as a spillover into overt waking behavior of impulses that no longer can find their usual discharge in sleep due to the experimental "capping" of the REM-sleep safety valve. Dement's results thus seem compatible with Freud's theory of the dream as an outlet for the discharge of tensions unable to find release in wakefulness.

More recent research has confirmed Dement's original findings on the sleep-cycle effects of systematic REM deprivation but has not supported his original observations of increased anxiety, increased appetite, or decreased concentration during periods of wakefulness immediately following REM-sleep deprivation.[7]

Employing awakenings made at the point of loss of tonus of neck muscles, a change generally preceding the onset of ascending stage 1 by a minute or so, it is possible to achieve greater REM-sleep deprivation (approximately 95 per cent) than is possible if awakenings are made using only EEG/EOG signs of the onset of this period. This method has been applied to two subjects who were REM sleep deprived for ten consecutive nights.[8] Psychological testing revealed little significant change in waking personality following the deprivation procedure. Similarly, Dement reports no significant waking behavioral effects for a subject who was deprived for eight consecutive nights of REM sleep by awakenings made at the point of loss of tonus of neck muscles, the presumed harbinger of the onset of REM sleep.[9]

In the case of two other subjects, however, who were deprived of REM sleep by this method for, respectively, fifteen and sixteen consecutive nights, Dement reports "rather dramatic" changes in personality after the fourteenth consecutive deprivation night. In one of these two cases, for instance:

> The subject, a taciturn and somewhat inhibited person with high moral standards, abruptly loosened up to the extent that he was becoming very garrulous, expressing annoyance and anger quite readily, and impulsively wanting to do a variety of things that he ordinarily would not have even considered. In the subject's own words, "I felt peculiarly uninhibited and carefree, not the least bit concerned with what others might be thinking. I was willing to try almost anything once. I wanted to go into all the night clubs, but especially the ones with the loudest, and better still, sexiest entertainment. To make it even more exciting, I thought I would go to a night club which had no cover charge and see how long I could stay before I was thrown out for not buying anything. When I was requested to leave, I felt no embarrassment whatsoever, which was rather incredible for me." [10]

This subject reverted to his normal waking-behavior patterns following the first "recovery" night, on which he achieved 60 per cent REM sleep, a value much in excess of his predeprivation amount.

Dement's second long-run REM-deprived subject also experienced a dramatic shift in personality following the fourteenth deprivation night, becoming almost paranoid in his suspicions of others. His deprivation nights were terminated, in fact, because of fears that the subject might develop a full-scale psychosis. Again, however, the changed behavioral symptoms disappeared during the recovery nights, on which the amount of REM sleep was markedly elevated over values achieved on predeprivation control nights.

It would seem from the experiences of these last two subjects that when REM deprivation is sufficiently complete and when the deprivation is extended to a period of at least two weeks, interference with normal REM sleep does lead to marked and deleterious changes in waking personality. These results, again, seem compatible with Freud's notion of the dream as a mechanism for the discharge of potentially harmful tensions that are unable to find release during waking experience. When this mechanism is blocked, these harmful tensions may accumulate and eventually force their way into waking expression in the form of symptoms of mental disturbance.

Do we, then, need to dream? Would we tend to go mad or show bizarre behavioral patterns if we did not have the opportunity afforded by the REM dream to discharge our tensions or to explore our problems? The evidence for such a proposition is, at best, equivocal. First of all, the early evidence of increased anxiety, appetite, and so on, following dream deprivation has, as noted, not been confirmed by subsequent research. Even Dement's two subjects with marked changes in personality following extended and nearly total dream deprivation did not show an increase in manifest anxiety in association with their other symptoms.

Secondly, the two undoubted positive cases of personality change after REM sleep deprivation are, as Dement himself has noted, open to other explanations than that which stresses the REM-sleep-depriving awakenings as the causal factor.[11] The number of awakenings required to suppress REM sleep became so prohibitive (over two hundred were required on the eighth night) for the subject dream-deprived for eight nights, that a drug (dexedrine) was used, in addition to experimental awakenings, to suppress REM sleep for these two subjects. It is at least possible that the administration, or effects, of this drug, rather than the REM sleep deprivation it helped to achieve, played some causal role in producing the personality changes ultimately observed. The subject with potentially psychotic symptoms of REM sleep deprivation had, moreover, a somewhat unstable personality pattern before the start of the experiment, and generalized nonspecific sleep deprivation might have played a role in producing the symptoms of the other subject.

Thirdly, REM sleep deprivation phenomena can be produced in cats by the successive awakening procedure employed with humans.[12] It seems unlikely that cats show these symptoms because they use their dreams as mechanisms for discharging tensions or repressed impulses that accumulate during the day. For one thing, cats just do not seem so inhibited in their waking life that they would need the kind of safety-valve during sleep postulated in Freudian theory. Since dream-deprivation phenomena seem as readily producible in cats as in men, it is difficult to accept them as unequivocal evidence for the tension-discharge function of dream experience.

Fourthly, REM-period deprivation and compensation phenomena may be observed in cats with all brain structures above the pons removed ("pontine" cats).[13] This evidence clearly suggests a minimal cortical, or psychological, involvement in REM-period deprivation phenomena.

Finally, Dement's evidence, even if the experimental treatment is judged responsible for the shifts in personality with which it was associated, does not show that it is necessarily dream deprivation that produces personality change. It is not shown by his procedure whether it is a deficit of physiological ascending stage-1 sleep or a deficit of the psychological concomitant of this stage, dreaming, that is responsible for any effects on personality. Dement, in fact, is now inclined to the view that dream deprivation is something of a misnomer for his experimental procedure and that so-called dream-deprivation effects are actually the result of the deprivation of *a stage of sleep* with a specific *biological* function—for instance, the discharge of some biochemical substance that accumulates during wakefulness and is ordinarily eliminated during REM sleep.[14]

Whatever one's speculations about the particular biological functions of REM sleep, there is good reason to believe that it and the biological need for it may be more primitive and primary than any need for the psychic associate of such sleep in the adult human. REM-period episodes appear regularly in the sleep of lower mammalian species,[15] and REM sleep is predominant in the human infant soon after birth.[16] Such evidence suggests that it has developed for evolutionary reasons as yet unknown but most likely somewhat remote from the psychological reasons specified by the safety-valve theory.

Apparently, at some point in the development of the human species and of particular members of our species, the REM period may become invested with mental content of a self-exploratory nature. It seems to partake of such content in the adult human. It seems doubtful, however, that such mentation is characteristic of the REM periods of the rat, for instance, or of the newborn human infant.

Once the REM period is so invested, how much does the organism come to need or rely upon the dream as a means of maintaining psychological stability? Will dream deprivation, in fact, cause the kind of interference with orderly adaptive behavior and with survival itself that interference with other basic human needs or drives produces? Or, is the opportunity for self-exploration, tension discharge, or whatever, provided in dream experience a luxury, one that the human organism finds somewhat useful but without which it could proceed to live its life pretty much unaffected in the long run by its loss of dream experience?

Psychoanalytic and other dream theories suggest the former alternative. Dement's dream-deprivation results are compatible with it. All available evidence, however, including the results of dream-deprivation research, is quite compatible with the latter alternative. Personality factors do not seem to be responsible, either in a phylogenetic or contemporary sense, for initiating REM periods. It is also possible that personality integration does not require the opportunity they afford for intensive self-exploration.

The best that can be said at present, then, about the functional value of the REM dream in relation to waking personality is that profound aspects of human personality are expressed in, and revealed by, the content of REM-period dreams. Whether this expression is a basic need of the human organism cannot be answered at present. For some reason there does seem to be a need for REM sleep, the biological state in which vivid dreaming occurs.

POSTSCRIPT

MUCH more is known about sleep and about mental activity during sleep than ever before. Most of the evidence, particularly that identifying different kinds of sleep and associating varying qualities of mental experience with these kinds of sleep, is of very recent origin. These accelerating developments hold forth great promise of still further gains in years to come.

From the perspective of the psychology of sleep, however, it should also be clear that much still remains to be discovered about the nature and functions of mental experience during this period. Indeed, there is a sense in which recent findings have only served to highlight just how ignorant we still are of the mind's operations during sleep.

It must be admitted that the promise of still further gains in knowledge of sleep does not extend equally well to its psychological investigation as to its physiological investigation. Ours is a century of tremendous advances in biological science, of ever greater expenditures in this area, and of the promise of still more impressive accomplishments in the future. Psychology's immediate past, present, and prospects for the future seem somewhat dim by comparison.

Yet, through fruitful collaboration with the burgeoning biological sciences, it may be possible for psychologists to shed much new light upon the age-old puzzles of human experience with which psychology contends. If I have any particular hopes for this book, it is that it may have pointed out that the tools are increasingly avaliable for the psychological investigation of sleep.

For there *are* many important and legitimate topics of psychological interest in the study of sleep. Sleep is not a field to be abandoned to the physiologist. For instance, we need, in addition to studies of the sleep cycle in mental illness, studies of mental activity during sleep in neurotics and psychotics; we need, in addition to developmental research into the sleep cycle, developmental research into the workings of the mind during sleep. These problems and many others like them are clearly psychological in nature, and they are now feasible objects of experimental investigation by the psychologist. Should he accept their challenge, future psychologies of sleep will prove much more rewarding than any now possible.

The psychology of sleep, in fact, may prove to be of great value in improving the understanding of the mind awake, particularly where adults have difficulty in comprehending styles of thought relatively foreign to their own daily experience: those of the mentally ill, for example, or of the young child. The psychology of sleep may be not only a topic of interest in its own right but also a broad pathway toward the more general goal of psychological science—the understanding of all forms of human behavior and experience.

NOTES

CHAPTER 1

1. These theories, and evidence pro and con, are reviewed by N. Kleitman, *Sleep and Wakefulness*, 2nd. ed. (Chicago: University of Chicago Press, 1963).

2. See, for instance: Kleitman, *op. cit.*; I. Oswald, *Sleeping and Waking* (Amsterdam: Elsevier, 1962); Ciba Foundation Symposium, *The Nature of Sleep* (Boston: Little, Brown and Company, 1961); D. B. Lindsley, "Attention, Consciousness, Sleep and Wakefulness," in J. Field (ed.), *Handbook of Physiology. Section 1. Neurophysiology* (Washington: American Physiological Society, 1960), Volume III, pp. 1553–1593; J. F. Delafresnaye (ed.), *Brain Mechanisms and Consciousness* (Springfield, Ill.: Charles C Thomas, Publisher, 1954); E. Gellhorn, *Physiological Foundations of Neurology and Psychiatry* (Minneapolis: University of Minnesota Press, 1953), chaps. 8–10.

3. Kleitman, *op. cit.*, chap. 22; Oswald, *op. cit.*, chap. 11.

4. Kleitman, *loc. cit.*

5. See, for instance: R. J. Lifton, *Thought Reform and the Psychology of Totalism* (New York: W. W. Norton & Company, Inc., 1961).

6. For example, F. A. Gibbs, H. Davis, and W. G. Lennox, "The Electro-encephalogram in Epilepsy and in Conditions of Impaired Consciousness," *Archives of Neurology and Psychiatry*, 34 (1935), 1133–1148.

7. E. Aserinsky and N. Kleitman, "Two Types of Ocular Motility Occurring in Sleep," *Journal of Applied Physiology*, 8 (1955), 1–10; W. Dement and N. Kleitman, "Cyclic Variations in EEG During Sleep and Their Relation to Eye Movements, Body Motility, and Dreaming," *Electroencephalography and Clinical Neurophysiology*, 9 (1957), 673–690.

8. D. B. Lindsley, "Psychophysiology and Motivation," in M. R. Jones (ed.), *Nebraska Symposium on Motivation, 1957* (Lincoln: University of Nebraska Press, 1957), pp. 44–105.

9. E. Jacobson, "The Electrophysiology of Mental Activities," *American Journal of Psychology*, 44 (1932), 677–694.

10. John S. Antrobus, Judith S. Antrobus, and J. L. Singer, "Eye Movements Accompanying Daydreaming, Visual Imagery, and Thought Suppression," *Journal of Abnormal and Social Psychology*, 69 (1964), 244–252.

11. D. Foulkes and G. Vogel, "Mental Activity at Sleep Onset," *Journal of Abnormal Psychology*, 70 (1965), 231–243; D. Foulkes, P. S. Spear, and J. D. Symonds, "Individual Differences in Mental Activity at Sleep Onset," *Journal of Abnormal Psychology*, in press.

12. I. Oswald, "Falling Asleep Open-Eyed During Intense Rhythmic Stimulation," *British Medical Journal*, 1 (1960), 1450–1455.

13. A. Rechtschaffen and D. Foulkes, "Effect of Visual Stimuli on Dream Content," *Perceptual and Motor Skills*, 20 (1965), 1149–1160.

14. Dement and Kleitman, *op. cit.*

15. Foulkes and Vogel, *op. cit.*; Foulkes, Spear, and Symonds, *op. cit.*

16. Foulkes and Vogel, *op. cit.*

17. W. Dement and N. Kleitman, "The Relation of Eye Movements During Sleep to Dream Activity: An Objective Method for the Study of Dreaming," *Journal of Experimental Psychology*, 53 (1957), 339–346; A. Rechtschaffen, P. Verdone, and J. Wheaton, "Reports of Mental Activity During Sleep," *Canadian Psychiatric Association Journal*, 8 (1963), 409–414.

18. Rechtschaffen, Verdone, and Wheaton, *ibid.;* Foulkes, Spear, and Symonds, *op. cit.*

19. Dement and Kleitman, "Cyclic Variations . . ." *op. cit.;* J. Kamiya, "Behavioral and Physiological Concomitants of Dreaming," progress report submitted to National Institute of Mental Health, 1962.

20. Kamiya, *op. cit.*

21. F. Snyder, *et al.*, "Changes in Respiration, Heart Rate, and Systolic Blood Pressure in Human Sleep," *Journal of Applied Physiology*, 19 (1964), 417–422.

22. *Ibid.*

23. Kamiya, *op. cit.*

24. Snyder, *et al.*, *op. cit.*

25. Kamiya, *op. cit.*

26. See Kleitman, *op. cit.*, chap. 8.

27. P. Verdone, "Variables Related to the Temporal Reference of Manifest Dream Content," unpublished Ph.D. dissertation, University of Chicago, 1963.

28. A. Rechtschaffen, P. Cornwell, and W. Zimmerman, "Brain Temperature Variations with Paradoxical Sleep in the Cat," paper presented to the Association for the Psychophysiological Study of Sleep, Washington, D.C., 1965.

29. E. Kanzow, "Changes in Blood Flow of the Cerebral Cortex and Other Vegetative Changes during Paradoxical Sleep Periods in the Unrestrained Cat," in Centre National de la Recherche Scientifique, *Aspects Anatomo-Fonctionnels de la Physiologie du Sommeil* (Anatomical and Functional Aspects of the Physiology of Sleep) (Paris: CNRS, 1965), pp. 231–237.

30. C. Fisher, J. Gross, and J. Zuch, "Cycle of Penile Erection Synchronous with Dreaming (REM) Sleep," *Archives of General Psychiatry*, 12 (1965), 29–45.

31. H. L. Williams, D. I. Tepas, and H. C. Morlock, "Evoked Responses to Clicks and Electroencephalographic Stages of Sleep in Man," *Science*, 138 (1962), 685–686.

32. *Ibid.*

33. *Ibid.*, p. 686.

34. H. L. Williams, *et al.*, "Responses to Auditory Stimulation, Sleep Loss, and the EEG Stages of Sleep," *Electroencephalography and Clinical Neurophysiology*, 16 (1964), 269–279.

35. E. V. Evarts, "Effects of Sleep and Waking on Activity of Single Units in the Unrestrained Cat," in Ciba Foundation Symposium, *op. cit.*, pp. 171–182; E. V. Evarts, "Neuronal Activity in Visual and Motor Cortex During Sleep and Waking," in Centre National de la Recherche Scientifique, *op. cit.*, pp. 189–209.

36. H. L. Williams, H. C. Morlock, and J. V. Morlock, "Discriminative Responses to Auditory Signals During Sleep," paper presented to the American Psychological Association, Philadelphia, 1963.

37. I. Oswald, A. M. Taylor, and M. Treisman, "Cortical Function During Human Sleep," in Ciba Foundation Symposium, *op. cit.*, pp. 343–348.

38. Kamiya, *op. cit.*

39. I. Oswald, *et al.*, "Melancholia and Barbiturates: A Controlled EEG, Body and Eye Movement Study of Sleep," *British Journal of Psychiatry*, 109 (1963), 66–78.

40. *Ibid.*, p. 77.

41. A. Rechtschaffen, D. R. Goodenough, and A. Shapiro, "Patterns of Sleep Talking," *Archives of General Psychiatry*, 7 (1962), 418–426.

42. R. J. Berger, "Tonus of Extrinsic Laryngeal Muscles During Sleep and Dreaming," *Science*, 134 (1961), 840.

43. A. Jacobson, *et al.*, "Muscle Tonus in Human Subjects During Sleep and Dreaming," *Experimental Neurology*, 10 (1964), 418–424.

44. Kamiya, *op. cit.*

45. A. Jacobson, *et al.*, "Somnambulism: All-Night Electroencephalographic Studies," *Science*, 148 (1965), 975–977.

46. Kamiya, *op. cit.*; A. M. Granda and J. T. Hammack, "Operant Behavior During Sleep," *Science*, 133 (1961), 1485–1486.

47. W. H. Emmons and C. W. Simon, "The Non-Recall of Material Presented During Sleep," *American Journal of Psychology*, 69 (1956), 76–81.

48. A. M. Granda and J. T. Hammack, *op. cit.*, p. 1486.

CHAPTER 2

1. E. Aserinsky and N. Kleitman, "Regularly Occurring Periods of Eye Motility, and Concomitant Phenomena, During Sleep," *Science*, 118 (1953), 273–274.

2. E. Aserinsky and N. Kleitman, "Two Types of Ocular Motility Occurring in Sleep," *Journal of Applied Physiology*, 8 (1955), 1–10.

3. *Ibid.*, p. 6.

4. *Ibid.*, p. 9.

5. E. Jacobson, *Progressive Relaxation*, 2nd ed. (Chicago: University of Chicago Press, 1938).

6. *Ibid.*, pp. 339–340.

7. J. B. Watson, *Behaviorism* (Chicago: University of Chicago Press, "Phoenix Books," 1959).

8. *Ibid.*, p. 241 (italics in original).

9. L. W. Max, "An Experimental Study of the Motor Theory of Consciousness. III. Action-Current Responses in Deaf-Mutes During Sleep, Sensory Stimulation and Dreams," *Journal of Comparative Psychology*, 19 (1935), 469–486.

10. W. Dement and N. Kleitman, "The Relation of Eye Move-

ments During Sleep to Dream Activity: An Objective Method for the Study of Dreaming," *Journal of Experimental Psychology*, 53 (1957), 339–346.

11. *Ibid.*, p. 344.

12. W. Dement, "An Essay on Dreams," in T. M. Newcomb (ed.), *New Directions in Psychology II* (New York: Holt, Rinehart, & Winston, Inc., 1965), pp. 135–257.

13. Dement and Kleitman, *op. cit.*

14. *Ibid.*

15. *Ibid.*, p. 344.

16. *Ibid.*

17. *Ibid.*

18. W. Dement and E. A. Wolpert, "The Relation of Eye Movements, Body Motility, and External Stimuli to Dream Content," *Journal of Experimental Psychology*, 55 (1958), 543–553.

19. *Ibid.*

20. P. Verdone, "Variables Related to the Temporal Reference of Manifest Dream Content," unpublished Ph.D. dissertation, University of Chicago, 1963.

21. R. J. Berger and I. Oswald, "Eye Movements During Active and Passive Dreams," *Science*, 137 (1962), 601.

22. H. P. Roffwarg, *et al.*, "Dream Imagery: Relationship to Rapid Eye Movements of Sleep," *Archives of General Psychiatry*, 7 (1962), 235–258.

23. Dement and Wolpert, *op. cit.*

24. E. A. Wolpert and H. Trosman, "Studies in Psychophysiology of Dreams. I. Experimental Evocation of Sequential Dream Episodes," *Archives of Neurology and Psychiatry*, 79 (1958), 603–606.

25. E. A. Wolpert, "Studies in Psychophysiology of Dreams. II. An Electromyographic Study of Dreaming," *Archives of General Psychiatry*, 2 (1960), 231–241.

26. N. E. Knopf, "A Study of Heart and Respiration Rates Dur-

ing Dreaming," unpublished Master's thesis, University of Chicago, 1962.

27. Verdone, *op. cit.*

28. A. Shapiro, *et al.*, "Dream Recall and the Physiology of Sleep," *Journal of Applied Physiology*, 19 (1964), 778–783.

29. Dement and Wolpert, *op. cit.*

30. *Ibid.*, p. 550.

31. W. Dement, "The Physiology of Dreaming," unpublished Ph.D. dissertation, University of Chicago, 1958.

32. Dement, "An Essay on Dreams," *op. cit.*

33. A. Rechtschaffen and P. Verdone, "Amount of Dreaming: Effect of Incentive, Adaptation to Laboratory, and Individual Differences," *Perceptual and Motor Skills*, 19 (1964), 947–958.

34. H. P. Roffwarg, W. Dement, and C. Fisher, "Preliminary Observations of the Sleep-Dream Pattern in Neonates, Infants, Children and Adults," in E. Harms (ed.), *Problems of Sleep and Dream in Children* (New York: Pergamon Press, Inc., 1964), pp. 60–72.

35. D. R. Goodenough, *et al.*, "A Comparison of 'Dreamers' and 'Nondreamers': Eye Movements, Electroencephalograms, and the Recall of Dreams," *Journal of Abnormal and Social Psychology*, 59 (1959), 295–302; Judith S. Antrobus, W. Dement, and C. Fisher, "Patterns of Dreaming and Dream Recall: An EEG Study," *Journal of Abnormal and Social Psychology*, 69 (1964), 341–344. Antrobus, *et al.*, do report that the "dreamer's" REM periods are reliably longer than those of the "non-dreamers" (an average of 105 minutes REM sleep as opposed to 83 minutes REM sleep for a period of 7.3 hours), but the magnitude of this difference hardly seems to account for the very large variation in dream recall between the two groups.

36. Goodenough, *et al.*, *op. cit.*

37. Dement and Kleitman, *op. cit.*, p. 342.

38. Wolpert and Trosman, *op. cit.*

39. A. Rechtschaffen, "Discussion of Dr. William Dement's Pa-

per," in J. H. Masserman (ed.), *Science and Psychoanalysis. Vol. VII.* (New York: Grune & Stratton, Inc., 1964), pp. 162–170.

40. W. Penfield, "Studies of the Cerebral Cortex of Man: A Review and an Interpretation," in J. F. Delafresnaye (ed.), *Brain Mechanisms and Consciousness* (Springfield, Ill.: Charles C Thomas, Publisher, 1954), pp. 284–304.

41. Goodenough, *et al., op. cit.*

42. Judith S. Antrobus, *et al., op. cit.*

43. A. Shapiro, D. R. Goodenough, and R. B. Gryler, "Dream Recall as a Function of Method of Awakening," *Psychosomatic Medicine*, 25 (1963), 174–180; D. R. Goodenough, *et al.*, "Dream Reporting Following Abrupt and Gradual Awakenings from Different Types of Sleep," *Journal of Personality and Social Psychology*, 2 (1965), 170–179; D. R. Goodenough, *et al.*, "Some Correlates of Dream Reporting Following Laboratory Awakenings," *Journal of Nervous and Mental Disease*, 140 (1965), 365–373.

44. R. A. Schonbar, "Some Manifest Characteristics of Recallers and Nonrecallers of Dreams," *Journal of Consulting Psychology*, 23 (1959), 414–418; J. L. Singer and R. A. Schonbar, "Correlates of Daydreaming: A Dimension of Self-Awareness," *Journal of Consulting Psychology*, 25 (1961), 1–6; C. T. Tart, "Frequency of Dream Recall and Some Personality Measures," *Journal of Consulting Psychology*, 26 (1962), 467–470.

45. D. Foulkes, P. S. Spear, and J. D. Symonds, "Individual Differences in Mental Activity at Sleep Onset," *Journal of Abnormal Psychology*, in press.

CHAPTER 3

1. A subject in the study by D. Foulkes, "Dream Reports From Different Stages of Sleep," *Journal of Abnormal and Social Psychology*, 65 (1962), 14–25.

2. S. Freud, *The Interpretation of Dreams* (New York: Basic Books, Inc., Publishers, 1955).

3. C. S. Hall, *The Meaning of Dreams* (New York: Dell Publishing Co., Inc., 1959).

4. Freud, *op. cit.*

5. Hall, *op. cit.*

6. *Ibid.*

7. S. Freud, "Three Contributions to the Theory of Sex," in *The Basic Writings of Sigmund Freud* (New York: The Modern Library, Inc., 1938), pp. 553–629.

8. D. Day, "Dream Interpretation as a Projective Technique," *Journal of Consulting Psychology*, 13 (1949), 416–420.

9. Hall, *op. cit.*

10. J. L. Framo, J. Osterweil, and I. Boszormenyi-Nagy, "A Relationship Between Threat in the Manifest Content of Dreams and Active-Passive Behavior in Psychotics," *Journal of Abnormal and Social Psychology*, 65 (1962), 41–47.

11. D. Foulkes, "Dream Reports From Different Stages of Sleep," unpublished Ph.D. dissertation, University of Chicago, 1960.

12. The findings of P. Verdone ("Variables Related to the Temporal Reference of Manifest Dream Content," unpublished Ph.D. dissertation, University of Chicago, 1963) are in accord with those cited in the text on differences between long-REM-period and short-REM-period awakenings, even in the failure to find a distinction between the two classes in the area of plausibility of dream content.

13. Although the difference in sampling conditions between home and laboratory dream collection renders the data somewhat ambiguous, there have been some studies that have attempted to compare home and laboratory dreams; for example, B. Domhoff and J. Kamiya, "A Comparison of Home and Laboratory Dream Reports," *Archives of General Psychiatry*, 11 (1964), 519–524.

14. D. Foulkes and A. Rechtschaffen, "Presleep Determinants of Dream Content: Effects of Two Films," *Perceptual and Motor Skills*, 19 (1964), 983–1005.

15. There is an ambiguity inherent in the use of a simple rating scale for "volitional" control that necessitates cautious interpretations of any results obtained with such a scale. Volitional control may be interpreted by the subject as implying voluntary control over the course of his thoughts and images or as implying an active role for the self character in what is basically an involuntary hallucinatory drama.

16. H. Trosman, *et al.*, "Studies in Psychophysiology of Dreams. IV. Relations Among Dreams in Sequence," *Archives of General Psychiatry*, 3 (1960), 602–607; W. Offenkrantz and A. Rechtschaffen, "Clinical Studies of Sequential Dreams. I. A Patient in Psychotherapy," *Archives of General Psychiatry*, 8 (1963), 497–508.

17. W. Dement and E. A. Wolpert, "Relationships in the Manifest Content of Dreams Occurring on the Same Night," *Journal of Nervous and Mental Disease*, 126 (1958), 568–578.

CHAPTER 4

1. W. Dement and N. Kleitman, "The Relation of Eye Movements During Sleep to Dream Activity: An Objective Method for the Study of Dreaming," *Journal of Experimental Psychology*, 53 (1957), 339–346.

2. D. R. Goodenough, *et al.*, "A Comparison of 'Dreamers' and 'Nondreamers': Eye Movements, Electroencephalograms, and the Recall of Dreams," *Journal of Abnormal and Social Psychology*, 59 (1959), 295–302.

3. J. Kamiya, "Behavioral and Physiological Concomitants of Dreaming," progress report submitted to National Institute of Mental Health, 1962.

4. *Ibid.*, p. 11.

5. D. Foulkes, "Dream Reports From Different Stages of Sleep," unpublished Ph.D. dissertation, University of Chicago, 1960; also, in abridged form, in *Journal of Abnormal and Social Psychology*, 65 (1962), 14–25.

6. A. Rechtschaffen, P. Verdone, and J. Wheaton, "Reports of Mental Activity During Sleep," *Canadian Psychiatric Association Journal*, 8 (1963), 409–414.

7. D. Foulkes and A. Rechtschaffen, "Presleep Determinants of Dream Content: Effects of Two Films," *Perceptual and Motor Skills*, 19 (1964), 983–1005.

8. From D. Foulkes, "Theories of Dream Formation and Recent Studies of Sleep Consciousness," *Psychological Bulletin*, 62 (1964), 236–247.

9. *Ibid.*

10. From Foulkes, "Dream Reports . . . ," *op. cit.*

11. *Ibid.*

12. This report was contributed by a subject in the study by Foulkes and Rechtschaffen, *op. cit.*

13. L. J. Monroe, *et al.*, "Discriminability of REM and NREM Reports," *Journal of Personality and Social Psychology*, 2 (1965), 456–460.

14. D. R. Goodenough, *et al.*, "Dream Reporting Following Abrupt and Gradual Awakenings From Different Types of Sleep," *Journal of Personality and Social Psychology*, 2 (1965), 170–179.

15. *Ibid.*

16. Rechtschaffen, Verdone, and Wheaton, *op. cit.*, p. 412.

17. Foulkes and Rechtschaffen, *op. cit.*

18. A. Rechtschaffen, G. Vogel, and G. Shaikun, "Interrelatedness of Mental Activity During Sleep," *Archives of General Psychiatry*, 9 (1963), 536–547.

19. *Ibid.*, p. 544.

20. *Ibid.*, p. 546.

21. Foulkes, "Dream Reports . . . ," *op. cit.*, and "Theories of Dream Formation . . . ," *op. cit.*

22. From Foulkes, "Theories of Dream Formation . . . ," *op. cit.*

CHAPTER 5

1. G. Vogel, "Studies in Psychophysiology of Dreams. III. The Dream of Narcolepsy," *Archives of General Psychiatry*, 3 (1960), 421–428; A. Rechtschaffen, *et al.*, "Nocturnal Sleep of Narcoleptics," *Electroencephalography and Clinical Neurophysiology*, 15 (1963), 599–609.

2. L. Maron, A. Rechtschaffen, and E. A. Wolpert, "The Sleep Cycle During Napping," *Archives of General Psychiatry*, 11 (1964), 503–508.

3. For example, L.-F. A. Maury, *Le Sommeil et les Rêves* (Sleep and Dreams) (Paris: Didier, 1878); D. Slight, "Hypnagogic Phenomena," *Journal of Abnormal and Social Psychology*, 19 (1924), 274–282; W. Archer, "'Hypnagogic Illusions,' or Dozing-Off Dreams," in R. L. Woods (ed.), *The World of Dreams* (New York: Random House, Inc., 1947), pp. 753–760.

4. W. Archer, *op. cit.*

5. L. Maron, A. Rechtschaffen, and E. A. Wolpert, *op. cit.*

6. For example, F. Snyder, "The New Biology of Dreaming," *Archives of General Psychiatry*, 8 (1963), 381–391.

7. D. Foulkes and G. Vogel, "Mental Activity at Sleep Onset," *Journal of Abnormal Psychology*, 70 (1965), 231–243.

8. W. Dement and N. Kleitman, "Cyclic Variations in EEG During Sleep and Their Relation to Eye Movements, Body Motility, and Dreaming," *Electroencephalography and Clinical Neurophysiology*, 9 (1957), 673–690.

9. J. Kamiya, "Behavioral, Subjective, and Physiological Aspects of Drowsiness and Sleep," in D. W. Fiske and S. R. Maddi (eds.), *Functions of Varied Experience* (Homewood, Ill.: Dorsey Press, 1961), pp. 145–174.

10. D. Foulkes, "Dream Reports From Different Stages of Sleep," *Journal of Abnormal and Social Psychology*, 65 (1962), 14–25.

11. *Ibid.*

12. D. Foulkes, P. S. Spear, and J. D. Symonds, "Individual Differences in Mental Activity at Sleep Onset," *Journal of Abnormal Psychology*, in press.

13. Subject 8 in the Foulkes and Vogel study, *op. cit.*

14. Subject 4, *ibid.*

15. Dement and Kleitman, *op. cit.*

16. I. Oswald, *Sleeping and Waking* (Amsterdam: Elsevier, 1962).

17. L. Kubie, "The Use of Induced Hypnagogic Reveries in the Recovery of Repressed Amnesic Data," *Bulletin of the Menninger Clinic*, 7 (1943), 172–182.

18. See, for example, H. P. Roffwarg, *et al.*, "Dream Imagery: Relationship to Rapid Eye Movements of Sleep," *Archives of General Psychiatry*, 7 (1962), 235–258.

19. Data of Foulkes and Vogel, *op. cit.*, and of Foulkes, Spear, and Symonds, *op. cit.*

20. G. Vogel, unpublished observations.

21. This analysis derives from, but is not identical to, that put forth by G. Vogel, D. Foulkes, and H. Trosman in "Ego Functions and Dreaming During Sleep Onset," *Archives of General Psychiatry*, in press.

CHAPTER 6

1. A. Rechtschaffen and L. Maron, "The Effect of Amphetamine on the Sleep Cycle," *Electroencephalography and Clinical Neurophysiology*, 16 (1964), 438–445.

2. I. Oswald, *et al.*, "Melancholia and Barbiturates: A Controlled EEG, Body and Eye Movement of Sleep," *British Journal of Psychiatry*, 109 (1963), 66–78.

3. S. C. Gresham, W. B. Webb, and R. L. Williams, "Alcohol and Caffein: Effect on Inferred Visual Dreaming," *Science*, 140 (1963), 1226–1227.

4. *Ibid.*

5. J. M. Stoyva, "Posthypnotically Suggested Dreams and the Sleep Cycle," *Archives of General Psychiatry*, 12 (1965), 287–294.

6. C. T. Tart, "Effects of Posthypnotic Suggestion on the Process of Dreaming," unpublished Ph.D. dissertation, University of North Carolina, 1963.

7. A. Rechtschaffen and P. Verdone, "Amount of Dreaming: Effect of Incentive, Adaptation to Laboratory, and Individual Differences," *Perceptual and Motor Skills*, 19 (1964), 947–958.

8. P. Wood, "Dreaming and Social Isolation," unpublished Ph.D. dissertation, University of North Carolina, 1962.

9. P. Hauri, Ph.D. dissertation in progress, Department of Psychology, University of Chicago.

10. D. Foulkes and A. Rechtschaffen, "Presleep Determinants of Dream Content: Effects of Two Films," *Perceptual and Motor Skills*, 19 (1964), 983–1005.

11. R. J. Berger and I. Oswald, "Effects of Sleep Deprivation on Behaviour, Subsequent Sleep, and Dreaming," *Journal of Mental Science*, 108 (1962), 457–465.

12. W. Dement, "The Effect of Dream Deprivation," *Science*, 131 (1960), 1705–1707.

13. H. W. Agnew, W. B. Webb, and R. L. Williams, "The Effects of Stage Four Sleep Deprivation," *Electroencephalography and Clinical Neurophysiology*, 17 (1964), 68–70.

14. L. J. Monroe, "Psychological and Physiological Differences between Good and Poor Sleepers," unpublished Ph.D. dissertation, University of Chicago, 1965.

15. Rechtschaffen and Verdone, *op. cit.*

16. H. P. Roffwarg, W. Dement, and C. Fisher, "Preliminary Observations of the Sleep-Dream Pattern in Neonates, Infants, Children and Adults," in E. Harms (ed.), *Problems of Sleep and Dream in Children* (New York: Pergamon Press, Inc., 1964), pp. 60–72.

17. Rechtschaffen and Verdone, *op. cit.*

18. R. M. Whitman, C. M. Pierce, and J. Maas, "Drugs and Dreams," in L. Uhr and J. G. Miller (eds.), *Drugs and Behavior* (New York: John Wiley & Sons, Inc., 1960), pp. 591–595.

19. R. M. Whitman, *et al.*, "Drugs and Dreams. II. Imipramine and Prochlorperazine," *Comprehensive Psychiatry*, 2 (1961), 219–226.

20. See, for example, D. Rapaport (ed.), *Organization and Pathology of Thought* (New York: Columbia University, Bureau of Publications, 1951).

21. Stoyva, *op. cit.*

22. C. T. Tart, " A Comparison of Suggested Dreams Occurring in Hypnosis and Sleep," *International Journal of Clinical and Experimental Hypnosis*, 12 (1964), 263–289.

23. Wood, *op. cit.*

24. Hauri, *op. cit.*

25. Foulkes and Rechtschaffen, *op. cit.*

26. An unpublished pilot study conducted by Norman Robertson at the University of Chicago, 1963–1964, under the supervision of Allan Rechtschaffen.

27. Unpublished observations.

28. C. S. Hall, *The Meaning of Dreams* (New York: Dell Publishing Co., Inc., 1959). An apparent exception is the frequent appearance of laboratory imagery in dreams collected from experimental subjects, particularly during early nights of service (see R. M. Whitman, *et al.*, "The Dreams of the Experimental Subject," *Journal of Nervous and Mental Disease*, 134 [1962], 431–439).

29. Reprinted as O. Poetzl, "The Relationship Between Experimentally Induced Dream Images and Indirect Vision," *Psychological Issues*, 2 (1960), no. 3, 41–120.

30. See C. Fisher, "Introduction," *Psychological Issues*, 2 (1960), no. 3, 1–40.

31. H. Johnson and C. W. Eriksen, "Preconscious Perception: A Re-examination of the Poetzl Phenomenon," *Journal of Abnormal*

and Social Psychology, 62 (1961), 497–503; S. E. Waxenberg, R. Dickes, and H. Gottesfeld, "The Poetzl Phenomenon Reexamined Experimentally," *Journal of Nervous and Mental Disease*, 135 (1962), 387–398; S. E. Pulver and B. Eppes, "The Poetzl Phenomenon: Some Further Evidence," *Journal of Nervous and Mental Disease*, 136 (1963), 527–534.

32. D. Foulkes and G. Vogel, "Mental Activity at Sleep Onset," *Journal of Abnormal Psychology*, 70 (1965), 231–243.

CHAPTER 7

1. See, for example, the studies reviewed in S. Freud, *The Interpretation of Dreams* (New York: Basic Books, Inc., Publishers, 1955).

2. W. Dement and E. A. Wolpert, "The Relation of Eye Movements, Body Motility, and External Stimuli to Dream Content," *Journal of Experimental Psychology*, 55 (1958), 543–553.

3. These examples were contributed by a subject in the study by D. Foulkes, P. S. Spear, and J. D. Symonds, "Individual Differences in Mental Activity at Sleep Onset," *Journal of Abnormal Psychology*, in press.

4. E. Gellhorn, *Physiological Foundations of Neurology and Psychiatry* (Minneapolis: University of Minnesota Press, 1953), chaps. 8–10.

5. J. H. Mendelson, *et al.* "Physiological and Psychological Aspects of Sensory Deprivation—A Case Analysis," in P. Solomon, *et al.*, *Sensory Deprivation* (Cambridge, Mass.: Harvard University Press, 1961), pp. 91–113.

6. For example, G. Moruzzi and H. W. Magoun, "Brain Stem Reticular Formation and Activation of the EEG," *Electroencephalography and Clinical Neurophysiology*, 1 (1949), 455–473.

7. M. Jouvet, "Recherches sur les structures nerveuses et les mécanismes responsables des différentes phases de sommeil physiologique" (Investigations of the nervous structures and the mechanisms responsible for different phases of physiological

sleep), *Archives of Italian Biology*, 100 (1962), 125–206; M. Jouvet, "Telencephalic and Rhombencephalic Sleep in the Cat," in Ciba Foundation Symposium, *The Nature of Sleep* (Boston: Little, Brown and Company, 1961), pp. 188–206; M. Jouvet, "Étude de la dualité des états de sommeil et des mécanismes de la phase paradoxale" (Study of the duality of states of sleep and of the mechanisms of the paradoxical phase), in Centre National de la Recherche Scientifique, *Aspects Anatomo-Fonctionnels de la Physiologie du Sommeil* (Anatomical and Functional Aspects of the Physiology of Sleep) (Paris: CNRS, 1965), pp. 397–446.

8. D. Foulkes, "Theories of Dream Formation and Recent Studies of Sleep Consciousness," *Psychological Bulletin*, 62 (1964), 236–247.

9. See, for example, the studies reviewed in Freud, *op. cit.*

10. Dement and Wolpert, *op. cit.*

11. I. Oswald, A. M. Taylor, and M. Treisman, "Cortical Function During Human Sleep," in Ciba Foundation Symposium, *op. cit.*, pp. 343–348.

12. R. J. Berger, "Experimental Modification of Dream Content by Meaningful Verbal Stimuli," *British Journal of Psychiatry*, 109 (1963), 722–740.

13. This example was contributed by a subject in the study by D. Foulkes, "Dream Reports From Different Stages of Sleep," *Journal of Abnormal and Social Psychology*, 65 (1962), 14–25.

14. C. Fisher, J. Gross, and J. Zuch, "Cycle of Penile Erection Synchronous with Dreaming (REM) Sleep," *Archives of General Psychiatry*, 12 (1965), 29–45.

15. J. Money, "Phantom Orgasm in Dreams of Paraplegic Men and Women," *Archives of General Psychiatry*, 3 (1960), 373–383.

16. Dement and Wolpert, *op. cit.*

17. A. Keys, *et al.*, *The Biology of Human Starvation* (Minneapolis: University of Minnesota Press, 1950).

18. F. Michel, *et al.*, "Sur les mécanismes de l'activité de pointes

au niveau du système visuel au cours de la phase paradoxale du sommeil" (On the mechanisms of spikes in the visual system during the paradoxical phase of sleep), *Comptes Rendus des Séances de la Société de Biologie* (Accounts of the Society of Biology Meetings), 158 (1964), 103–106.

19. G. T. Ladd, "Contribution to the Psychology of Visual Dreams," *Mind,* New Series, 1 (1892), 299–304.

20. A. Rechtschaffen and D. Foulkes, "Effect of Visual Stimuli on Dream Content," *Perceptual and Motor Skills,* 20 (1965), 1149–1160.

21. D. Foulkes and G. Vogel, "Mental Activity at Sleep Onset," *Journal of Abnormal Psychology,* 70 (1965), 231–243.

CHAPTER 8

1. A. Rechtschaffen and P. Verdone, "Amount of Dreaming: Effect of Incentive, Adaptation to Laboratory, and Individual Differences," *Perceptual and Motor Skills,* 19 (1964), 947–958: Judith S. Antrobus, W. Dement, and C. Fisher, "Patterns of Dreaming and Dream Recall," *Journal of Abnormal and Social Psychology,* 69 (1964), 341–344.

2. Rechtschaffen and Verdone, *op. cit.*

3. L. J. Monroe, "Psychological and Physiological Differences between Good and Poor Sleepers," unpublished Ph.D. dissertation, University of Chicago, 1965.

4. Rechtschaffen and Verdone, *op. cit.*

5. Judith S. Antrobus, *et al., op. cit.*

6. R. A. Schonbar, "Some Manifest Characteristics of Recallers and Nonrecallers of Dreams," *Journal of Consulting Psychology,* 23 (1959), 414–418: J. L. Singer and R. A. Schonbar, "Correlates of Daydreaming: A Dimension of Self-Awareness," *Journal of Consulting Psychology,* 25 (1961), 1–6; C. T. Tart, "Frequency of Dream Recall and Some Personality Measures," *Journal of Consulting Psychology,* 26 (1962), 467–470.

7. For example, Singer and Schonbar, *op. cit.*

8. W. Dement, "Dream Recall and Eye Movements During Sleep in Schizophrenics and Normals," *Journal of Nervous and Mental Disease*, 122 (1955), 263–269.

9. I. Feinberg, *et al.*, "Sleep Electroencephalographic and Eye Movement Patterns in Schizophrenic Patients," *Comprehensive Psychiatry*, 5 (1964), 44–53.

10. *Ibid.;* and R. L. Koresko, F. Snyder, and I. Feinberg, " 'Dream Time' in Hallucinating and Non-Hallucinating Schizophrenic Patients," *Nature*, 199 (1963), 1118–1119.

11. P. Onheiber, *et al.*, "Sleep and Dream Patterns of Child Schizophrenics," *Archives of General Psychiatry*, 12 (1965), 568–571.

12. C. Fisher and W. Dement, "Studies on the Psychopathology of Sleep and Dreams," *American Journal of Psychiatry*, 119 (1963), 1160–1168.

13. H. P. Roffwarg, W. Dement, and C. Fisher, "Preliminary Observations of the Sleep-Dream Pattern in Neonates, Infants, Children and Adults," in E. Harms (ed.), *Problems of Sleep and Dream in Children* (New York: Pergamon Press, Inc., 1964), pp. 60–72.

14. W. Offenkrantz and A. Rechtschaffen, "Clinical Studies of Sequential Dreams. I. A Patient in Psychotherapy," *Archives of General Psychiatry*, 8 (1963), 497–508.

15. *Ibid.*, p. 506.

16. S. Freud, *The Interpretation of Dreams* (New York: Basic Books, Inc., Publishers, 1955), p. 608.

17. D. Foulkes and A. Rechtschaffen, "Presleep Determinants of Dream Content: Effects of Two Films," *Perceptual and Motor Skills*, 19 (1964), 983–1005.

18. D. Foulkes, P. S. Spear, and J. D. Symonds, "Individual Differences in Mental Activity at Sleep Onset," *Journal of Abnormal Psychology*, in press.

19. *Ibid.*

20. *Ibid.*

21. D. Foulkes and G. Vogel, "Mental Activity at Sleep Onset," *Journal of Abnormal Psychology*, 70 (1965), 231–243.

CHAPTER 9

1. D. Foulkes and A. Rechtschaffen, "Presleep Determinants of Dream Content: Effects of Two Films," *Perceptual and Motor Skills*, 19 (1964), 983–1005.

2. A. Rechtschaffen, P. Verdone, and J. Wheaton, "Reports of Mental Activity During Sleep," *Canadian Psychiatric Association Journal*, 8 (1963), 409–414. It should be noted that these authors quickly point out the inappropriateness of this comparison for the many NREM reports that contain more dreamlike properties than the comparison implies.

3. R. J. Berger and I. Oswald, "Effects of Sleep Deprivation on Behaviour, Subsequent Sleep, and Dreaming," *Journal of Mental Science*, 108 (1962), 457–465.

4. D. Foulkes, "Dream Reports From Different Stages of Sleep," unpublished Ph.D. dissertation, University of Chicago, 1960.

5. S. Freud, *The Interpretation of Dreams* (New York: Basic Books, Inc., Publishers, 1955).

6. W. Dement, "The Effect of Dream Deprivation," *Science*, 131 (1960), 1705–1707.

7. A. Kales, *et al.*, "Dream Deprivation: An Experimental Reappraisal," *Nature*, 204 (1964), 1337–1338; W. Dement, "Studies on the Function of Rapid Eye Movement (Paradoxical) Sleep in Human Subjects," in Centre National de la Recherche Scientifique, *Aspects Anatomo-Fonctionnels de la Physiologie du Sommeil* (Anatomical and Functional Aspects of the Physiology of Sleep) (Paris: CNRS, 1965), pp. 571–608.

8. Kales, *et al., op. cit.*

9. Dement, "Studies on the Function . . . ," *op. cit.*

10. *Ibid.*, p. 592.

11. *Ibid.*

12. M. Jouvet, "Étude de la dualité des états de sommeil et des mécanismes de la phase paradoxale" (Study of the duality of states of sleep and of the mechanisms of the paradoxical phase), in Centre National de la Recherche Scientifique, *op. cit.*, pp. 397–446; J. Siegel and T. P. Gordon, "Paradoxical Sleep: Deprivation in the Cat," *Science*, 148 (1965), 978–980.

13. M. Jouvet, *op. cit.*

14. Dement, "Studies on the Function . . . ," *op. cit.*

15. For example: W. Dement, "The Occurrence of Low Voltage, Fast, Electroencephalogram Patterns During Behavioral Sleep in the Cat," *Electroencephalography and Clinical Neurophysiology*, 10 (1958), 291–296; J. E. Swisher, "Manifestations of 'Activated' Sleep in the Rat," *Science*, 138 (1962), 1110; E. D. Weitzman, *et al.*, "Cyclic Activity in Sleep of Macaca Mulatta," *Archives of Neurology*, 12 (1965), 463–467; W. R. Adey, R. T. Kado, and J. M. Rhodes, "Sleep: Cortical and Subcortical Recordings in the Chimpanzee," *Science*, 141 (1963), 932–933.

16. H. P. Roffwarg, W. Dement, and C. Fisher, "Preliminary Observations of the Sleep-Dream Pattern in Neonates, Infants, Children and Adults," in E. Harms (ed.), *Problems of Sleep and Dream in Children* (New York: Pergamon Press, Inc., 1964), pp. 60–72.

BIBLIOGRAPHY

Asterisks indicate works of either wide scope or relatively non-technical style that are recommended to the general reader who may wish to pursue his interest in sleep or dreams beyond the present volume.

Adey, W. R., Kado, R. T., and Rhodes, J. M. "Sleep: Cortical and Subcortical Recordings in the Chimpanzee," *Science,* 141 (1963), 932–933.

*Adler, A. *What Life Should Mean to You.* New York: "Capricorn Books," 1958, chap. 5.

Agnew, H. W., Webb, W. B., and Williams, R. L. "The Effects of Stage Four Sleep Deprivation," *Electroencephalography and Clinical Neurophysiology,* 17 (1964), 68–70.

Antrobus, John S., Antrobus, Judith S., and Singer, J. L. "Eye Movements Accompanying Daydreaming, Visual Imagery, and Thought Suppression," *Journal of Abnormal and Social Psychology,* 69 (1964), 244–252.

Antrobus, Judith S., Dement, W., and Fisher, C. "Patterns of Dreaming and Dream Recall: An EEG Study," *Journal of Abnormal and Social Psychology,* 69 (1964), 341–344.

Archer, W. " 'Hypnagogic Illusions,' or Dozing-Off Dreams." In Woods, R. L. (ed.). *The World of Dreams.* New York: Random House, Inc., 1947. Pp. 753–760.

BIBLIOGRAPHY

Aserinsky, E., and Kleitman, N. "Regularly Occurring Periods of Eye Motility, and Concomitant Phenomena, During Sleep," *Science,* 118 (1953), 273–274.

————. "Two Types of Ocular Motility Occurring in Sleep," *Journal of Applied Physiology,* 8 (1955), 1–10.

Berger, R. J. "Tonus of Extrinsic Laryngeal Muscles During Sleep and Dreaming," *Science,* 134 (1961), 840.

————. "Experimental Modification of Dream Content by Meaningful Verbal Stimuli," *British Journal of Psychiatry,* 109 (1963), 722–740.

Berger, R. J., and Oswald, I. "Effects of Sleep Deprivation on Behaviour, Subsequent Sleep, and Dreaming," *Journal of Mental Science,* 108 (1962), 457–465.

————. "Eye Movements During Active and Passive Dreams," *Science,* 137 (1962), 601.

*Bonime, W. *The Clinical Use of Dreams.* New York: Basic Books, Inc., Publishers, 1962.

Ciba Foundation Symposium. *The Nature of Sleep.* Boston: Little, Brown and Company, 1961.

Day, D. "Dream Interpretation as a Projective Technique," *Journal of Consulting Psychology,* 13 (1949), 416–420.

Delafresnaye, J. F. (ed.). *Brain Mechanisms and Consciousness.* Springfield, Ill.: Charles C Thomas, Publisher, 1954.

Dement, W. "Dream Recall and Eye Movements During Sleep in Schizophrenics and Normals," *Journal of Nervous and Mental Disease,* 122 (1955), 263–269.

————. "The Occurrence of Low Voltage, Fast, Electroencephalogram Patterns During Behavioral Sleep in the Cat," *Electroencephalography and Clinical Neurophysiology,* 10 (1958), 291–296.

————. "The Physiology of Dreaming." Unpublished Ph.D. dissertation, University of Chicago, 1958.

————. "The Effect of Dream Deprivation," *Science,* 131 (1960), 1705–1707.

*————. "An Essay on Dreams." In Newcomb, T. M. (ed.). *New Directions in Psychology II.* New York: Holt, Rhinehart, & Winston, Inc., 1965. Pp. 135–257.

————. "Studies on the Function of Rapid Eye Movement (Paradoxical) Sleep in Human Subjects." In Centre National de la Recherche Scientifique, *Aspects Anatomo-Fonctionnels de la Phys-*

iologie du Sommeil (Anatomical and Functional Aspects of the Physiology of Sleep). Paris: CNRS, 1965. Pp. 571–608.

Dement, W., and Kleitman, N. "Cyclic Variations in EEG During Sleep and Their Relation to Eye Movements, Body Motility, and Dreaming." *Electroencephalography and Clinical Neurophysiology,* 9 (1957), 673–690.

————. "The Relation of Eye Movements During Sleep to Dream Activity: An Objective Method for the Study of Dreaming," *Journal of Experimental Psychology,* 53 (1957), 339–346.

Dement, W., and Wolpert, E. A. "The Relation of Eye Movements, Body Motility, and External Stimuli to Dream Content," *Journal of Experimental Psychology,* 55 (1958), 543–553.

————. "Relationships in the Manifest Content of Dreams Occurring on the Same Night," *Journal of Nervous and Mental Disease,* 126 (1958), 568–578.

Domhoff, B., and Kamiya, J. "A Comparison of Home and Laboratory Dream Reports," *Archives of General Psychiatry,* 11 (1964), 519–524.

Emmons, W. H., and Simon, C. W. "The Non-Recall of Material Presented During Sleep," *American Journal of Psychology,* 69 (1956), 76–81.

Evarts, E. V. "Effects of Sleep and Waking on Activity of Single Units in the Unrestrained Cat." In Ciba Foundation Symposium. *The Nature of Sleep.* Boston: Little, Brown and Company, 1961. Pp. 171–182.

————. "Neuronal Activity in Visual and Motor Cortex During Sleep and Waking," in Centre National de la Recherche Scientifique, *Aspects Anatomo-Fonctionnels de la Physiologie du Sommeil* (Anatomical and Functional Aspects of the Physiology of Sleep). Paris: CNRS, 1965. Pp. 189–209.

Feinberg, I., et al. "Sleep Electroencephalographic and Eye Movement Patterns in Schizophrenic Patients," *Comprehensive Psychiatry,* 5 (1964), 44–53.

Fisher, C. "Introduction," *Psychological Issues,* 2 (1960), no. 3, 1–40.

Fisher, C., and Dement, W. "Studies on the Psychopathology of Sleep and Dreams," *American Journal of Psychiatry,* 119 (1963), 1160–1168.

Fisher, C., Gross, J., and Zuch, J. "Cycle of Penile Erection Synchronous with Dreaming (REM) Sleep," *Archives of General Psychiatry,* 12 (1965), 29–45.

Foulkes, D. "Dream Reports From Different Stages of Sleep." Unpublished Ph.D. dissertation, University of Chicago, 1960.

————. "Dream Reports From Different Stages of Sleep," *Journal of Abnormal and Social Psychology,* 65 (1962), 14–25.

————. "Theories of Dream Formation and Recent Studies of Sleep Consciousness," *Psychological Bulletin,* 62 (1964), 236–247.

Foulkes, D., and Rechtschaffen, A. "Presleep Determinants of Dream Content: Effects of Two Films," *Perceptual and Motor Skills,* 19 (1964), 983–1005.

Foulkes, D., Spear, P. S., and Symonds, J. D. "Individual Differences in Mental Activity at Sleep Onset," *Journal of Abnormal Psychology,* in press.

Foulkes, D., and Vogel, G. "Mental Activity at Sleep Onset," *Journal of Abnormal Psychology,* 70 (1965), 231–243.

Framo, J. L., Osterweil, J., and Boszormenyi-Nagy, I. "A Relationship Between Threat in the Manifest Content of Dreams and Active-Passive Behavior in Psychotics," *Journal of Abnormal and Social Psychology,* 65 (1962), 41–47.

*French, T. M., and Fromm, Erika. *Dream Interpretation.* New York: Basic Books, Inc., Publishers, 1964.

*Freud, S. *The Interpretation of Dreams.* New York: Basic Books, Inc., Publishers, 1955.

————. "Three Contributions to the Theory of Sex." In *The Basic Writings of Sigmund Freud.* New York: Modern Library, Inc., 1938. Pp. 553–629.

*Fromm, Erich. *The Forgotten Language.* New York: Grove Press, Inc., 1957.

Gellhorn, E. *Physiological Foundations of Neurology and Psychiatry.* Minneapolis: University of Minnesota Press, 1953.

Gibbs, F. A., Davis, H., and Lennox, W. G. "The Electro-encephalogram in Epilepsy and in Conditions of Impaired Consciousness," *Archives of Neurology and Psychiatry,* 34 (1935), 1133–1148.

Goodenough, D. R., *et al.* "Dream Reporting Following Abrupt and Gradual Awakenings From Different Types of Sleep," *Journal of Personality and Social Psychology,* 2 (1965), 170–179.

Goodenough, D. R., *et al.* "Some Correlates of Dream Reporting

Following Laboratory Awakenings," *Journal of Nervous and Mental Disease,* 140 (1965), 365–373.

Goodenough, D. R., *et al.* "A Comparison of 'Dreamers' and 'Nondreamers': Eye Movements, Electroencephalograms, and the Recall of Dreams," *Journal of Abnormal and Social Psychology,* 59 (1959), 295–302.

Granda, A. M., and Hammack, J. T. "Operant Behavior During Sleep." *Science,* 133 (1961), 1485–1486.

Gresham, S. C., Webb, W. B., and Williams, R. L. "Alcohol and Caffein: Effect on Inferred Visual Dreaming," *Science,* 140 (1963), 1226–1227.

*Hadfield, J. A. *Dreams and Nightmares.* Baltimore: Penguin Books, 1954.

*Hall, C. S. *The Meaning of Dreams.* New York: Dell Publishing Co., Inc., 1959.

Hauri, P. Unpublished Ph.D dissertation in progress. University of Chicago.

Jacobson, A., *et al.* "Muscle Tonus in Human Subjects During Sleep and Dreaming," *Experimental Neurology,* 10 (1964), 418–424.

———. "Somnambulism: All-Night Electroencephalographic Studies," *Science,* 148 (1965), 975–977.

Jacobson, E. *Progressive Relaxation.* Chicago: University of Chicago Press, 2nd ed., 1938.

———. "The Electrophysiology of Mental Activities," *American Journal of Psychology,* 44 (1932), 677–694.

Johnson, H., and Ericksen, C. W. "Preconscious Perception: A Reexamination of the Poetzl Phenomenon," *Journal of Abnormal and Social Psychology,* 62 (1961), 497–503.

Jouvet, M. "Telencephalic and Rhombencephalic Sleep in the Cat." In Ciba Foundation Symposium, *The Nature of Sleep.* Boston: Little, Brown and Company, 1961. Pp. 188–206.

———. "Recherches sur les structures nerveuses et les mécanismes responsables des différentes phases de sommeil physiologique" (Investigations of the nervous structures and the mechanisms responsible for different phases of physiological sleep). *Archives of Italian Biology,* 100 (1962), 125–206.

———. "Étude de la dualité des états de sommeil et des mécanismes de la phase paradoxale" (Study of the duality of states of sleep and of the mechanisms of the paradoxical phase). In Centre National de la Recherche Scientifique, *Aspects Anatomo-Fonctionnels de la Physiologie du Sommeil* (Anatomical and Functional Aspects of the Physiology of Sleep). Paris: CNRS, 1965. Pp. 397–446.

*Jung, C. G. *Modern Man in Search of a Soal.* New York: "Harvest Books," Harcourt, Brace & World, Inc., n.d., chap. 1.

Kales, A., *et al.* "Dream Deprivation: An Experimental Reappraisal," *Nature,* 204 (1964), 1337–1338.

Kamiya, J. "Behavioral, Subjective, and Physiological Aspects of Drowsiness and Sleep." In Fiske, D. W., and Maddi, S. R. (eds.). *Functions of Varied Experience.* Homewood, Ill.: Dorsey Press, 1961. Pp. 145–174.

————. "Behavioral and Physiological Concomitants of Dreaming." Unpublished progress report submitted to National Institute of Mental Health, 1962.

Kanzow, E. "Changes in Blood Flow of the Cerebral Cortex and Other Vegetative Changes during Paradoxical Sleep Periods in the Unrestrained Cat." In Centre National de la Recherche Scientifique, *Aspects Anatomo-Fonctionnels de la Physiologie du Sommeil* (Anatomical and Functional Aspects of the Physiology of Sleep). Paris: CNRS, 1965. Pp. 231–237.

Keys, A., *et al. The Biology of Human Starvation.* Minneapolis: University of Minnesota Press, 1950.

*Kleitman, N. *Sleep and Wakefulness.* Chicago: University of Chicago Press, 2nd ed., 1963.

Knopf, N. "A Study of Heart and Respiration Rates During Dreaming." Unpublished Master's thesis, University of Chicago, 1962.

Koresko, R. L., Snyder, F., and Feinberg, I. " 'Dream-Time' in Hallucinating and Non-Hallucinating Schizophrenic Patients," *Nature,* 199 (1963), 1118–1119.

Kubie, L. "The Use of Induced Hypnagogic Reveries in the Recovery of Repressed Amnesic Data," *Bulletin of the Menninger Clinic,* 7 (1943), 172–182.

Ladd, G. T. "Contribution to the Psychology of Visual Dreams," *Mind,* new series 1 (1892), 299–304.

Lifton, R. J. *Thought Reform and the Psychology of Totalism.* New York: W. W. Norton & Company, Inc., 1961.

Lindsley, D. B. "Psychophysiology and Motivation." In Jones, M. R.

(ed.). *Nebraska Symposium on Motivation, 1957.* Lincoln: University of Nebraska Press, 1957. Pp. 44–105.

———. "Attention, Consciousness, Sleep and Wakefulness." In Field, J. (ed.). *Handbook of Physiology. Section 1. Neurophysiology.* 3 vols. Washington: American Physiological Society, Vol. III, 1960. Pp. 1553–1593.

Maron, L. Rechtschaffen, A., and Wolpert, E. A. "The Sleep Cycle During Napping," *Archives of General Psychiatry,* 11 (1964), 503–508.

Maury, L.-F. A. *Le Sommeil et les Rêves* (Sleep and Dreams). Paris: Didier, 1878.

Max. L. W. "An Experimental Study of the Motor Theory of Consciousness. III. Action-Current Responses in Deaf-Mutes During Sleep, Sensory Stimulation and Dreams," *Journal of Comparative Psychology,* 19 (1935), 469–486.

Mendelson, J. H., *et al.* "Physiological and Psychological Aspects of Sensory Deprivation—A Case Analysis." In Solomon, P., *et al.* (eds.). *Sensory Deprivation.* Cambridge, Mass.: Harvard University Press, 1961. Pp. 91–113.

Michel, F., *et al.* "Sur les mécanismes de l'activité de pointes au niveau du système visuel au cours de la phase paradoxale du sommeil" (On the mechanisms of spikes in the visual system during the paradoxical phase of sleep), *Comptes Rendus des Séances de la Société de Biologie* (Accounts of the Society of Biology Meetings), 158 (1964), 103–106.

Money, J. "Phantom Orgasm in Dreams of Paraplegic Men and Women," *Archives of General Psychiatry,* 3 (1960), 373–383.

Monroe, L. J. "Psychological and Physiological Differences between Good and Poor Sleepers." Unpublished Ph.D. dissertation, University of Chicago, 1965.

Monroe, L. J., *et al.* "Discriminability of REM and NREM Reports," *Journal of Personality and Social Psychology,* 2 (1965), 456–460.

Moruzzi, G., and Magoun, H. W. "Brain Stem Reticular Formation and Activation of the EEG," *Electroencephalography and Clinical Neurophysiology,* 1 (1949), 455–473.

Offenkrantz, W., and Rechtschaffen, A. "Clinical Studies of Sequential Dreams. I. A Patient in Psychotherapy," *Archives of General Psychiatry,* 8 (1963), 497–508.

Onheiber, P., *et al.* "Sleep and Dream Patterns of Child Schizophrenics," *Archives of General Psychiatry,* 12 (1965), 568–571.

Oswald, I. "Falling Asleep Open-Eyed During Intense Rhythmic Stimulation," *British Medical Journal,* 1 (1960), 1450–1455.

———. Sleeping and Waking. Amsterdam: Elsevier, 1962.

Oswald, I., *et al.* "Melancholia and Barbiturates: A Controlled EEG, Body and Eye Movement Study of Sleep," *British Journal of Psychiatry,* 109 (1963), 66–78.

Oswald, I., Taylor, A. M., and Treisman, M. "Cortical Function During Human Sleep." In Ciba Foundation Symposium, *The Nature of Sleep.* Boston: Little, Brown and Company, 1961. Pp. 343–348.

Penfield, W. "Studies of the Cerebral Cortex of Man: A Review and an Interpretation," in Delafresnaye, J. F. (ed.). *Brain Mechanisms and Consciousness.* Springfield, Ill.: Charles C Thomas, Publisher, 1954. Pp. 284–304.

Poetzl, O. "The Relationship Between Experimentally Induced Dream Images and Indirect Vision," *Psychological Issues,* 2 (1960), no. 3, 41–120.

Pulver, S. E., and Eppes, B. "The Poetzl Phenomenon: Some Further Evidence," *Journal of Nervous and Mental Disease,* 136 (1963), 527–534.

Rapaport, D. (ed.). *Organization and Pathology of Thought.* New York: Columbia University, Bureau of Publications, 1951.

Rechtschaffen, A. "Discussion of Dr. William Dement's Paper." In Masserman, J. H. (ed.). *Science and Psychoanalysis. Vol. VII.* New York: Grune & Stratton, Inc., 1964. Pp. 162–170.

Rechtschaffen, A., Cornwell, P., and Zimmerman, W. "Brain Temperature Variations with Paradoxical Sleep in the Cat." Paper presented to the Association for the Psychophysiological Study of Sleep, Washington, D.C., 1965.

Rechtschaffen, A., and Foulkes, D. "Effect of Visual Stimuli on Dream Content," *Perceptual and Motor Skills,* 20 (1965), 1149–1160.

Rechtschaffen, A., Goodenough, D. R., and Shapiro, A. "Patterns of Sleep Talking," *Archives of General Psychiatry,* 7 (1962), 418–426.

Rechtschaffen, A., and Maron, L. "The Effect of Amphetamine on the Sleep Cycle," *Electroencephalography and Clinical Neurophysiology,* 16 (1964), 438–445.

Rechtschaffen, A., and Verdone, P. "Amount of Dreaming: Effect of Incentive, Adaptation to Laboratory, and Individual Differences," *Perceptual and Motor Skills,* 19 (1964), 947–958.

Rechtschaffen, A., Verdone, P., and Wheaton, J. "Reports of Mental Activity During Sleep," *Canadian Psychiatric Association Journal,* 8 (1963), 409–414.

Rechtschaffen, A., Vogel, G., and Shaikun, G. "Interrelatedness of Mental Activity During Sleep," *Archives of General Psychiatry,* 9 (1963), 536–547.

Rechtschaffen, A., *et al.* "Nocturnal Sleep of Narcoleptics," *Electroencephalography and Clinical Neurophysiology,* 15 (1963), 599–609.

Roffwarg, H. P., Dement, W., and Fisher, C. "Preliminary Observations of the Sleep-Dream Pattern in Neonates, Infants, Children and Adults." In Harms, E. (ed.). *Problems of Sleep and Dream in Children.* New York: Pergamon Press, Inc. 1964. Pp. 60–72.

Roffwarg, H. P., *et al.* "Dream Imagery: Relationship to Rapid Eye Movements of Sleep," *Archives of General Psychiatry,* 7 (1962), 235–258.

Schonbar, R. A. "Some Manifest Characteristics of Recallers and Nonrecallers of Dreams," *Journal of Consulting Psychology,* 23 (1959), 414–418.

Shapiro, A., Goodenough, D. R., and Gryler, R. B. "Dream Recall as a Function of Method of Awakening," *Psychosomatic Medicine,* 25 (1963), 174–180.

Shapiro, A., *et al.* "Dream Recall and the Physiology of Sleep," *Journal of Applied Physiology,* 19 (1964), 778–783.

Siegel, J., and Gordon, T. P. "Paradoxical Sleep: Deprivation in the Cat," *Science,* 148 (1965), 978–980.

Singer, J. L., and Schonbar, R. A. "Correlates of Daydreaming: A Dimension of Self-Awareness," *Journal of Consulting Psychology,* 25 (1961), 1–6.

Slight, D. "Hypnagogic Phenomena," *Journal of Abnormal and Social Psychology,* 19 (1924), 274–282.

Snyder, F. "The New Biology of Dreaming," *Archives of General Psychiatry,* 8 (1963), 381–391.

Snyder, F., *et al.* "Changes in Respiration, Heart Rate, and Systolic Blood Pressure in Human Sleep," *Journal of Applied Physiology,* 19 (1964), 417–422.

BIBLIOGRAPHY

Stoyva, J. M. "Posthypnotically Suggested Dreams and the Sleep Cycle," *Archives of General Psychiatry*, 12 (1965), 287–294.

Swisher, J. E. "Manifestations of 'Activated' Sleep in the Rat," *Science*, 138 (1962), 1110.

Tart, C. T. "Frequency of Dream Recall and Some Personality Measures," *Journal of Consulting Psychology*, 26 (1962), 467–470.

———. "Effects of Posthypnotic Suggestion on the Process of Dreaming." Unpublished Ph.D. dissertation, University of North Carolina, 1963.

———. "A Comparison of Suggested Dreams Occurring in Hypnosis and Sleep," *International Journal of Clinical and Experimental Hypnosis*, 12 (1964), 263–289.

Trosman, H., et al. "Studies in Psychophysiology of Dreams. IV. Relations Among Dreams in Sequence," *Archives of General Psychiatry*, 3 (1960), 602–607.

Verdone, P. "Variables Related to the Temporal Reference of Manifest Dream Content." Unpublished Ph.D. dissertation, University of Chicago, 1963.

Vogel, G. "Studies in Psychophysiology of Dreams. III. The Dream of Narcolepsy," *Archives of General Psychiatry*, 3 (1960), 421–428.

Vogel, G., Foulkes, D., and Trosman, H. "Ego Functions and Dreaming During Sleep Onset," *Archives of General Psychiatry*, in press.

Watson, J. B. *Behaviorism*. Chicago: University of Chicago Press (Phoenix Books), 1959.

Waxenberg, S. E., Dickes, R., and Gottesfeld, H. "The Poetzl Phenomenon Re-examined Experimentally," *Journal of Nervous and Mental Disease*, 135 (1962), 387–398.

Weitzman, E. D., et al. "Cyclic Activity in Sleep of Macaca Mulatta," *Archives of Neurology*, 12 (1965), 463–467.

Whitman, R. M., Pierce, C. M., and Maas, J. "Drugs and Dreams." In Uhr, L., and Miller, J. G. (eds.). *Drugs and Behavior*. New York: John Wiley & Sons, Inc., 1960. Pp. 591–595.

Whitman, R. M., et al. "Drugs and Dreams. II. Imipramine and Prochlorperazine," *Comprehensive Psychiatry*, 2 (1961), 219–226.

———. "The Dreams of the Experimental Subject," *Journal of Nervous and Mental Disease*, 134 (1962), 431–439.

Williams, H. L., et al. "Responses to Auditory Stimulation, Sleep

Loss, and the EEG Stages of Sleep," *Electroencephalography and Clinical Neurophysiology,* 16 (1964), 269–279.

Williams, H. L., Morlock, H. C., and Morlock, J. V. "Discriminative Responses to Auditory Signals During Sleep." Paper presented to the American Psychological Association, Philadelphia, 1963.

Williams, H. L., Tepas, D. I., and Morlock, H. C. "Evoked Responses to Clicks and Electroencephalographic Stages of Sleep in Man," *Science,* 138 (1962), 685–686.

Wolpert, E. A. "Studies in Psychophysiology of Dreams. II. An Electromyographic Study of Dreaming," *Archives of General Psychiatry,* 2 (1960), 231–241.

Wolpert, E. A., and Trosman, H. "Studies in Psychophysiology of Dreams. I. Experimental Evocation of Sequential Dream Episodes," *Archives of Neurology and Psychiatry,* 79 (1958), 603–606.

Wood, P. "Dreaming and Social Isolation." Unpublished Ph.D. dissertation, University of North Carolina, 1962.

*Woods, R. L. (ed.). *The World of Dreams.* New York: Random House, Inc., 1947.

GLOSSARY

Action Potential electrical potential of a muscle or nerve fiber.

Affect experienced emotion.

Afferent referring to nerve fibers that carry impulses from sensory receptors at the periphery of the body to the brain.

ARAS (*Ascending Reticular Activating System*) a network of cell bodies and fibers arising in the brain-stem reticular formation and projecting diffusely to the cerebral cortex. Its function appears to be the arousing or alerting of the organism.

Autonomic referring to the autonomic nervous system and/or the visceral structures it activates.

Autonomic Nervous System nervous structures directly responsible for the activation of visceral organs of vegetative function such as the heart, lungs, liver, and so on.

Barbiturate any of several salts of barbituric acid, most often used medically for sedation or pain relief.

Brain Waves a popular term for recorded brain potentials (see EEG) or particular patternings of such recorded potentials. The most important brain-wave patterns include:

Alpha Waves an approximately 10 cps EEG rhythm characteristic of relaxed wakefulness, but also seen, generally at a somewhat slower frequency, during REM sleep.

Delta Waves 1–3 cps high-voltage EEG rhythms, characteristic of EEG sleep stages 3 and 4.

K-Complexes sharp, high-voltage EEG wave forms occurring spontaneously during NREM sleep, most prominently during stage-2 sleep, and also seen during NREM sleep as evoked responses to external stimuli.

Spindles 12–14 cps spindle-shaped EEG wave forms characteristic of stage-2 and -3 sleep.

Theta Waves 4–6 cps spikelike EEG wave forms prominent during sleep onset (descending EEG sleep stage 1).

Cathexis an investment of energy, attention, or interest in or toward something.

Central Nervous System the brain and spinal cord.

Cerebral Cortex the convoluted surface of the cerebrum.

Cerebrum the largest lobe of the human brain, divided into two hemispheres (left and right) and four regions (*frontal, temporal, parietal, occipital*).

Conceptual (of mental activity) lacking in concrete or pictorial symbols; without sensory imagery; see *Perceptual.*

Control Night a night on which an experimental treatment—for example, drug administration or selective sleep deprivation—under evaluation is omitted, so that a base-line value may be established for the variable that it is supposed may be affected by the treatment.

Correlation an association of one variable with another, so that the one is at least partially predictable from the other; if *positive*, high indexes of one variable tend to be associated with high indexes of the other variable; if *negative*, high indexes of one variable tend to be associated with low indexes of the other variable; a *zero* correlation indicates no tendency for two variables to be associated with one another.

cps (cycles per second) in brain-wave measurement, the number of wave peaks per second, a measure of brain-wave frequency.

Day Residue a memory of the dream-day that, in Freud's theory, constitutes part of the raw material from which the dream is constructed.

Decathexis a transfer of energy, attention, or interest away from something.

Defense Mechanism any technique adopted, often unconsciously, by the individual to ward off potentially traumatic confrontations with his own feelings, desires, and so on; *Projection* is one example of such a technique.

Desynchronous (of brain waves) lacking regularity of frequency, so-called because the lack of a regular rhythm in the EEG is supposed to indicate desynchronous firing of adjacent brain cells.

Dexedrine a psychic-energizing drug that tends to suppress REM sleep.

Dream-Day the day immediately preceding the night's sleep from which a dream is recalled.

Dream Deprivation the selective deprivation of ascending stage-1 sleep with REMs, accomplished by awakening a subject each time he enters such sleep or by administering drugs or other treatments that selectively suppress this stage of sleep.

Dream Symbolism the representation by one element of manifest dream content of some thought, feeling, and so on, that is not present, as such, in the manifest dream. The supposed symbolism of dream content is the reason why it is often felt that dreams cannot be taken at face value but rather require interpretation.

"Dreamer" a person who claims, outside the laboratory, to dream frequently (also known as a *recaller*).

EEG (*Electroencephalogram*) a recording of *brain potentials* (moment-to-moment shifts in energy level between adjacent cells or regions of the cerebral cortex).

Electrode (in electroencephalography) a tiny silver disk affixed to the subject's scalp for the detection of brain-wave activity.

Electroencephalograph an apparatus for detecting, amplifying, and producing a graphic record, EEG, of brain potentials.

EOG (*Electrooculogram*) a recording of the movement of the eyeball.

Evoked Response an EEG response to an external stimulus, used

as an indication of whether such a stimulus has elicited any
cortical reaction, and, if so, to determine the cortical locus
of that reaction.

Extrinsic Ocular Muscles   muscles responsible for the movement
of the eyeball in its socket.

First-Night Effect   a reliably lower than average REM-time value
often observed on the subject's initial night in a sleep laboratory.

Free Association   a psychoanalytic technique in which the patient associates rapidly and without conscious deliberation
to his manifest dream content.

Functional Deafferentiation   a state in which the organism is insensitive to external sensory stimulation as if afferent neural
fibers had been interfered with so that they were no longer
able to propagate nervous impulses to the cerebral cortex.

GSR (*Galvanic Skin Response*)   a sudden decrease in the electrical
resistance of the skin, often associated with emotional states.

Hallucination   a false perception; that is, a perception in the
absence of appropriate sensory excitation in whose reality
the perceiver believes.

Hypnagogic   referring to events occurring during the act of
falling off to sleep.

Hypnopompic   referring to events occurring during the act of
awakening from sleep.

Incorporation   the inclusion, either directly or indirectly, of a
stimulus in manifest dream content.

Kinesthetic Imagery   actual or imagined muscular sensations.

Latent   not directly manifest in overt behavior.

Latent Dream Content   see *Manifest Dream Content.*

Manifest Dream Content   the dream as immediately experienced;
distinguished in Freudian theory from latent dream content,
the dream's meaning as revealed by the interpretation of the
supposed symbolism of the manifest dream.

Median   the central observation of a series, used as a descriptive
measure of the central tendency of that series (the arithmetic
mean of the series of observations 1, 2, 100, 200, 697 is

1000/5 or 200; the median, or middle, observation in the series, is 100).

Microvolt   a millionth of one volt, a unit of measurement of brain-wave intensity.

Narcolepsy   a disease in which the afflicted individual periodically finds it impossible to stay awake during the daytime, even though he may be engaged in activities requiring wakefulness and apparently wishes to remain awake.

Neuron   a single nerve cell; the basic unit of all structures of the nervous system.

Neurosis   a relatively nonacute form of personality maladjustment or disturbance; see *Psychosis*.

"Nondreamer"   a person who claims, outside the laboratory, to dream seldom or not at all (also known as a *nonrecaller*).

NREM (*Non-Rapid Eye Movement*)   referring to EEG sleep stages 2, 3, and 4 (and sometimes also descending stage 1), which are without REMS.

Paranoid   characterized by delusions of being the object of persecution.

Passive Theory (of sleep)   the viewpoint that sleep is simply the absence of wakefulness and requires no special explanations over and above those evolved to account for wakefulness.

Perceptual   of or pertaining to the experience of sensory—visual, kinesthetic, and so on—imagery.

Phylogenetic   referring to the evolutionary development of the human species.

Placebo   a substance having no known physical effect upon the organism, given in drug research to control for psychological effects that may attend the administration of any substance whatsoever to the organism.

Poetzl Phenomenon   the supposed appearance in manifest dream imagery of imperfectly perceived waking impressions.

Pons   a hindbrain structure, one part of which (*nucleus reticularis pontis caudalis*) appears to be responsible for the periodic appearance of episodes of REM sleep.

Posthypnotic Suggestion   a suggestion given during a hypnotic trance as to behavior the subject will manifest some time after the trance state is abolished.

Primary Process (of thought processes) characterized by disorder, the lack of logical connections, extraneous intrusion of impulses or wishes, hallucination, regression, and so on; see *Secondary Process.*

Projection the attribution to others of what is actually characteristic of one's self.

Projective Test any set of psychological test materials that are poorly structured, either in a perceptual (inkblots) or thematic (Thematic Apperception Test pictures) sense, to which the subject is to give structure by his identifications or interpretations of the materials. The subject's responses, ostensibly descriptions of the stimuli, are examined as possible projections of his own thoughts, feelings, impulses, and so on.

Proprioceptive referring to feedback from sensory cells excited by movements of the organism.

Psychoanalysis treatment of patients based on Freud's theory of mental illness; more generally, his theory of personality and human behavior.

Psychosis a relatively acute form of personality maladjustment or disturbance in which the patient is fundamentally out of touch with the world as it is known by others.

Psychosomatic referring to physical complaints or disorders of psychological causation.

Psychotherapy a generic term for any form of psychological (or nonmedical) treatment of mental illness.

r (symbol for Pearson product-moment correlation coefficient) a measure of the degree of correlation between two variables whose possible value ranges from +1.00 (perfect positive correlation) through .00 (no correlation) to −1.00 (perfect negative correlation).

Recovery Nights nights of undisturbed sleep immediately following nights of generalized or selective sleep deprivation.

Regressive reverting to content or modes of thinking character-

istic of an earlier, particularly an infantile or childish, period
of personal development.

Reliable   referring to the consistency, across time, or across observers at one point in time, of a set of observations; see
Valid.

REM *(Rapid Eye Movement)*   such movements are seen during
wakefulness and during ascending EEG stage-1 sleep; also
used to refer to ascending EEG stage-1 sleep.

REM *Period*   a period, generally of 10–30 minutes duration and
bounded on both sides by NREM sleep, of ascending EEG stage-
1 sleep with its accompanying REMs.

REM *Time*   the proportion of a night's total sleep time spent in
ascending stage-1 sleep.

Retinal   pertaining to the *retina*, the light-sensitive image-
forming structure of the eye.

Reticular Formation   a system of nerve cells extending from the
base of the brain to the forebrain (see also ARAS).

Schizophrenia   a psychotic disorder characterized by withdrawal
from, and a lack of interest in, the everyday world.

Secondary Process (of thought processes)   characterized by ra-
tionality, ordered logic, freedom from extraneous intrusion
of impulses or wishes, reality orientation, and so on.

SEM *(Slow Eye Movement)*   such movements are seen at sleep
onset.

Sensory Deprivation   a condition of drastic restriction of stimulus intensity and variety available to an organism.

[*Statistically*] *Significant*   as evaluated by probability statistics,
a probably genuine and replicable difference or effect.

Sleep Deprivation   (1) *generalized sleep deprivation* a condition
in which an organism is prevented from experiencing any kind
of sleep whatsoever; (2) *selective sleep deprivation* a condition in which an organism is prevented from experiencing
some particular stage of sleep—see, for example, *Dream
Deprivation*—without being deprived of other stages of
sleep.

Somnambulism   sleep walking.

Stages of Sleep qualitatively different patterns of EEG/EOG activity occurring during sleep. The several stages of EEG/EOG sleep are:

> *STAGE 1* a low-voltage, random EEG pattern: (1) *descending stage 1* occurs at sleep onset, is generally of brief duration, accompanied either by SEMS or ocular quiescence, and is characterized by the periodic appearance of theta waves; (2) *ascending stage 1* occurs after a period of NREM sleep, is generally of fairly sustained duration, accompanied by REMS, and is associated with the experiencing of especially vivid and sustained dream imagery (also called REM sleep).
>
> *STAGE 2* an EEG pattern characterized by the presence of spindles and K-complexes and by the relative absence of alpha and delta waves (an NREM sleep stage).
>
> *STAGE 3* an EEG pattern characterized by the presence of spindles in conjunction with fairly considerable delta activity (an NREM sleep stage).
>
> *STAGE 4* an EEG pattern characterized by the almost total dominance of delta activity (an NREM sleep stage).

Standard Deviation a measure of the dispersion or scatter of a series of observations about their mean (the square root of the averaged squared deviation of individual observations from the mean).

Synchronous (of brain waves) characterized by regularity of frequency, named this because such regularity is supposed to indicate the synchronous firing of adjacent brain cells.

Valid referring to the accuracy or truthfulness of an observation, interpretation, and so on; see *Reliable*. An interpretation may be reliable—two independent observers agree upon it—but inaccurate, hence invalid.

Vasoconstriction a decrease in the diameter of blood vessels.

Viscera the internal organs of the body, especially those of the thoracic and abdominal regions, for example, heart, lungs, liver, and intestines.

INDEX

INDEX

ABOUT THE AUTHOR

D AVID Foulkes is Assistant Professor in the Department of Psychology and Philosophy at the University of Wyoming, Laramie. In 1965, he was the recipient of a $70,000 three-year research grant from the National Science Foundation for studies of dream content. He is an active contributor to scientific journals and is a member of the American Psychological Association, the Association for the Psychophysiological Study of Sleep, and the Midwestern Psychological Association.

Dr. Foulkes received his B.A. degree from Swarthmore College, Swarthmore, Pennsylvania, and his doctorate from the University of Chicago, Illinois. His past affiliations include: Research Associate, Departments of Psychology and Psychiatry, University of Chicago (1963–1964), and Instructor, Department of Psychology, Lawrence University, Appleton, Wisconsin (1960–1963). He now lives, with his wife and son, in Laramie.